Finding the Gospel

A Pastor's Disappointment and Discovery

✻

J. Daniel Day

© 2020
Published in the United States by Nurturing Faith Inc., Macon GA,
www.nurturingfaith.net.

Nurturing Faith is the book-publishing arm of Good Faith Media (goodfaithmedia.org).

Library of Congress Cataloging-in-Publication Data is available.

ISBN: 978-1-63528-118-7

All rights reserved. Printed in the United States of America.

All scripture quotations, unless otherwise noted, are from the New Revised Standard Version.

Cover photo by J. Daniel Day

"Dan Day has provided us a front-row seat witnessing his tenacious journey to make meaning of an inherited theology whose usefulness had worn thin and shallow. Holding scripture central, while engaging the messiness of life, he chronicles a personal theological transformation, and a joyful discovery of a new direction in proclaiming and living out the gospel. All who enter the pulpit Sunday after Sunday would benefit from examining their theological presumptions with the same courage and humility as exhibited in these pages. And in doing so, God's dream for the world is realized!"

—*Paula Dempsey*
Director of Partnership Relations
Alliance of Baptists

"Drawing on years of active and insightful ministry, Dan Day offers this important survey of issues and actions that have shaped his life and his life's vocation in the church. At a time when Christian identity often seems in permanent transition, Day calls us to reflect on what it means not only to enter into faith, but also to be formed by faith throughout our lives."

—*Bill J. Leonard*
Founding Dean and Professor of Divinity Emeritus
Wake Forest University School of Divinity

"Here is a book that will cause you to reflect on your inherited gospel and ponder the question, 'Is the church really interested in what interested Jesus?' Without disowning 'The Plan,' Dan Day shows us a better way to understand the gospel. Speaking hard truths with humor and humility, Day keeps us kingdom-focused. As he states, many of us know how to do church, but we don't know how to do kingdom. This book gives us a good starting place."

—*Lynn Brinkley*
Associate Director
Baptist Women in Ministry

"Dan Day captures the transformation ethos of the gospel. Over time, thoughtful Christians are transformed by a living gospel that challenges our preconceived ideas regarding faith. Faith is not a stagnant concept, but a living philosophy adapting to time and circumstances shining the gospel's light and justice. Day's book says it in an extraordinary way."

—*R. Mitch Randall*
Chief Executive Officer
Good Faith Media

"This is a wonderful book. I hope it will receive the very wide readership it surely deserves."
—*Fisher Humphreys*
Professor Emeritus
Beeson Divinity School, Samford University

"In the Old Testament they were called 'hoary' heads—an adjective we don't use in the twenty-first century. It meant gray or white hair that comes with age. The Old Testament and New Testament God-followers considered these hoary-headed ones to be sages, priests, and prophets. Dan Day is one of these 'hoary heads.' And, rather than sinking into a retired dotage, he has continued to be a pastor in heart and head. If I were still leading seminary-level courses in ecclesial ethics, this book would be a required text. For those who haven't had the opportunity of seminary or other theological education, take this one as a must-read primer."

—*Bill Tillman*
Retired Christian Ethics Professor
Coordinator of the Center for Congregational Ethics

Contents

Acknowledgments vii
Introduction ix

Part 1: Disappointment 1
"Our little systems have their day ..."

    CHAPTER 1 3
    Second Thoughts about an Inherited Gospel

    CHAPTER 2 11
    When First Thoughts Must Be Rethought

    CHAPTER 3 15
    A Summary of Suspicions

Part 2: Discovery 31
"... and thou, O Lord, art more than they."

    CHAPTER 4 33
    The Elephant in the Sanctuary: God's Kingdom

    CHAPTER 5 39
    The Kingdom They Wanted

    CHAPTER 6 45
    The Urgency of Now

    CHAPTER 7 49
    The Now (but Not Really?) Kingdom
        Excursus: One Key Verse and Two Linguistic Worlds 53

    CHAPTER 8 55
    God's Dream: The Kingdom by Another Name

    CHAPTER 9 61
    One Billboard Outside David's Royal City

CHAPTER 10 65
Farewell to Saturday's World

CHAPTER 11 69
The King Who Saves by His Life

CHAPTER 12 75
The King Who Saves by His Death

CHAPTER 13 85
The Good News of the Reign of God

CHAPTER 14 89
Speaking Better Things

Part 3: Discernment 103
"We have but faith: we cannot know … A beam in darkness: let it grow."

CHAPTER 15 105
Church: Premature Ambassador of the Now and Future King

CHAPTER 16 117
Worship: Painful Party of the Woke

CHAPTER 17 127
Bible: Archives of the Kingdom

CHAPTER 18 135
Race: *One* Nation … with Liberty and Justice for *All*?

CHAPTER 19 147
Sex/Gender: Below the Belt, Between the Sheets, and Beyond Reason

CHAPTER 20 159
Politics: Avoiding the Pilate Syndrome
    Excursus: Hitler's Reich (Kingdom) and the Church 170

CHAPTER 21 179
Coda: Here Ends the Status Report

For Further Reading 183

Acknowledgments

My helpers in the writing of this book were many. Those who tried to offer guidance, correction, and encouragement from the scholar's corner (some of whom may groan with what I failed to do with their counsel) are: Curtis Freeman, Derek Hogan, Fisher Humphreys, Mikeal Parsons, Walter Shurden, and Bill Tillman.

Friends who read portions and offered their comments at various stages in the development of the book: Lynn Brinkley, Mattie Compton, Gary W. Cook, Trey Davis, Barry Diehl, Jim Drennan, Diane Hill, Chris Malone, Jill Martin-Prouty, Stephanie Parker, Daryll Powell, Lawrence Powers, Mike Eddinger, Ron Poythress, Dave Stratton, and Gordon Whitaker. I owe them much for their most helpful reflections, especially my three special amigos: Mike, Ron, and Dave:

In addition, Jennifer Carlyle Davis proved to be a timely and most skillful coach and editor in the latter days of this endeavor. Also a profound thank you goes to Jackie Riley and Vickie Frayne of Nurturing Faith / Good Faith Media for their skills and great patience in bringing this book to press. And last, but probably not least since nothing happens nowadays without technology, I thank Wendy Tingle for making computer magic happen more than once.

I also extend thanks to three churches that, while this book was either playing in some unknown backroom of my mind or being dropped into the files of my laptop, displayed their bravery by asking me to serve as their interim pastor: First Baptist Church of New Bern, North Carolina; Broadway Baptist Church of Fort Worth, Texas; and First Baptist Church of Clayton, North Carolina. Each church is wonderfully different, but all were alike in their warm reception, patient collaboration, and teaching power:

Again, I acknowledge the goodness of life with Mary Carol Rogers Day, my wife of fifty-five years, peerless cheerleader and soulmate always—even when I was absent though present while writing this book.

Finally, I dedicate this endeavor to all the pastors who, especially in this time of whirligig change and demonic polarization, are steadily attempting to teach the faith, nurture hope, and model love. My continuing admiration and prayers are with you!

Introduction

Finding the Gospel is a book about changing one's mind. Or, more accurately, it is a book about how I have changed my mind about some portions of the Christian faith—especially its central message. Apparently, I am not the only one caught up in this rethinking endeavor. Some people suggest Christianity itself is undergoing one of its every 500-year "rummage sales" when all manner of doctrines and practices are dragged out to the driveway for disposal.[1] I don't know if that's true—and I will be long dead before the historians settle the question—but what I do know is that as I enter the fourth quarter of my life, my own faith doesn't look like it did in the first quarter, or, for that matter, in any previous quarter. It is still a work in progress. Perhaps it is so for you, too. If so, I'd like for this book to be my way of sharing notes with you.

There's one thing I learned very soon in my process: Change is hard work. Intellectually and emotionally, it is hard work. If we were talking about something less emotionally charged—such as changing from cable to satellite TV—it would be so much simpler. But when the change has to do with what you think about God and everything south thereof, the stakes are much higher. If you are a pastor, it can even feel suicidal. You begin to worry that you might wind up like the Reverend Jim Casy in John Steinbeck's *The Grapes of Wrath*. Casy is quick to clarify that he used to be the Rev. Jim Casy, but now he is just Jim Casy:

> Ain't got the call no more. I wouldn't take the good ol' gospel that was just layin' there to my hand. I got to be pickin' at it an' workin' at it until I got it all tore down. Here I got the sperit sometimes an' nothin' to preach about.[2]

Nobody wants a faith that's "all tore down" and leaving you with "nothin' to preach about"—or to trust in. But then, nobody wants a faith that doesn't make sense either. And when that clash begins inside you, the hard work of change has already begun—like it or not.

So perhaps a helpful first note to share is an encouragement to put aside your fear of giving fresh thought to what you believe—or more specifically, to what you were taught. It's inescapable that we all begin this life with a passel of other folks' conclusions as our orthodoxy. (Some of us even go to seminary to have more orthodoxy laid on us.) We predictably drink in Mama's morals or Daddy's worldview as being the gospel truth. And it was—for them. This is where we all begin, with inherited orthodoxies about everything from religion to how to bake a ham, from what patriotism means to how frequently to bathe. But others' orthodoxies have a sneaky way of eventually colliding with our own meaning-making, and when that collision occurs, we are faced with the challenge of sticking with what we picked up from others or forging our own orthodoxies—with changing our minds, or not.

When reaching that crossroad, I take heart from the Bible's reports that even God risks some changes of mind (see Exod. 32:14, Jer. 18:1-11, Jon. 3:1-10). Surely, changing one's mind can't be all bad if even God has done it.

I also find encouragement in God's repeated cry for us to repent. Though repentance is usually associated with tearful regret, the principal Hebrew and Greek words (*teshuva* and *metanoia*, respectively) that are translated as repentance literally mean to turn or turn around and to change your mind. Repentance, then, isn't just a cathartic religious experience of feeling horribly sorry. It is a change of mind that leads to a new direction.

Life, if lived as a learner and with any degree of humility, will be a series of repentances, a succession of mind changes and consequent life changes. Every plateau of life brings new vistas, vistas that require us to recalibrate our course based upon what we now can see. What seemed like True North yesterday now appears to be three degrees left or right of True North, and, if we wish to reach our destination, it is today's reading we had better follow.

I will admit up front the brashness of this project, as though you really care or need or want to review my baggage-laden journey, or as though I had such a unique story to tell or was such a prominent character that my theological journey would be of interest. The truth is that I am not that different from a great many Protestant clergy persons—neither scandal nor great honors have been mine.

For more than fifty years I have been a Baptist pastor, minding the store at several different churches across America's southland, facing Sunday sermon deadlines, tending to parishioners' hurts and hopes—while also trying to carve out a life of meaning for myself. As a capstone to that deployment, I taught seminarians in a divinity school for five years. I want to believe that across those decades I learned some things about life, myself, God, and what makes the world tick—that I gained some "sage-ing" with my "age-ing." And now, in the fourth quarter of my life, it is important to me to say what I think I have learned—to voice some second thoughts about my theological inheritance and to say as clearly as possible how my mind has changed.

Why be so self-revealing, one may ask. I would reply with two principal reasons. First, I'd like to share notes with some of you who are wrestling with your faith, or lack of it. Perhaps I can suggest a new tune for some who have grown weary of the church's same old song. It could be that the song you learned was helpful for a while, but as your life has unfolded, that song now has too many sour notes or not enough stanzas (that is, it quits long before your questions do). If so, I'd like for you to hear something possibly better.

I write also because of the current state of things in our nation and its churches. Where America stands today (angry, divided, suspicious) and where the church in America stands today (angry, divided, suspicious) is not what I thought I was giving my life to, nor where I thought I was leading in all those Sunday sermons, pastoral conversations, and church meetings. So I write because I'd like for the church to start singing a new, a better song. I'd like for her to learn new ways to read her scriptures and to live her life. I'd like for her gospel to be more fully engaged with life this side of heaven.

Introduction

There are many today who would call themselves "seekers," or persons who doggedly hope there is more to the Christian faith than many of our Sunday experiences reveal. Without trying to be cute or sensational, these pages are my attempt to tell you, sometimes with embarrassment, what one preacher/pastor has found thus far.

In Part 1, "Disappointment," you will find the story of my growing disenchantment with the understanding of the gospel I formed from my early teachers. No doubt some of those teachers would be disappointed if they knew how I heard them and would protest that what I heard was not what they were trying to convey. Perhaps the fog of fundamentalism was so thick within me that it concealed the fine distinctions some tried to offer me. Perhaps I was just not listening. But "Disappointment" tells you why I had to find a better gospel or quit. I have intentionally kept this part of the book as brief as possible, believing you already have heard or lived enough tales of eroding faith. Besides, that is not the message I want to tell you.

Part 2, "Discovery," is the heart of the book, the message I want to tell you. In this section I state my convictions about the gospel Jesus preached, the kingdom of God. My thesis throughout this book is that this message of God's kingdom is the good news, the better gospel needed for this hour—at least I know it has "saved" this sinner. This section is, admittedly, more demanding than the first, but I have done my best to explain my convictions in sequential, bite-size units rather than in convoluted professorial paragraphs. But I cannot reduce the mystery of faith to child's play. I warned you that this is hard work!

In Part 3, "Discernment," my intent is to show you how a gospel of the kingdom has influenced my thinking about three theological topics and three ethical issues. This is the "So what?" section of the book; for some readers it may be the most important section. If nothing more, these chapters illustrate once again that theology and ethics, belief and behavior, are always linked.

Some readers will recognize that I have attached some lines from Alfred Lord Tennyson's "In Memoriam A.H.H." onto these section headings. Tennyson (1809–1892), like many of us, also struggled for his faith in times of great cultural and theological turmoil, and, thankfully, left us better for his search. I can only hope that a sentence or two within this book might do the same for some who read it.

Notes

[1] Phyllis Tickle, *The Great Emergence: How Christianity is Changing and Why* (Grand Rapids, MI: Baker Books, 2008) offers this analogy. Representative of this trend, see Brian D. McLaren, *The Great Spiritual Migration: How the World's Largest Religion is Seeking a Better Way to be Christian* (New York: Convergent Books, 2016) or Richard Rohr, *The Universal Christ: How a Forgotten Reality Can Change Everything We See, Hope For, and Believe* (New York: Convergent Books, 2019).

[2] John Steinbeck, *The Grapes of Wrath* (New York: Penguin Books, 1999), 20-21.

PART 1

※

Disappointment

"Our little systems have their day ..."

As early as 1995, the Christian writer Philip Yancey was worried because "when I ask a stranger, 'What is an evangelical Christian?' I get an answer like this: 'Someone who supports family values and opposes homosexual rights and abortion.'" Yancey found this perception lamentable "because the gospel of Jesus was not primarily a political platform."[1]

His distinction raises the question: "Well, can you then tell me what his gospel was about, primarily?" That question is the burden of this book. What *is* the gospel? And, more specifically, what was the gospel in its first-century dress, and what is it now, for this off-kilter hour when politics has become all-consuming and Jesus and his gospel appear to be wholly conscripted into the armies of right-wing politics? Do Christians in fact have any good news to offer anyone today when so many seem fed up with all religionists or are absolutely sure their way is God's only way?

The first section of this book is my lover's quarrel with the gospel of the faith tradition that bore and trained me. That faith tradition is the one that troubled Yancey and that has more than troubled me. It has compelled me to find a better gospel than the one it gave me. That's the story you will find in the next pages. Even if your story is quite different from mine, I suspect you will recognize some of the terrain. The details may differ, but the landscape is familiar enough. For seekers, the road is often much the same.

Note

[1] Philip Yancey, *The Jesus I Never Knew* (Grand Rapids, MI: Zondervan Publishing, 1995), 246-47. Nineteen years later Yancey updated his concern in his aptly titled book, *Vanishing Grace: What Ever Happened to the Good News?* (Grand Rapids, MI: Zondervan, 2014).

CHAPTER 1

✻

Second Thoughts about an Inherited Gospel

I cut my preaching teeth as a youth evangelist. I never was that good at it, but the demand was great enough among Oklahoma Baptist churches in the early 1960s that even so-so ministerial students like myself could stay busy preaching our four sermons in weekend youth-led revivals. A host church sponsored these Friday–Sunday events. Although they were meant to reach teenagers, the entire church was expected to attend all four revival services.

One summer I was even invited to "lead a meeting" at a couple of churches in Texas and one in Arkansas. That flush of success got me to wondering if Billy Graham should be urged to take early retirement. I thought better of that, however, when I realized that my pay, raised in "love offerings" taken in each church, wasn't all that impressive. Even so, that summer I made enough to buy some natty clothes and a pre-owned, but beautiful, powder-blue-and-white 1957 Chevrolet Bel Air, with a four-barrel carburetor on a V8 engine that ran like a cheetah on steroids! But I digress.

The content of my four sermons was predictable 1960s evangelistic stuff:

- a gripping story or nicely turned phrase from the King James Version of the Bible as my text
- a melodramatic tale or two taken from a sermon illustration book
- a smattering of shocking statistics about teenagers' drinking and dancing habits (and the hanky-panky we all knew that led to) or a reference to the Doomsday Clock set by nuclear scientists of the day
- a legitimizing, theological-sounding quote from a real evangelist such as D.L. Moody
- a sprinkling of Bible verses about hell and heaven
- a full pedal-to-the-metal emphasis upon accepting Jesus as your personal Lord and Savior tonight while there is still time

That was what I preached each weekend, but the only thing that set my sermon apart from the local pastor's last or next Sunday sermon was the age of the preacher. This was a standard sermonic soundtrack long after the '60s were visible only in the rearview mirror.

Occasionally, the pastor or youth leader would ask me to go with him to try to "win a teenager to Christ." I was always quite willing to go and just as willing to share with a young person the gospel as I had received it. In those conversations, I always used a four-point outline called The Plan of Salvation. For each point there was a verifying Bible verse (printed here in the King James Version then in use). Here is that plan and the Bible verses:

- Point 1: All have sinned (including you, of course). "There is none righteous, no, not one." Romans 3:10.
- Point 2: The wages of sin is death (not just biologically, but eternally in hell). "For the wages of sin is death...." Romans 6:23a.
- Point 3: Jesus died for your sins that you might be forgiven and go to heaven. "... while we were yet sinners, Christ died for us." Romans 5:8. "... but the gift of God is eternal life through Jesus Christ...." Romans 6:23b.
- Point 4: You must accept Jesus as your personal Lord and Savior to be saved. "That if thou shalt confess with thy mouth the Lord Jesus, and shalt believe in thine heart that God hath raised him from the dead, thou shalt be saved ... For whoever shall call upon the name of the Lord shall be saved." Romans 10: 9, 13.

After I made this presentation, my task was to urge the teenagers to invite Jesus into their heart then and there, and, if they were hesitant, to rebut their "no" with persuasive arguments and good reasons to get themselves saved immediately. Sometimes youngsters actually did say "yes," and I led them in praying what was called "the sinner's prayer" for forgiveness and salvation.

This particular plan I used was known to insiders as The Roman Road to Salvation because all its biblical citations were found within just a page or two from one another in Paul's Letter to the Romans. That helped to "keep it simple" for those of us who really didn't know much about the Bible; all we had to do was underline the verses and turn two or three pages to the next reference. (In another chapter I will look more critically at the biblical basis of The Roman Road.) Actually, there were several iterations of The Plan, but every version attempted to distill the gospel to a short series of bullet points to be affirmed. A full-page, seven-point Plan of Salvation (and labeled as such at the top of the page) is published in *The Baptist Hymnal, 1991*.[1]

This trip down memory lane is not unique. It represents the gist of American evangelical belief and practice in the twentieth century. Allowing for local differences in style, emphasis, and fervor, this is still the bottom-line theological base of hundreds of thousands of churches and their members. Using these methods and concepts, they have reached untold thousands and built churches that provide lives of meaning and hope for generations past and present. This is the message I responded to as an eight-year-old when I "accepted Jesus" and was baptized. This tradition is my home, and these are my people. And in one sentence, here is the gospel as I received it from them and as I

Second Thoughts about an Inherited Gospel

preached it: *God sent Jesus into this world to die for the punishment of my sins so that I might be forgiven and go to heaven when I die.*

Long ago, however, this particular way of understanding the gospel lost its hold on me.

Let me hurriedly add that I am in agreement with what this sentence is attempting to express. I do most truly believe Jesus is the Savior this world desperately needs! But I disagree with the way this sentence states my belief, and with what it fails to say—and I very much regret the problems created by saying it this way. But, as I said, this particular way of understanding the gospel lost its hold on me long ago.

Perhaps it would be just as true to say I lost my hold on it. It is difficult now to reconstruct just how and when this loosening began, but by my mid-twenties I had certainly joined the company of the confused. Most likely it began with my puzzlement during those youth revival days with some of the words of Jesus printed in red in my Bible, words that seemed to contradict The Plan. The Plan promised, "Believe these three things, and you will be saved." But Jesus' red-letter words said: "If any want to become my followers, let them deny themselves and take up their cross and follow me. For those who want to save their life will lose it, and those who lose their life for my sake will find it" (Matt. 16:24-25). That's Jesus talking. But a central plea of my sermons was for people to "save their life." Unquestionably, whatever Jesus was talking about, it sounded a whole lot scarier than most of what I was preaching.

Jesus' words caused me to wonder if maybe there were two classes of Christians: (1) the "believers in Jesus" category for average folks and (2) the category of "followers of Jesus" for the super-spiritual folks—something akin to economy and first-class tickets into heaven. How, I wondered, could salvation be so simple and easy on one hand but be so demanding on the other? "Only believe" and "Take up a cross" were a difficult combination! It is worth mentioning, too, that those were also the days when I was hearing for the first time about a German theologian named Bonhoeffer who had written something about "cheap grace." I didn't know what he meant, but it sounded intriguing. But I let my wonderment rest. "All of this is the kind of thing they will explain to me in seminary," I told myself.

My early faith-changing journey also included a professor at Oklahoma Baptist University and his course in the philosophy of religion. My world was recast by both. Some might say, "See, this is what happens when those smart-aleck college professors start attacking youngsters' faith." The truth is, my philosophy professor, Gregory Pritchard, attended church more faithfully than some of us ministerial students; he was there every Sunday, modeling the best of churchmanship. And, for that matter, I do not remember him ever challenging any student's views, even if they were so naïve that students in the class would. He simply exposed us to a wider world of thought than any of us had ever seen or heard of before, and, by letting us wrestle with that wider world, he modeled the best of teaching in addition to his model churchmanship. I learned from him that inquiry and commitment weren't enemies, that the best belief was thoughtful belief.

Then, finally, I went to seminary. Some people think that is where they load you up with doctrine and the ability to say confidently, "the Bible says." There was some of that in my seminary, to be sure, and for some of my classmates that is all they wanted and all they received. But for others of us, the greatest gift that seminary gave us was the library. Acres of books and journals filled with the thoughts and second thoughts, the prayers and testimonies and wonderings of the saints and not-so-saintly across the centuries. That place humbled me. It awakened me to the variety of ways the Bible had been interpreted through the ages, and to the deep, wide sea of God's working, removing from me the silliness of assuming I could pin God down like a butterfly and definitively dissect the mysteries of the Almighty. Those endless bookshelves reminded me that countless others before me had wrestled with the Holy—and had written reports of their encounter, reports I could read and learn from. My sense of wonder widened.

One book in that library that I now realize left a lasting impression upon me was written by a British New Testament scholar, C.H. Dodd.[2] Apparently motivated by some of the same questions I was asking (albeit on a much higher academic level), Dodd had carefully studied the speeches of the apostle Peter that are reported in the Book of Acts. From them he distilled the recurring themes of the proclamation of this first Christian preacher. He called this distillation the *kerygma*, a Greek word also used by the Apostle Paul to refer to the message he was preaching. According to Dodd, the speeches of Peter consistently dealt with six themes:

1. The age of fulfillment of the messianic promises has dawned.
2. This has taken place through the ministry, death, and resurrection of Jesus, the Christ.
3. This Jesus has been exalted to the right hand of God as the messianic head of the new Israel.
4. The Holy Spirit now at work in the church is the authenticating sign that this is true.
5. The messianic age will soon be consummated in the return of the Christ.
6. Therefore, repent and receive God's forgiveness, Spirit, and salvation.

These six themes, said Dodd, formed the earliest *kerygma*, the heart of the first Christian gospel message.

My professors introduced me to Dodd and to the *kerygma*. But I did not connect the dots. Or my teachers did not show me how the dots connected with my inherited gospel. All I saw was that Jesus and his cross and resurrection were at the center of it—and this only confirmed the ideas I had brought with me from childhood. I paid no attention to the breathtaking historical sweep of the *kerygma* and its basis in the fulfillment of promises I'd never really studied, and I did not give attention to its grounding and

Second Thoughts about an Inherited Gospel

consummation in an eternal purpose. The *kerygma's* semi-hidden hint that Jesus was one part (the colossally big part, to be sure) of a divine, cosmic redemption plot—this hint went unheard. This deafness to the new will come up again in my story, but for the time being I will simply say that as the years of my life passed, I began to hear Dodd's findings as a key to all I was searching for.

So, after five years of study (seven, if I include the two spent writing a dissertation), not only did seminary not explain to me how there could be economy and first-class tickets into heaven, but it also didn't hand me a cocksure guarantee that I had "the real deal" gospel in my grasp—even though I now possessed two fancy embossed seminary diplomas. Yes, "my easy God was gone," but in that idol's place there was a worshipful yearning, still churning today, to be a more thoughtful believer.

This said, I must report I had already seen enough of church life and read enough books (including the Bible) to form some disturbingly stern opinions about the gospel I had been preaching. It seemed to me that this gospel of mine was offering a salvation that was:

… so *commodified* that it was valued mostly as an after-death life insurance policy.
… so *divorced* from its giver that you could grab the gift and diss the Giver.
… so *cheap* that it was "purchasable" for no more than whispering a prayer or walking an aisle.
… so *diluted* that a six-year-old who knew no more about life than an onion could be "born again."

And I was now theologically aware enough that it bothered me that this gospel offered a salvation that was also:

… so *individualized* that it contained no expected ties to neighbor or any "other."
… so *privatized* that the church and its worship, instruction, or discipline were unnecessary.
… so *violence-based* that God appeared as a bloodthirsty monster demanding his pound of flesh.
… so *spiritualized* that injustice was usually shrugged off as unsolvable "till we all get to heaven."
… so *dumbed down* that anti-intellectualism too often found a warm hiding place within it.

That was a devastating load of negativism and questioning for a young minister to carry into his early pastoral work—and I list it now not as an accusation but as a report of disappointments that were rumbling within me, even if I wasn't yet able to describe them as I have here. But in those days the theological journals, along with the daily newspapers and weekly news magazines, were filled with articles about Christian theologians talking seriously about God's death, the church's irrelevance in our increasingly secular society, and the questionable justification for American armies in Vietnam. "What is the gospel?" was only one of many two-ton questions confronting seminarians like me in those days.

Once seminary pushed me from its womb, another large library was waiting for me: life. This, I discovered, is the subject pastors deal with most of all. Good books are God-sent, but so is life, and both are here to be our teachers. So, I began my efforts to listen to and learn from both. Across the next half-century, …

- I sat with families through long night hours as the life of loved ones crept away.
- On many Sunday mornings I spoke welcoming words of blessing upon pink newborns.
- I listened to stories of pain and stammered prayers for help.
- I got to know remarkable women, often dismissed as "little old ladies," who endowed churches with holy presence and meaning.
- I dealt with a few remarkably "little" men whose will-to-power had yet to meet Jesus.
- I once baptized a man so huge I could not immerse him—he knelt in the baptistry and I poured water over him.
- On one occasion, standing in the sluggish waters of the Red River, clad in a t-shirt, shorts, and sneakers, I baptized a trembling mother of teenagers.
- By request, I prayed over everything from Wal-Mart openings to AIDS marches to the dedication of a state fairgrounds water fountain.
- Sometimes I let arrogance and ignorance rule me and lived to regret my pettiness and to attempt apologies.
- I served a hitch on my city's Human Rights Commission, pulled jury duty on a paternity trial, and led unsuccessful campaigns to defeat liquor-by-the-drink and state-sponsored lotteries.
- I greeted Easter sunrise worshipers and knelt with them at midnight on Christmas Eve.
- I crept home after many a Sunday sermon, disappointed that the sermon had gone so badly, wishing I might never have to get up there again, but then thanked God I had another chance to do so.
- I officiated giddy weddings and witnessed ugly divorces.
- I dealt with beggars and bigots and big-name egos and more than once was blown away by the wisdom, courage, and compassion of everyday saints.
- I felt the anger of members who were mad about something I'd said or written or did or failed to do.
- I received thank-you notes from those whose thoughtfulness healed me.

A bit of math informs me that I have been stepping up to a pulpit somewhere north of 2,700 Sundays now, trying to speak Sunday words to Monday's world.

And what a world it has been! In my pulpit days I witnessed the Cuban Missile Crisis, the Silent Majority, Selma, Silicon Valley, Wounded Knee, Apollo 11, Iran-Contra, Da Nang, Chappaquiddick, Kent State, Kuwait, *I'm OK—You're OK*, Watergate, Branch Davidians, Whitewater, Stonewall, 9/11, Sandy Hook, shock and awe, Viagra, trickle-down, Roe v. Wade, hanging chads, Paris Accords, Berlin Wall, Desert Storm—and that's just a bit of the national news. And then there was the river of acronyms: ERA, NAFTA, AARP, NRA, IRA, GPS, KKK, MADD, PFLAG, SALT, NAACP, ISIS, TSA, LGBTQ+, and now MAGA.

Through it all, sometimes with low-burner interest and at other times intensely, I kept looking for a satisfactory answer to my early question about the gospel. Year by year, event by event, book by book, my mind was changing about many things, including the question of the good news I was to be preaching and living. How could my mind not be churning? For anyone to go out thinking what we thought coming in is a waste of life! All those years, all those experiences, all those places visited, books read, persons met, danced with, and battled against—how could anyone still be the same? I cannot imagine it. I am today so little like my youth evangelist self that I chuckle when I remember him. But I respect him, just as I respect, but do not truly understand, the many people who today are still satisfied with his world of thought and faith. But I am no longer of their number. My mind has changed about these matters. The library of life and print has led me to new convictions.

I seriously doubt, however, that I ever would have written about that journey had it not been for a rhetorical question that hooked me in 2018.

Notes

[1] *The Baptist Hymnal* (Nashville: Convention Press, 1991), 667.
[2] C.H. Dodd, *The Apostolic Preaching and Its Developments* (London: Hodder & Stoughton, 1936).

CHAPTER 2

✻

When First Thoughts Must Be Rethought

In March of 2018 I was seated at a folding table, listening to a presentation in a preacher-type meeting. Ten minutes into his presentation, the speaker asked a question and then immediately answered it with a rhetorical question. I cannot recall his initial question, but the follow-up question was: "Well, what's the gospel?"

The word "gospel" is, of course, often used as a reference to Christianity in general or even to the Bible in its totality, as though everything in the Bible is "good news"—which anyone who has ever read all 31,102 verses of it will readily tell you is poppycock! But this speaker was not speaking in generic terms. He was being quite specific,[1] and I am sure he assumed his questions were no-brainers for this crowd. Therefore, he paused only a moment before pushing on to his next point.

Unfortunately, I was unable to travel with him. He had led me back to the question I first began gnawing on in youth revival days. Time and tide may have washed away the theologians' questions about God's demise, but the question of what this God would have us hear and share as good news was still very much alive.

What, indeed, *is* the gospel? The good news that sixteenth-century Bible translator William Tyndale said "signyfyth good, mery, glad and joyfull tydings, that maketh a mannes hert glad, and maketh him synge, daunce, and leepe for joye."[2]

The branch of the Baptist river I knew best would say the proper reply to the speaker's question would be The Plan. But when I trotted out that answer, I did not "daunce and leepe for joye" as Tyndale would have me do. I frowned. I frowned because, among other things, this meeting had been called to discuss the shape of Christian fidelity in America's toxic political climate and, as I tried to put that inherited gospel into serious dialogue with our childish, tweeted political polarization, my heart sank. The two seemed to be speaking different languages. And, to my dismay, many of the most ardent believers in The Plan did not seem too concerned or see a theological challenge within the childishness.

Then, as I looked around the room, I saw faces—unfortunately, all of them were white—of leaders in churches where strife was predictably as present as glad hearts and dancing feet (much of this created by the very divisive political climate that had prompted this meeting). I saw good people with tired blood, leaders whose lives and presence at the meeting demonstrated they were persuaded of the relevance of God and the gospel but who were also fending off the emptiness of feeling themselves less and less relevant to this present hour, men and women whose sermonic "good news" too often landed with a thud rather than with a gasp or an amen—or even an appreciative nod. Still, whatever may

Finding the Gospel

have been true about my colleagues, my old question about the content of the gospel was shoving its way to the forefront once again.

Then, with a deep sense of gratitude, I realized that what I now understand as the gospel is significantly different from the gospel I inherited. The gospel according to The Plan had long ago been retired, at least in my own thought-world. Without even giving me the courtesy of an official notice, the library of life and print had erased that inherited gospel and given to me another understanding that I was convinced did have something to say to these times—and all times! In those stunned moments of realization, I determined to write an account of how I'd come to this new place and to describe its features.

My hesitancy, however, at that moment, and even as I now write, is that my testimony may be heard as arrogance—as though I, of all the mortals on earth, have the final word. Far from it! I am confident that many people throughout history have understood and preached this better gospel even as I am confident that my present understanding remains laughably less than the whole gospel.[3]

The truth is, no one has ever gotten the gospel completely right—it is so immense, and our thimbles are so small. But we can edge closer. We can come nearer to God's trumpets and echoing angel-song. Indeed, I believe the greatest challenge facing the American church today is the recovery of a biblical gospel—a declaration from and about God that puts a smile on one's face because it brings lively hope and keener wisdom to our soul. The church and certainly this world is in desperate need of heartening announcements of God's past and present work throughout history—ours included. Absent such credible, vision-lifting declarations, our energies are consumed in feisty fulminations or frittered away in sulking resignation to the inevitable. Our need is a reclaimed Hallelujah, a recovery of "glad and joyfull tydings that maketh a mannes hert glad."

Thomas Long, a life-long Presbyterian and arguably America's foremost teacher of preaching, appears to share my concern about the absence of the sound of good news in our churches—if it is to be measured by much current preaching. Speaking to the faculty and students of Yale Divinity School in 2006, Long admitted his judgment might be "overly harsh," but he challenged his audience to "listen to sermons being preached these days in the broad mainline churches, and see if they do not often have the hollow sound of an old oak whose living center has died and rotted away." These sermons are "an act of nostalgia," he said, with "plenty of God-talk and religious chatter …, but what seems absent is the vibrant sense of the living, divine reality.… [They are] holy sounding talk with all the edges filed away … [with] plenty of morality and good counsel but no desert bush bursting into flame." He quoted one of his keenest student's complaint that many of the sermons she heard were "like listening to something on National Public Radio, well researched, very well written prose, clever and witty in places, well voiced, but oral religious essays, nevertheless."[4]

Though my question has been about the adequacy of the gospel according to The Plan, Long was searching for *any* gospel from mainline pulpits. How could sermons be so bland if they uttered God's good news? Long titled his lecture "No News Is Bad News: God in the Present Tense." This title, surely, was a not-so-subtle wordplay that his divinity school auditors would have caught. They knew our word "gospel" translates the Greek word meaning "good news." Long was asking about the gospel content of these sermons. What *is* our gospel? Raphael Warnock, pastor of the historic Ebenezer Baptist Church in Atlanta, Georgia, in his book *The Divided Mind of the Black Church*, documents that America's black church, in its own way and forms, is also wrestling with the same question.[5]

So, the sinking heart I felt when I tried to place my inherited gospel in dialogue with our present environment is not restricted to a Baptist of Bible-belt origin like me. There is a widespread dis-ease in Christ's many-splintered church, and it has something to do with the loss of a true and credible gospel. The message heard from America's pulpits—of whatever stripe—is not registering as *important* news, let alone *good* news, or even as *news*. Though our various traditions have their own histories and explanations as to how they find themselves in this gospel-less situation, the plight is shared broadly. In consequence, our people gnaw on nutrient-free scraps of vacated hopes, smothered by the banalities of dutiful religion, solemnly awaiting the realtors' best bids for our already emptying buildings.

Is there no "word from the Lord"? I think so.

Notes

[1] Desiring to protect the multifaceted good news of the Christian message (per the Sufi saying: "The ways of God are as the number of the souls of men"), some may challenge my assumption that Christian faith has only one gospel. I would respond by agreeing that the gospel *is* multifaceted, but in its essence, it is one coherent message. Thus, how important it is to see the thing whole and correctly, lest we omit or misrepresent any attractive facet.

[2] William Tyndale, *Prologue to the New Testament, 1525.*

[3] "The evil habit of men in all times to criticize their predecessors for having seen only half of the truth hides from them their own partiality and incompleteness." H. Richard Niebuhr, *The Kingdom of God in America* (New York: Harper Torchbook, 1959), xv.

[4] Thomas G. Long, *Preaching from Memory to Hope* (Louisville, KY: Westminster John Knox, 2009), 34.

[5] Raphael G. Warnock, *The Divided Mind of the Black Church: Theology, Piety & Public Witness* (New York: New York University Press), 2014. For another assessment of the North American pulpit, see Canadian homiletician Paul Scott Wilson, *Setting Words on Fire: Putting God at the Center of the Sermon* (Nashville: Abingdon Press, 2008); his subtitle reveals his diagnosis of the problem.

CHAPTER 3

❊

A Summary of Suspicions

I have taken some ribbing across the years for my choice of reading material. Though I consider myself an avid reader, not a few of my acquaintances have been disappointed that I was not up to date on the latest, greatest book written on a subject, especially a theological subject. I plead guilty to the charge. Once upon a time I tried harder to keep up than I do now. But I eventually decided that truly good books had staying power and that they would wait for me. Besides, for a fellow who has spent his life talking from a two-thousand-year-old book, the charge of being behind the times no longer stings as much as it once did.

This said, I want now to share something I first read in 1969. In Paul Scherer's still-worthy 1965 book (See, I was four years late getting to it!), *The Word God Sent*, he referred[1] to criteria found in a still-older book published by Cambridge University Professor of Divinity, Herbert Farmer (1892–1981). Farmer released this book, *The Healing Cross*,[2] in the frantic months before the Nazi Luftwaffe began its frightful blitzkrieg upon the British mainland in 1940. In his introduction, he offered three criteria any formulation of the gospel must meet—especially in those climactic days. In my estimation, his checklist still resonates as valid and instructive:

1. *Our gospel must not be too small to be true.* It must be commensurate "with the great forces sweeping through the modern world." Those forces were and are hurricane-force international geo-political winds carrying unprecedented cultural changes, meaning that within the gospel there must be a "cosmic note ... of the Christian fellowship being called of God to be the organ of His purpose in relation to the whole process of history." Any so-called gospel that "does not ... lift men's eyes—not incidentally but inevitably—beyond the limits of their parish or their denomination, or even their own individual salvation, crucial as that is, will seem *too small to be true.*"

2. *Our gospel must not* sound *too confident to be true*. It must be marked by humility, by a readiness to admit our imperfect knowledge. The gospel's light does not banish the darkness; rather, its glory is the light it gives amid the darkness. Life and God still remain filled with mystery. "God has indeed spoken in Christ—that is the everlasting Gospel," said Farmer, "but it is *God* who has spoken" and God's fallible listeners comprehend only partially. Our proclamation is a witness, not a decree. Smugness is impermissible if our gospel is not to be judged *too confident to be true.*

3. *Our gospel must not be too easy to be true.* It must be so presented that the note of austerity is heard. "This is but to say that the Cross must be at the centre of the Message. The Cross is healing, but it does not cease to be—Cross." If our message lacks a "come and die" ingredient within its summons, it is only ecclesiastical twaddle. "If the Gospel is to fit the modern scene and to seem other than a mere twittering of birds over a volcano" the note of a "call to adventure, to danger, to heroic and costly enterprise must be heard." Otherwise, it will seem too easy to be true.

When I first read these criteria, I found them to be both devastating indictments and illuminating beacons. In the simplest of terms Farmer had put his finger on why I was struggling with my inherited gospel and also had given me guidance in my search for a better one. I can do no better now than to offer you the summary of suspicions Dr. Farmer's words began to clarify for me long ago. And, because my search for a better gospel has stretched across decades, this summary includes some of the findings and themes that inform everything else I have found.

If it's all about me, isn't it too small to be true?

When I say that my inherited gospel was too small, I am gesturing toward the high-degree of self-interest that permeates it. The crassest expression of this, of course, was in the appeal to get saved so that hell would not be one's eternal destiny. Soft-pedal my evangelistic presentations as I would, they still came down to unabashed appeals to our basic animal instincts for survival and the avoidance of suffering—especially the kind of eternal flesh-burning suffering some of my colleagues preached. I will leave it to others to haggle over what we are to believe about hell. My point is that ultimately my good news was how to escape the wrath of a bad-news God. My evangelism was anchored, therefore, in pleading with people to act in their own self-interest. But this gave me a very wobbly foundation when I then told them that its opposite—self-sacrifice—was really the will and way of God.

The same me-centered dead end appeared when I urged people to accept Jesus as their "personal" Savior and Lord. (Had we in fact stressed the *Lord* aspect of this phrase half as much as the Savior aspect, some of my objections would have evaporated. As it was, the trump card of hell dictated that the emphasis be upon Jesus as your personal SAVIOR and Lord.)

In fairness, the personally experienced aspect of faith that the word "personal" was pointing to was and is essential, a truth I will return to in a moment. But is "personal" the right word to use here, especially when, in practice, "personal" means "individual"? In other contexts, the word "personal" has connotations of one's private possession, such as a "personal" savings account. You use the word to speak of your "personal" identification number or PIN, or even your "personal" trainer. "Personal" carries overtones of something that is uniquely your own, something stored on your cell phone or in a safe-deposit box as your private possession. It is yours alone. But neither Jesus nor salvation are things we own. If anything, they own us!

The word "personal" began to be of serious concern to me when I discovered it was nowhere used in this manner in the New Testament. Scripture speaks of our Lord as the savior of the world and of us as fortunate beneficiaries of his universal grace. We are among the throngs he personally saves, but he is not just our personal savior. He is bigger than that. He is the savior of the world, and we are invited to give our little selves away to this cosmic, everlasting One. The summons is outward toward the Greater One.

However, no sooner had I begun to question the word "personal," than two other words began to disturb me even more. The verbs "accept" and "receive" were most often paired with "personal Lord and Savior." To the best of my researching skills, however, the New Testament never reports anyone "accepting" Jesus and only once speaks of "receiving" Jesus (John 1:14). In the Gospels, persons follow Jesus or give themselves to Jesus, and Paul writes of persons obeying Jesus or the gospel, or of being called to or by Jesus, but "accepting" Jesus is unheard of, and "receiving" him almost so. If it matters, Jesus' twelve disciples are never said to have "received" or "accepted" him as their personal Savior and Lord.

The discrepancy between the verbs I and my church friends were using and the verbs the New Testament used was upsetting, to say the least. All the biblical verbs had an out-going force to them; the persons being written about follow or obey or give themselves to Jesus. The direction of these biblical verbs was outward toward the Greater One, not inward toward "me." That pattern was reversed, however, when I spoke of "receiving" or "accepting" Jesus.

In day-to-day speech, when you accept or receive something, you take possession of it or agree to be responsible for it. This would suggest that Jesus is "taken in" as our possession and is made to "fit" within our life. The directional field is inward. All is flowing into "me," and "I" am the great repository! It is only one short mental step from here to a conception of myself as the larger entity, the host, and Christ as my pocketed *personal* genie—not the Lord of all that exists!

To summarize, this gospel of mine seemed to be predicated as much upon self-preservation and self-enhancement as upon God's work in Jesus of Nazareth. My sermons may outwardly have been about Jesus, but the sales pitch was all about "me." And who, in their right mind, would not want their own pocketed, personal god with promised forever-protective powers?

Martin Luther used the Latin words *incurvatus se* (curved in upon oneself) to describe unredeemed human nature. To me, too much of my gospel began to seem like a baptized version of the same malady. How was it possible to build lives that truly love

God and care for others upon a "me" foundation? This was a gospel that was just "too small."

(Examples of a too-small gospel today are "prosperity gospel" churches whose appeal is to enrich and enhance "me," and religiously laced nationalist/racist/white supremacy groups that strive to protect and preserve "me" and "my" group's dominance in society.)

On the other hand—and this is a most important counterbalance—there is an essential "me-ness" within the gospel of God! First-person possessive pronouns play a crucial role in our faith.

I must give my mother credit for reminding me of this even through her death. In the notes she left for her funeral, she made a request that the congregation sing the gospel song "I've Found a Friend." I am so glad she did; even in death she still spoke to her faith-sifting son about the personal in our faith. Because this song is unknown to most people today, here are the words of the first two stanzas:

> I've found a Friend, oh, such a Friend!
> He loved me ere I knew Him;
> He drew me with the cords of love,
> And thus He bound me to Him.
> And round my heart still closely twine
> Those ties which naught can sever,
> For I am His, and He is mine,
> Forever and forever.
>
> I've found a Friend, oh, such a Friend!
> He bled, he died to save me;
> And not alone the gift of life,
> But His own self He gave me.
> Naught that I have my own I call,
> I hold it for the Giver;
> My heart, my strength, my life, my all,
> Are His and His forever.[3]

This is one of the countless testimony songs I grew up with and still love. They are filled with first-person singular pronouns recalling the goodness of God to "me" and exulting in "my" relationship with Jesus. It is one of the great wonders of our faith that "I" matter to God. As a preacher of my youth said, "With God, no one gets lost in the crowd." Or, as the Apostle Paul left us record, it is immensely important for us to know "the Son of God who loved *me* and gave himself for *me*" (Gal. 2:20).

But notice how finely this hymn expresses this individualism. It is a two-way relationship in which Jesus has the upper hand. Note: "He loved me ere I knew Him … He drew me … He bound me … I am His … Naught that I have my own I call … My heart, my strength, my life, all, are His and His forever." Even before the declaration that "He is mine," there is the confession "I am His." Though "I" may have found Him, from that discovery onward this song is all about Him and his doing. Central to the excellence of this song is that it opens the believer to honor the "other," be they a stranger, the beggar, the prisoner, or the immigrant. "Naught that I have my own I call; I hold it for the Giver." Here "I" am empowered by "my" friendship with Jesus to be a friend to others. This religious individualism is healthily open to the "other." It displays concern for "us" and the common good of all rather than just "me."

When I was a "wet behind the ears" pastor, I did not yet recognize the downstream effects of self-centered religious individualism. I now know this is a virus that creates more than pastoral headaches and church splits. If the religious orientation of thousands is an unchecked "me" orientation, painful cultural consequences follow. It can lead to the selfish and potentially self-righteously vicious, me-centered politics indicted by David Brooks, columnist for the *New York Times*. Brooks says that for the last sixty years "the worship of the self has been the central preoccupation of our culture—molding the self, investing in the self, expressing the self," creating a societal "catastrophe."

> When a whole society is built around self-preoccupation, its members become separated from one another, divided and alienated. And that is what has happened to us.… The rot we see in our politics is caused by a rot in our moral and cultural foundations—in the way we relate to one another, in the way we see ourselves as separable from one another, in the individualistic values that have become the water in which we swim.[4]

Brooks goes on to note that people eventually rebel against the isolation and meaninglessness of this "hyper-individualism" by joining a partisan tribe—a group whose glue is mutual distrust of the "other," a tribalism where "it is always us versus them, friend or enemy, destroy or be destroyed. Anger is the mode."[5] Clearly, he is describing the current state of our culture. To my ears he is also voicing the need for a gospel that is not as me-centered as the culture.

Looking back, I must wonder if the gospel of The Plan, preached in all good faith and sincerity by pastors like me, did not do much to fund our sad societal tribalism. Yes, the gospel according to The Plan gave us an explainable and marketable gospel, but it was a gospel that carried within it the seeds of selfishness. Rather than calling others to give themselves away, the message was to get themselves "saved" and thereby assure themselves of heaven's joys without a drop of sweat for, or even interest in, others. This gospel saved "souls"—whatever that means—but left the saved as lost as ever in a wide, deep sea of self-centeredness. And it baptized the whole package in the name of the Father, Son, and Holy Spirit! If this verdict be extreme, I nonetheless read with embarrassed contrition Jesus' words about Pharisees who "cross sea and land to make a single convert, and … make the new convert twice as much a child of hell" (Matt. 23:15).

If it's Bible-lite, isn't it too confident to be true?

Years ago, after attending a large convocation of Baptists during which the gospel song "Saved! Saved! Saved!" was sung, a church musician friend of mine erupted in disgust: "There is nothing more repulsive than hearing three thousand Baptists braying at the top of their lungs: 'I'm Saved! Saved! Saved!'"

He knew, of course, the blessing of deep assurance of God's forgiving mercy. It was just the "braying" about it that aggravated him so.[6] (And it could be that he'd done business with enough of them to know that not all three thousand acted like the saved are supposed to!) Maya Angelou said she was always taken aback when people walked up to her and told her they were Christians. Her first response was the question "Already?" It seemed to her "a lifelong endeavor to try to live the life of a Christian," and that it was "in the search itself that one finds the ecstasy."[7]

There is indeed an essential modesty, a reverential humility, if you will, that clothes true Christian spirituality. Big-britches swaggering never fits. We walk by faith and not by sight. A cocksure "been there, done that" attitude that checks off spiritual accomplishments as a mountain climber checks off peaks scaled is unseemly. Though the Bible nourishes strong, deep convictions, it also urges us to keep doors and windows open for more light and more wisdom, admonishing us to "never be rash with your mouth, nor let your heart be quick to utter a word before God, for God is in heaven, and you upon earth" (Eccl. 5:2). It seems to me that, if nothing else, the Bible is an extended plea to walk humbly with God.

So my church musician friend had a very valid point. There is a fine but most important line between quiet confidence in the gracious promises of God and a presumptuous arrogance that reveals questionable respect for God. Quiet confidence in God comes from trusting the word of a capable Friend. Presumptuous arrogance comes from having a notarized contract.

As I lived my way into the role of pastor, the gospel of The Plan seemed more and more to be most at home in the latter category. It was as though salvation were a transactional "deal" made with God to assure one's heavenly hereafter. ("God, I will believe these three things and you—in exchange—will see to it that I don't go to hell.") And, of course, if that really is the "deal," no ensuing relationship with God is needed or expected.

The contract has been agreed to. You are "saved"—case closed. It all seems so neat, tidy, final, ... and suspicious!

On the other hand, the more I lived into the role of pastor, the more I learned of the richness, the density, and the mystery of God's ways with humankind. The Bible was proving to be ever so much more fascinating and multi-layered than the gospel according to The Plan indicated. I'd already determined that "personal" and "accept" and "receive" were not dominant New Testament words. So, I began to wonder just how biblical The Plan itself really was.

My first discovery about that question came from the discipline of church history. There I learned that The Plan of salvation came to birth only in nineteenth-century American revivalism. (I have a good friend who insists it appeared first in the thought of the British evangelist George Whitefield [1714–1770]. I will let my friend duke it out with other scholars who date it to the revivalists of the next century. Either way, the gospel of The Plan is a "Johnny come lately" to the story of Christianity.) It is the shorthand form of the message preached by evangelists such as Charles Finney (1792–1875) and later Dwight L. Moody (1837–1899) and Billy Sunday (1862–1935) and more recently Billy Graham (1918–2018).

From the 1,189 chapters of the Bible and nearly 2,000 years of Christian existence, zealous evangelical pioneers distilled a terse, four-point summary of the Christian message. Never in Christian history had anyone attempted such a feat, but a bustling nation needed the Savior, and the American entrepreneurial mindset was determined to provide a quick and easily understood statement or, to be crass about it, a straightforward "sales pitch." The Plan of Salvation was the result.

With this birth certificate in hand, I next noticed with some surprise the creedal nature of The Plan. It was an evangelistic creed with a concluding action step! The creedal, catechetical affirmations are: All have sinned, the wages of sin is death, and Christ died for your sins. The action step is: Accept Jesus as your personal Lord and Savior. A heartfelt "I believe" is required for each proposition. An irony of this is that the creators of The Plan were from that branch of the church most suspicious of the use of creeds—especially when persons harbored the notion that believing right doctrines could save you.[8]

I encountered a greater irony, however, when I realized that The Plan, which I had assumed was a distillation of the New Testament's gospel, was only a fragment from the gospel according to Paul. The Plan's statements rest upon four verses selected from Paul's letter to the Romans. Jesus the Savior is never cited. The Plan, therefore, gives us the gospel according to Paul, not Jesus. This fact alone certainly did not render The Plan worthless—after all, Paul was the Lord's apostle and I had no reason to question his worthiness as a spokesperson for his Lord—but it did put a question mark around The Plan.

That question mark began to flash with warning lights for me during a series of sermons on the Roman letter that I preached to a longsuffering congregation in the

1970s. I am confident those sermons were not the clearest or most interesting homiletic exercises that flock had ever heard, but their preacher profited immensely from preparing them! Among the many things I learned in the course of studying for those sermons was that the verses The Plan excerpts and elevates are not the pivotal verses in Romans. When read in context, those verses play an important role, but not the ultimate role. They are not the summit; they are stepping stones *to* the summit, paving stones *toward* Paul's understanding of the Christian gospel.

That gospel according to Paul, which I began to discover in my Romans immersion and then from countless other studies, is the message that the God of the Jews had proved God's lovingkindness to all persons—not just to God's chosen people, the Jews!—in the person and work of Jesus, the Jewish messiah, creating in this messiah "one new humanity" (Eph. 2:15) from the many tribes and tongues of this festering world (consider Ephesians, Galatians, 1 and 2 Corinthians, along with Romans). Paul's good news was that ancient dividing walls between God and humankind—and between all the earth's peoples—were abolished in Christ who now reigns as "the firstborn within a large family" (Rom. 8:29) drawn from all these disparate peoples. Paul's gospel was the announcement of the fruition of God's steadfast, ages-old intention to shower blessing upon all the people of the world or, as he put it in his opening paragraph, to bring "salvation to *everyone* who has faith, to the *Jew* first and *also to the Greek*" (Rom. 1:16, emphases added).

Unfortunately, not a hint of this wider-screen view surfaces in The Plan. Its creators selected four or five verses that supported a "personal Lord and Savior" salvation and ignored Romans' global, audacious, "every nation and tribe and color and tongue" gospel of reconciliation.[9] Unheard is the news of God overcoming ancient barriers of race and sex and culture and nation and economic class, a gospel about a "new creation" of the whole cosmos! All we hear from The Plan is an atomistic "personal" gospel of "just Jesus and me."

My conclusion was that The Plan's propositions find their proper place as stout timbers within the scaffolding of this grander gospel; they are worthy planks used in the building of a greater superstructure, but they are an inadequate summary of it. Indeed, cherry-picked from their context, they become a hollowing reduction of Paul's big picture concept of God's plan for the cosmos. They become prooftexts to bolster a concept of salvation that has more in common with a legal contract than the discovery of "a Friend, oh such a Friend, who not alone the gift of life, but His own self he gave me."

With some jubilation and not a little anxiety, it was becoming clearer and clearer to me that the gospel of The Plan was too much a child of human contrivance. It was Bible-lite, and the cocksure business-like way it was deployed seemed contradictory to the Bible's amazed but quiet confidence in God's surprising grace.

In subsequent years I awakened to yet another facet of the Bible-lite nature of my inherited gospel. In all my growing-up years the Old Testament had seemed like a foreign land, so very distant from my Jesus-centered New Testament. Sure, the Old Testament had some beautiful psalms within it and some great tales—as Hollywood proved with blockbuster films about Samson and Delilah and Moses and the Ten Commandments—and an occasional useful passage for inclusion in Christmas and Easter devotions, but for the most part the Old Testament was a tedious encyclopedia of ancient wars, palace intrigues, and unhappy prophets raging about everybody's sins. They were interesting stories perhaps, if such stuff interested you—and interminably long—but what they had to do with the gospel of The Plan was difficult to see. In all those endless pages, getting saved never came into clear view!

But eventually I came to see that the problem was not with the Old Testament; the problem was with The Plan! It did not mesh well with its surroundings; it was a foreign "thing" stitched onto the Bible's continuous Old Testament-New Testament story. In that story Jesus is the culmination of the Old Testament's story and what Jesus says is in continuity with what his prophet ancestors had said. The people who were there and listened to Jesus surmised he was "John the Baptist [raised from the dead], but others Elijah, and still others Jeremiah or one of the prophets" (Matt. 16:14). They knew he fit within the prophetic stream of voices calling for public and personal righteousness, for a people who live in God-fearing respect for one another. But my inherited gospel said Jesus was the soul-saving, heaven-guaranteeing personal Savior I needed—which, indeed, he was and is—but little if anything was said by my gospel about what the man stood for and preached, which was a righteousness even more searing and soaring than his prophet-predecessors had preached. Sadly, I was beginning to understand that my concentration upon The Plan not only sidelined 70 percent of the Bible from me, but it also misrepresented Jesus. This supremely confident, downsized gospel was biblically askew.

A few years' distance from these discoveries has, however, permitted me to see that this Bible-lite gospel did and does have the great virtue of simplicity. It speaks in clear words a crucial, central portion of the Christian gospel, namely, that Jesus died for our sins. The theme of God's love and grace for sinners, the assurance of God's forgiveness, the hope of eternal life—all these basic facts are within The Plan. Even a child can grasp the story that is told in this presentation, and, as one who "accepted" Jesus and was baptized at age eight, I remain grateful for the simple gate into the gospel world that the Bible-lite Plan provided. It continues to do so for many seekers, and therefore I cannot speak contemptuously of it.

I can, however, add a warning that this simplicity carries a danger within it. It can lull one into imagining that this is all there is, that in having said "yes" to The Plan all is resolved and our God-relationship is now taken care of. I will have much more to say about this, but here I note that by early adulthood my own understanding of the faith had expanded so greatly that I seriously wondered if I ought to seek re-baptism. The watery experience of an eight-year-old now seemed almost like a baptism into a foreign faith, bearing faint resemblance to what I later understood to be the gospel of Jesus. Simplism, in other words, has its virtue in providing a toehold, but it too often becomes a dead end, concealing the necessity of the journey it must launch. To be sure, Bible-lite beginnings have launched some grand and ever-deepening lives of faith, but it is worth asking why we would continue to distribute maps that we know life and the Lord will have to correct.

Duke Divinity School's Ellen Davis has a clarifying light to shine into this thicket, light that would have been wonderfully liberating to me years ago. Even so, her words are a welcome late confirmation of my conclusion about the Bible-lite character of my inherited gospel. Davis challenges any reading of the Bible that understands the question "Are you saved?" to be the single theme of the gospel and the Christian life. That question, she insists, "puts me, or what God has done for me, at the center of religious interest." However,

> [T]he Old Testament clarifies the fact that the Bible as a whole is relentlessly *theo*centric. Its pervasive focus is not on salvation, either personal or corporate, but rather revelation of the nature and will of God. From a biblical perspective, salvation is a subcategory of revelation—or better, salvation is a consequence of revelation fully received. This is a regular pattern in the Bible: when God's Person or Presence is made known to some human agent and God's will is fully accepted and therefore becomes operative in our world, then salvation is what happens for God's people. The culmination of the pattern is Jesus' perfect knowledge of his Father, demonstrated in his obedient life and his death, through which salvation comes to the whole world.[10]

The truth and helpfulness of Davis' statement will be illustrated often in the following pages. For the moment, I commend her wisdom to you as a scholar's confirmation of what this fumbling pastor was sensing: Any gospel worthy of my confidence must be anchored not in doctrinal propositions but in the person, character, and work of the God revealed in holy scripture. I must read those scriptures listening for what they were telling me about God and what God was up to.

If it leapfrogs today, isn't it too easy to be true?

During my years as a pastor I was asked on a few occasions to conduct a funeral service for a person who, sadly, had no known church connection and scant record of ever extending himself for anyone's aid or comfort. Yet, if blessed Aunt Sally could conjure up some foggy memory of dead Arnold "giving his heart to Jesus" in a revival meeting out at

A Summary of Suspicions

Mount Pisgah Church when he was six or seven, the family members breathed easier and commissioned me to preach dead Arnold into heaven. Their only apparent interest was getting Arnold inside the pearly gates. In stupefaction I asked myself: Does no one care about Arnold's forfeiture of a life of potentially caring influence, the tragedy of this man's underlived existence? It would seem the only reason anyone might concern themselves with God was to avoid hell. And, God help me, I often surmised that was all the family thought God was interested in.

This ugly surmise became a burning issue for me: What *is* God interested in? The gospel of The Plan surely taught that God was interested in clean living (according to local, middle-class virtue), tithing, and charitable deeds, but the overall message was that what really, truly interested God was rescuing souls from hell and receiving them into heaven. This was the relentless emphasis and drumbeat of my denomination and churchly ethos. Young pastors like me quickly learned that an annually impressive wad of heaven-assuring baptisms was like aces in a gambler's hand. If you had enough of 'em, you couldn't lose! Crochety deacons were muzzled if the baptistry was in frequent use. My church's baptistry, however, was never that crowded. I could not with good conscience fan hell's flames hot enough to activate listeners' survival instincts, nor could I adorn heaven with enough fine furniture and lovely angels to make it a must-see destination.

In fact, heaven itself began to be a puzzle to me. I noticed that most every funeral service I conducted included a reading from John 14: "In my Father's house there are many dwelling places ... I go to prepare a place for you ... so that where I am, there you may be also." When I asked myself why these words were so frequently read, I had to admit that the reason was more profound than that these are overwhelmingly beautiful and reassuring words. The additional, stunning reason was that they were about the only memorable words we have from Jesus about heaven!

The plain truth is, Jesus did not say that much about heaven. The Gospels indicate he said more about many other subjects—prayer, obedience, fear, wealth, etc.—than about heaven. But if getting into heaven is the main goal of our lives, would not he have given greater attention to it than this? Thankfully, other voices within the New Testament addressed this void—at least enough to assure me that heaven was not a hoax. I was and am content to believe that the God who raised Jesus from the dead does not allow death to end our existence. There is more to come! But still, I had to ask why—if this is the major goal and endpoint—why Jesus himself talked so little about the heaven we sang and talked about so much.[11] Thus I returned to the question of what God was really interested in.

By this time, I had ventured into the world of the American Baptist Churches of the USA. When I was a boy we had called them "Northern Baptists," and, in those earlier days, they were numerically strongest in the North and Northeast. But in the 1980s I became the pastor of a church in Missouri that had a Northern Baptist heritage. By that date the Northern Baptists had changed their name to American Baptist Churches

USA. What changed for me, though, as I lived and worked among them, was my way of hearing the Bible. For the first time in my church life I began to hear the word "justice."

Justice, I discovered, is like a bell that cannot be unrung. Justice is a word that cannot be unheard, once it is ever heard. The prophet Amos said it best: "Let justice roll down like waters, and righteousness like an everflowing stream" (5:24). Though that verse had always been in my Bible; American Baptists helped me hear it ringing throughout the Bible.

They helped me hear it in Moses' laws, in the Psalmist's songs and prayers, in the prophets' anguish, in Jesus' teachings, in the Epistles, and certainly in the Revelation to John. From across the Bible I began to learn that God's passion for seeing justice practiced on earth was a theme more frequently heard than promises of life everlasting. I became convinced that somewhere in all our salvation talk something must be said about the God whose cries for justice, integrity, mercy, and neighborliness are audible on page after page of the book. This world, this life, this creation, this history, this wondrous-tenuous mixture of peoples and cultures and needs—this also was surely a part of what God was interested in! Justice demanded a hearing.

And that brings me back to poor Arnold, that fabricated fellow I was commissioned to preach into heaven a few paragraphs ago. I finally came to a painful conclusion about the gospel that young Arnold had heard out there at the Mount Pisgah revival. It had done him a double injustice.

First, it had done him the injustice of removing God as an essential actor in his life. By granting a seven-year-old his guaranteed transfer ticket from hell to heaven, it told him the one big God-issue of his life was taken care of, forever. So I ask you, who really needs God if you've already got the biggie taken care of? With one "yes," young Arnold had hit the jackpot—and this, before finishing the second grade! In terms of spiritual vitality and life experience, he had simultaneously been "born again" and also rendered "dead on arrival" by that revival decision. God as a dynamic factor and guide for his life was left as an option, not a necessity.

This way of getting saved still seems to me like a cruel spiritual version of the "curse" that often leads children of the super-rich to dissipation and even suicide. "My life was never destined to be quite happy," lamented William K. "Willie" Vanderbilt, grandson of the fabulously wealthy Commodore Vanderbilt. All that familial wealth "left me with nothing to hope for, with nothing definite to see or strive for."[12] The title of "poor little rich kids" might well fit many Christians who came to faith through the kind of gospel Mount Pisgah and I had been preaching. We got our converts all dressed up for a party that wouldn't commence until they died!

The second injustice Arnold suffered was parallel to the first. The significance of the rest of his life had just been leapfrogged. Everything between Mount Pisgah Church and the mortuary was now shorn of lustrous consequence; Arnold was "just passin' through."

This was because salvation according to The Plan spoke only of rescue *from* the clutches of evil; it spoke very little about being called *to* useful engagement in the good work of God. Salvation in biblical perspective, as I was beginning to learn, means receiving an earthly vocation just as much as it means making a heavenly reservation! It means receiving a life with meaning and with meaningful work to do.

The assignment given to Adam/Eve to serve as God's image (that is, representatives and reflectors of God into the world) and as caretakers of God's garden tells me God meant for humans to function as priests and as stewards of creation. This is the human purpose, our vocation/calling. The same vocation/calling was, in different words, given to Israel. It was to be "a priestly kingdom and a holy nation" (Exod. 19:6), a people whose way of life witnessed to and gave flesh to God's character and work. God rescued Israel for meaningful work, not just to rest in the Promised Land.

So, in this additional way, Arnold was cheated—cheated out of an understanding of God's this-worldly purpose for us. The gospel he heard was about what God could do for "me" rather than the good work God might be calling Arnold to do and, in its doing, to find life at its fullest. Therefore, the great potential of Arnold's earthly life was discounted. He did not hear the word "justice" as God's call to divine service.

Indeed, one of the saddest aspects of the gospel according to The Plan is its silence concerning a holy, divine purpose running through history, the purpose I had begun to call "justice." God's purpose is more than this, of course, but "justice" at least refers to a holistic, earth-and-heaven vision and concern. And, though it is not well enough known, many of America's evangelistic pioneers included "justice" concerns within their evangelistic witness. Some, like Charles Grandison Finney, were ardent opponents of slavery. Finney's ministry was also characterized by notable embryonic steps toward women's rights, racial equality, and education reform. But Finney's bi-focal vision (and not his alone, by any means!) of a gospel that was both "personal" in the deepest sense and "social" in even a political sense did not endure.[13]

In its place there emerged an exclusive interest in a personal salvation dealing only with "me" and my after-death destiny, a salvation that has been described as having a "detached spirituality (a heavenly mindedness with a questionable earthly use) and an escapist eschatology (leaving the world and going to heaven)."[14]

By the time I became a pastor in 1962, pastors knew that swift and often fierce criticism—and more!—could come from the pews if their sermons included any "justice" references. I first experienced this in the form of anonymous letters protesting favorable comments I made from the pulpit about Martin Luther King Jr. and against the forms of racism he and all Americans were then confronting. However, no burning crosses ever showed up on my lawn, nor was I awakened in the middle of the night by threatening phone calls as many others were. No doubt that was because the churches I served had been previously served by courageous pastors who had taken much of that heat.

A story told about one of those pastors concerned a well-known church member who angrily exited a Sunday service in which, for the second time, a black man was present. On his way out the member growled to the head usher: "I'll be back when you get that son-of-a-bitch out of here!" "That colored guy?" the usher asked. "No! That blankety-blank preacher!"

My first experience with this kind of anger came the day after I preached a sermon in which I said there was no reason women should not serve as deacons in the church. (I did not dare suggest they might also serve as pastors!) A red-faced rebuke from Deacon Dunn awaited me at nine o'clock the next morning. He spoke, I knew, for many. It should not surprise you, therefore, that my tenure in that church was short and his rebuke was enough, I confess, for me to forego much further agitation in that church for sharing leadership with women. I knew, as did all of us within the orbit of The Plan, that if we dabbled too much outside The Plan's parameters, we would hear the protest: "Stick to the gospel and stay away from these 'social issues'!" Translated, that meant, "Leapfrog the present. Talk about the tomorrow-world of heaven and hell." And, of course, that was and remains the easy way out. It is the way that leaves "the world" free to go to hell, unchallenged.

Too little has changed since then. Take any "social issue" of America's more recent history, and it is likely that most Plan-conversant pulpits were and are silent concerning them, or, if vocal, they advocate only traditional, change-averse positions.[15] Generally speaking, "social issues" are still considered an unnecessary distraction from the gospel and certainly a threat to the unity of the church. To my mind, the culprit throughout all of this was and remains an inadequate understanding of the gospel.

Said differently, I was becoming more and more impressed by the repeated pattern of God's coming to us rather than our going to God. If I dare to express this in questionable spatial terms, the biblical pattern seemed to be God's "descent" *into* this world rather than a human "ascent" *to* another world. For example, God's will and word for Israel at her birth came down from the heights of Mount Sinai. The words of her prophets are "as the rain and the snow [that] come down from heaven" (Isa. 55:10). And is not Jesus' incarnation the epicenter of this descent of God? Jesus "emptied himself and took on the form of a slave ... he humbled himself" (Phil. 2:7-8). The birthing hour of the church arrives when the Spirit comes down "from heaven" (Acts 2:2) on disciples. Jesus taught those disciples and us to pray: "Thy kingdom come; thy will be done on earth as in heaven." And our holy book concludes with John seeing "the holy city, New Jerusalem, coming down out of heaven from God" (Rev. 21:2). Once again, it is a matter of "lines of direction," and in this instance the Bible's major plot lines reveal a repeated pattern of "up there" coming "down here." In sum, the gist of the storyline seemed to be a descent of the heavenly, not an escape into the eternal. In God's book, today and here and now matter just as much as tomorrow. So, it was clear to me that what I was searching for was:

… a gospel that spoke of this one world and its social/political wounds along with our individual/spiritual brokenness
… a gospel that spoke of justice and of gracious inner healing
… a grander gospel that reunited these separated worlds
… a gospel that spoke to the individual self about the upward and inward dimensions of life (spiritual/devotional) and to the self-in-community about the outward dimensions of life (social/ethical)
… a gospel that would bring personal healing through the mercies of God and also generate social hope through the promises of God, assuring believers that not even death can terminate God's love affair with us and all God's creation

***

I have now told you some of my second thoughts, a summary of my suspicions about my own inherited ways of understanding the gospel. Its formulaic phrases and ideas were and are not heretical; God graciously has deigned to use them in amazing ways—indeed, I would not be writing these words now had God not worked through them to reach me. But with every passing year I became more deeply convinced that this way of framing and speaking the gospel was marred by limited and limiting concepts.

Where then was I to turn for a more adequate gospel? Well, in that same book in which Herbert Farmer provided the three criteria used here, I found additional help. Farmer insisted there that the gospel's meaning could not "be grasped by mere repetition of fixed and ancient formulae." Phrases that once carried powerful meaning, he said, lose their potency with the passing of time and the emergence of new cultural forms. "The adjustment of the Message to its environment," he wrote, "is partly a matter of terminology, but it is even more a matter of adjustment of emphasis, of bringing into the foreground what has hitherto been in the background, of making dominant what for a longer or shorter period has been a hardly noticed, though never truly absent, overtone."[16] Therefore, Farmer said, the church's enduring task is to practice the wisdom of the householder in Jesus' parable (Matt. 13:52) who brings out of his treasure things new and old, depending upon the present need.

In wonderful confirmation of Jesus' parable of treasures old and new, I discovered bit by bit and year by year the better gospel I sought. I discovered it in a treasure deposited in the biblical storehouse by no less than Jesus of Nazareth. That treasure is what he called the good news of the kingdom (or reign) of God.

Notes

[1] Paul Scherer, *The Word God Sent* (New York: Harper & Row, 1965), ch. 3, "The Credibility and Relevance of the Gospel."

[2] Herbert H. Farmer, *The Healing Cross: Further Studies in the Christian Interpretation of Life* (New York: Charles Scribner's Sons, 1939). All citations are taken from the "Introduction," pp. v-x.

[3] J.G. Small, "I've Found a Friend."

[4] David Brooks, *The Second Mountain: The Quest for a Moral Life* (New York: Random House, 2019), xx, xxii.

[5] Ibid., 299.

[6] Blunt Methodist that he is, Will Willimon writes: "When a pious kid smugly announced, just before pickup softball at fourth-grade recess, "Last night I got saved. I went and gave my life to Christ. I'm rede-e-e-med," I wondered, *why would you boast?* You can't give something to somebody who already owns what's being given. All that smart-ass little Baptist had done was to say yes to the obvious, to admit to the way things are, to allow himself to be loved." *Accidental Preacher: A Memoir* (Grand Rapids, MI: Eerdmans, 2019), 36-37.

[7] Maya Angelou, *Wouldn't Take Nothin' For My Journey Now* (New York: Random House, 1993), 173.

[8] In my "believer's church" tradition, membership in the church requires the individual's testimony of personal faith. Hence, a heartfelt "I do" to The Plan's statements regarding salvation was a natural fit for entrance into the church. For many people, however, such belief was a product of gentle nurture rather than of dramatic conversion.

[9] The Letter to the Romans continues to be a lively interpretive subject for New Testament scholars. Scot McKnight and Joseph B. Modica, eds., *Preaching Romans: Four Perspectives* (Grand Rapids, MI: Eerdmans, 2019) provides explanatory essays and sample sermons from four current perspectives: the "Lutheran," the "New," the "Apocalyptic," and the "Participationist." The perspective I have presented is within the "New" category. See also Beverly Roberts Gaventa, *When in Romans: An Invitation to Linger with the Gospel According to Paul* (Grand Rapids, MI: Baker Academic, 2016).

[10] Ellen F. Davis and Richard B. Hays, eds., *The Art of Reading Scripture* (Grand Rapids, MI: Eerdmans, 2003), 21.

[11] I subsequently came upon Canadian theologian Douglas John Hall's summation: "With only a few exceptions, and those tangential, biblical literature maintains an astonishing disinterest in the so-called afterlife. It is content to leave heaven to God, and hell too." That aptly sums up what I came to believe about the matter. Hall, *The Cross in Our Context: Jesus and the Suffering World* (Minneapolis: Fortress Press, 2003), 218.

[12] Cited by Michael McGerr, *A Fierce Discontent: The Rise and Fall of the Progressive Movement in America* (New York: Oxford University Press, 2003), 35.

[13] This "Great Reversal" came when followers of The Plan sensed that theological liberalism valued social betterment over personal regeneration. See George M. Marsden, *Fundamentalism and American Culture* (Oxford University Press, 2006).

[14] N.T. Wright, *The Day the Revolution Began* (New York: HarperOne, 2016), 35.

[15] Marvin A. McMickle, *Where Have All the Prophets Gone? Reclaiming Prophetic Preaching in America* (Cleveland, OH: Pilgrim Press, 2006), incisively notes the choice of conservative churches to champion safe, politically determined "moral values" rather than the broader and more indicting biblical insistence upon justice.

[16] Farmer, *The Healing Cross*, v.

PART 2

✽

Discovery

"... and thou, O Lord, art more than they."

"One phrase sums up the meaning of our Lord's mission and message. It is the Kingdom of God. If we can discover what Jesus meant by it, we have the key to the Gospels and, indeed, to the whole New Testament."[1]
—*Archibald Hunter,* The Work and Words of Jesus

I recently had the challenge of listening to a friend who had just purchased a new cellphone and was determined to tell me all about its cutting-edge features. That same week I winced my way through a report from an acquaintance who had discovered a new tattoo artist and wanted to show and tell me all the amazing things this guy could do with vulnerable flesh. In both cases, the reporters' enthusiasm was clearer than the explanations.

My goal in this section of the book is to convey to you my enthusiasm about the reign of God and also give you some understandable explanation of it—all the while hoping I will be more successful in both desires than my techie and tattooed friends were! Discovering this kingdom key to the Bible's message has been a gift from God to me, and I sincerely hope you hear that delight in my words. But I also want the next pages to contain enough substantive biblical content that you hear something more than just my delight. You deserve to know what I see in this teaching and why I think it speaks a better word than my inherited gospel.

So, I am about to put on an additional hat, that of an "explainer," in addition to the "fellow pilgrim" hat I've been wearing. This means I am inviting you to become a student, as I have been, and invest some grey matter in the material I'll be covering. This also means that on occasion I will cite a scholar's words to corroborate my statements. If you are sensitive about such things, you may even note that some of the sources I cite are "dated," meaning they were published before the year 2000. I do, of course, cite more recent authors (the thought of N.T. Wright, for instance, is more pervasive than the footnotes indicate), but ultimately this section of the book is not about demonstrating mastery of this season's academic debates but about telling you of a credible good new gospel to be found on the pages of a nineteen-hundred-year-old New Testament. All my "authorities," be they scholars or just everyday saints, were and remain a part of my story of discovery. They are bridges that have helped me cross deep rivers. I pray you will discover similar bridges—and that maybe this book might become one!

Here is my plan. I begin by asking why, if this kingdom idea is so central, we have heard so little about it and where Jesus himself got the idea (chs. 4–5). Then I'll try to explain what the New Testament means by this term (chs. 6–7). My next task is to show you how Jesus inaugurated this kingdom (chs. 8–11) and how its message for today might be restated (ch. 12). Finally, I'll offer some comparisons of this gospel with that of The Plan to demonstrate why I think this gospel is so much better (ch. 13).

Note

[1] Archibald Hunter, *The Work and Words of Jesus* (Philadelphia: Westminster Press, 1950), 68.

CHAPTER 4

✳

The Elephant in the Sanctuary: God's Kingdom

My first clash with the kingdom of God came when I was in my mid-thirties and only minutes after I had preached a sermon from the Sermon on the Mount. A deacon in this, my new pastorate, walked up to me and said: "That sermon you just preached has no place in our pulpit."

I was stunned. My mind raced back over the sermon, searching for unintended offensive content. Finding none, I stammered: "Really? I was just dealing with the Sermon on the Mount."

"Yes. But the Sermon on the Mount pertains only to the Kingdom Dispensation. We are in the Church, the Spirit Dispensation now, not the Kingdom Dispensation!"

In my best pastorally disguised bafflement, I said: "Huh?"

That is when I received my first lesson in what is known as Premillennial Dispensationalism, a schema of interpreting the Bible that professes to "rightly divide the word of truth" (2 Tim. 2:15 KJV). The operative word for this schema truly is "divide" because Premillennial Dispensationalism divides the biblical story into five dispensations or five successive periods of history, in each of which God displays a different way of relating to humankind. My error, according to my correcting deacon, was that I had used a text applicable only to the Kingdom Dispensation. He assured me we were not living in that dispensation!

I had, of course, heard of Premillennial Dispensationalism before. You could not grow up in an Oklahoma Baptist church in those days without hearing some of its ideas, even if not its tongue-twisting name. But I had never paid any attention to its teachings, and this meant, I can assure you, that my introduction to the kingdom was unpleasant—at least the kingdom as taught in the footnotes of the popular Scofield Reference Bible. Those footnotes were the Bible my self-appointed teacher was using to correct me. In my youthful impatience, I soon dismissed his complaint as foolishness. (That probably explains why he and I never "bonded," and why his followers did not grieve when soon "the Lord called me elsewhere.") And perhaps that also partially explains why the kingdom of God remained too long a non-starter for me. I heard it as being a divisive term mired in hair-splitting, fundamentalist gobbledygook.

From my classroom studies, though, I had learned a little about the kingdom. I knew, for instance, that there was no difference in meaning between the expressions "kingdom of God" and "kingdom of heaven." The latter phrase had come from the Jews' giant-size respect for the name and even the word "God." So, quite often, they would substitute "heaven" for God. Both meant the same thing, although, across the centuries, some readers incorrectly began to assume that "of heaven" signified that both terms were referring to life after death—in heaven.

Truth be told, I guess I was among that number. I understood both terms to be a fuzzy, Bible-pretty way of referring to heaven. Though I cannot remember when I began to question that assumption, it likely began as I understood how little Jesus said about some things (such as heaven) and how much he said about others (for example, justice and this kingdom).

That's when it began to soak in that the words kingdom, kingdom of God, and kingdom of heaven appear sixty-seven times in the first three Gospels—that's an average of almost once per chapter in sixty-eight chapters. Baseball hitters would kill for an average like that!

At some point I also noted that Mark, generally thought to be the first written of the gospels, says Jesus' first public words were kingdom of God words: "Jesus came to Galilee, proclaiming the good news of God, and saying, 'The time is fulfilled, and the kingdom of God has come near; repent and believe in the good news'" (1:14). The Gospel of Matthew says the same thing (4:17).

John, the fourth Gospel, joins in, most notably in Jesus' famous conversation with Nicodemus: "No one can see the kingdom of God without being born from above" (3:3). However, John seems to have preferred the expression "eternal life" to indicate the same thing the other three meant by the kingdom of God. If that is so, we can throw in seventeen more references to our tally, granting a grand total of eighty-four references to this kingdom in the four gospels!

Add to this that the Acts of the Apostles tells us the resurrected Jesus continued to speak about this kingdom (1:3) until the day of his ascension, and concludes its story of the exploits of the early church with the Apostle Paul in Rome "proclaiming the kingdom of God and teaching about the Lord Jesus Christ" (28:31). Clearly, neither the term nor the idea died in the four gospels. It was alive and well years later.

So, if frequency of appearances proves anything, I discovered that no other term or subject in the Gospels—not heaven or hell or salvation or church (not even the Stewardship Committee's favorite term "financial pledge card")—no other term or word or name except "Jesus" gets more New Testament ink than the kingdom of God.

I also assured myself that though the precise expression "kingdom of God" does not appear in the Old Testament, the idea of God as king is ubiquitous. "The LORD has established his throne in the heavens, and his kingdom rules over all" (Ps. 103:19) is a commonplace idea in that testament. "The LORD reigns!" is a similar, frequent refrain. Once my eyes had been opened to see it, I realized this kingdom idea was no outlier to the Bible. It was a dominant thread running through the entire book.

The Plan, however, never mentioned it. My inherited gospel gave it no ink at all—not even in the footnotes! I still did not know what the term meant, but its absence from my gospel was disturbing.

But for that matter, the term did not appear that much in the church life I knew. Yes, you might hear the phrase sprinkled occasionally into some prayers as almost a throwaway line and in the (then very infrequent) congregational recitation of the Lord's Prayer. And it found a voice in some of our hymns.

"Lead on, O King Eternal" comes to mind: "for not with swords loud clashing, nor roll of stirring drums; with deeds of love and mercy the heavenly kingdom comes." "A Mighty Fortress" also has that great line: "the body they may kill, God's truth abideth still; his kingdom is forever." And certainly, there was Timothy Dwight's 1801 hymn, "I Love Thy Kingdom, Lord," which unfortunately equates the kingdom with the church.

Still, not to be ugly about it, the hymns I knew mostly tipped their hat to this theme or cleverly used "kingdom" to complete the poet's rhyming scheme (it works well with wisdom, freedom, and ransom, or, if just one syllable is needed, it works with come, sum, or even dumb). Thus, mysteriously, the major theme of Jesus' teaching and preaching—and a major theme of the Bible itself—had slipped out of sight and sound in my sector of the church.

Homiletician David Buttrick drew attention to the same absence in the sermons and worship of mainline churches as long ago as 1996. That year he began his contribution to the prestigious Lyman Beecher Lectures on Preaching at Yale Divinity School by asking, "Whatever happened to the kingdom of God?" He continued: "All of a sudden in the twentieth century, the kingdom of God seems to have vanished from our preaching. Like Lewis Carroll's remarkable Cheshire cat, the kingdom has faded from sight, and not even a smile remains."[1]

The silence Buttrick noted has not been broken often, if it all, since he asked about it. Though I'm not aware of what is preached every Sunday in every church (thank God!), I must say I've not heard of many kingdom of God sermons recently.[2] So, for all intents and purposes, this dominant theme of the entire Bible, and certainly of Jesus' ministry, appears to be the ignored elephant in the sanctuary. Or, to use Herbert Farmer's intriguing metaphor, the theme of God's reign was biblical treasure awaiting recall.

A first question I had about all of this was why the kingdom had been relegated to a soundproof corner of the church's basement. Surely, not every pastor had a Premillennial Dispensationalist watchdog waiting in the vestibule, did they?

Clearer thinking led me to speculate that in America our silence might have something to do with the fact that monarchy and king had been booted off the continent by 1783. As the democratic experiment became more ingrained in our national character, our ability to understand or identify with kings or kingdom atrophied. It was truly foreign to us. Too, in America, in the earliest years of the twentieth century, the Baptist pastor/theologian Walter Rauschenbusch elevated the kingdom of God concept in his advocacy of what became known as the Social Gospel. However, conservatives dismissed his interpretation of the kingdom as too liberal, and liberals, after the disillusionment of the Great Depression and two world wars, critiqued his idealistic insights as naïve and too optimistic. So, America's political and theological history may have something to do with our Sunday silence.

Probably as much responsibility for the silence, however, was and is due to the unsettled state of New Testament studies. For more than a century, scholars have spawned a succession of ideas about the "historical Jesus" and what and who he really was and what he actually said as opposed to what was said about him and put in his mouth by later ecclesial scribes. This inevitably created no few differing ideas about the meaning of the kingdom he preached. E.P. Sanders in his 1993 book *The Historical Figure of Jesus* noted that "the word 'kingdom' is used in a diversity of ways in the Gospels" and that it remained "one of the most discussed issues in New Testament scholarship … [and] intensive efforts over the last hundred years to define the phrase [have left] the issue more confused rather than clearer."[3] More recently (2004), Frederick Dale Bruner, author of a two-volume commentary on Matthew, admits: "Most of us read something new on the kingdom almost every year, and we usually come away from our reading as confused as when we began."[4] One consequence of this has been that preachers and church musicians have been reticent to give much attention to a debated and still-to-be-understood kingdom.

Finally, about the time my own interest in the kingdom was forming, theologians became sensitive to gender issues. A first target in that discussion was our use of masculine pronouns to speak of God, and an obvious extension of this was the masculine reference within the word kingdom. Thus, "kingdom" was tried and found wanting, and now is commonly referred to as God's "rule" or "reign" or even the somewhat awkward "kin-dom." These options remove the male identifier in *king*dom, and they also helpfully guide us away from associating God's kingdom with any geographical or territorial dominion. In these pages I will often happily use "rule" or "reign." Even so, for the most part I choose to use the traditional term "kingdom"—in part because the translation of the Bible I read most often [NRSV] retains the term and in part because the kingdom idea exceeds the boundaries of any chosen term. Please feel free, however, to substitute your preferred term while giving me permission to use the more traditional one, a term that to my mind need not be rejected as sexist, though I certainly reject the idea that God is male—or female.

I am embarrassed to report, however, that for me personally, there was yet a more existential reason why the centrality of the kingdom of God did not register as important. All of the foregoing obstacles notwithstanding, there was a more personal reason why I did not acknowledge this elephant.

The Elephant in the Sanctuary: God's Kingdom

In the introduction to this section of the book there is a quote declaring that the expression "kingdom of God" is the key to the Gospels and the entire New Testament, a quote from A.M. Hunter (1906–1991), a well-known Scottish New Testament scholar of my seminary days. I could have cited more current scholars to establish the point Hunter made about the kingdom's centrality, because his assessment is as widely shared today as when he wrote it in 1950 or when I first read it in 1965. And that is just the point. I read Hunter's words—and even underlined them—more than fifty years ago, but they did little to reshape my understanding of Jesus or the gospel for decades.

As a twenty-something seminarian, I was already so firmly committed to the validity and sufficiency of my inherited gospel that Hunter's challenging and correcting words just did not break through my thick skull! My embedded theology of The Plan stayed intact. I suspect the same dynamic is true of all of us in many areas of our life. But in this instance, it meant I spent decades "reading around" Jesus' gospel, never letting his kingdom message expand my inherited way of hearing him. So, when I ask why his kingdom idea has received so little attention, I must add the embarrassing admission that hearing is difficult for those of us who are confident that we have already heard.

This is especially so when we begin to suspect that the gospel of the kingdom of God is the scary Jesus-stuff I first worried and wondered about in my youth revival days. As the coming pages will demonstrate, this kingdom gospel operates on a different wavelength than does The Plan. While The Plan offers four propositions to get us safely out of this world, the kingdom moves in precisely the opposite direction. It is not a way *out* of here; it is a way *into* this messy world. Its concern is with engagement, not escape; its agenda deals with all the greasy, no-easy-answer, often yucky stuff of getting God's will done "on earth as in heaven." Moreover, while The Plan operates with straight-up "Yes" or "No" theological propositions, the good news of the kingdom operates with puzzling calendars and multilayered parables whose meaning sometimes seems only two hairs short of madness. Hence, the kingdom of God is both simple in concept and mystery-laced in details. You can line the shelves of a good-sized library with books—unfortunately, written mostly by scholars for scholars—on this one subject.

This also means that I must paint with broad strokes and refuse the temptation to burrow down into every inviting cranny. That is the specialists' assignment. I refuse, however, to let this central theme of Jesus be placed in escrow until all scholars on all continents are in agreement on every detail. Yes, there is lively debate still going on in the hallowed halls of divinity schools about this subject. But in general meaning, the central matters are clear enough. It is long past time to let this elephant's trumpet be heard.

I begin with what Jesus' first hearers likely would have had in mind when he opened his mouth and said, "The time is fulfilled, and the kingdom of God has come near; repent, and believe in the good news" (Mark 1:15).

Notes

[1] David G. Buttrick, *Preaching the New and the Now* (Nashville: Abingdon Press, 1998), 7.

[2] The "Subject Index" of *20 Centuries of Great Preaching* (Waco, TX: Word Books,1971), edited by Clyde Fant and William Pinson, indicates that the terms kingdom of God or kingdom of heaven appear only 26 times within the sermons or biographical sketches of the 95 preachers, from Jesus to Martin Luther King Jr., included within its 13 volumes. Of those 26 entries, one is a quotation from Jesus and 15 are from or about Walter Rauschenbusch, the "father" of the Social Gospel.

[3] E.P. Sanders, *The Historical Figure of Jesus* (London: Allen Lane Penguin Press, 1993), 169-170.

[4] Frederick Dale Bruner, *Matthew: A Commentary, Vol. 1: The Christbook*, rev. ed. (Grand Rapids, MI: Eerdmans, 2004), 300.

CHAPTER 5

The Kingdom They Wanted

"May he [God] establish his kingdom in your lifetime and in your days, and in the lifetime of the whole house of Israel, speedily and at a near time."

That sentence appears in an ancient Jewish prayer (called the *Kaddish*), almost certainly prayed in Jesus' day and perhaps even prayed by him. It shows us that the idea of a coming kingdom ruled by God alone was widespread in Jesus' day. Of course, the Jewish people had long been adamant that their God was already king, king over all creation. Their songbook was filled with joyous assurances that "the LORD reigns" (Psalm 93, 96, 97, 99, etc.). However, this bold faith-claim had to coexist with an ever-present question of why: If God was in fact sovereign over all creation, why did so many ungodly events happen? If the LORD truly reigns, how could there be stillborn infants and broken families, thieves and floods, and wars and poverty and rape?

Added to Israel's perplexity was its long history of disappointing earthly kings and resulting divided/lost kingdoms, decades of identity-robbing exile, frustrating nation-rebuilding, and disgusting pagan military occupation troops. Finally, underlining the craziness of it all, was the Jews' bruised conviction that in all of this they were still the LORD'S chosen people. "If this is the way you treat your friends, who wants to be your enemy?" might well be the unspoken frustration seeping through many portions of the Old Testament.

Be this as it may, from this contested, anguished existence was born a yearning for a lasting, divine kingdom that would finally demonstrate the sovereignty of Israel's God along with its true status as God's chosen people. The *Kaddish* gave that undying longing a daily voice.

Even so, researchers have not yet found literary evidence from Jesus' day that his contemporaries called this yearned-for tomorrow the "kingdom of God." This specific expression seems to owe more to Jesus than to the common vocabulary of the day. Curiously, however, his listeners never are reported to have asked for a definition when he used the phrase. Apparently, they simply "got it"—and my assumption is that they "got it" in broad outline in terms of the *Kaddish* longing. Of course, Jesus gave it surprising new twists, and probing those is part of my assignment in these pages.

On the other hand, the *Kaddish* is not the only evidence we have of the presence of deep yearning for this gift from God. There were many messianic figures and movements in that era, although a review of this diversity is one of those tempting side trips I must not drag you through.[1] Suffice it to say the situation may be not unfairly likened to the gamut of opinions today about whether our only hope is the cataclysmic second coming of Jesus or that everything depends upon direct political action by the faithful or the belief that, in spite of all the bad news, the world is actually slowly getting better and better. The point is that there was in Jesus' day a lively hope for, and multiple ideas concerning, the coming of what Jesus called the kingdom of God.

Even so, we may gain insight from asking. "When the Jews prayed the *Kaddish*, what came to their minds as being the answer to their prayers?" Can we be more specific about what they were praying for? How would they know the kingdom's presence when they saw it? This can best be determined by giving attention to the word pictures Israel's prophets had painted of that good time coming.

In our church life, these are the passages we usually hear only once a year and unfortunately pay too little attention to them since they are read during the pre-Christmas weeks of Advent when many of us are already thinking about Mary and Joseph (or, God help us, Rudolph and our credit card limit). The upshot is that we most likely miss one great dimension of Christmas. So, even if you never have before, do give careful attention to the passages below; they tell the ideas and scenes that most likely came to mind for people such as Simon Peter, Mary Magdalene, Zaccheus, Martha, James—and Mary and Joseph—when Jesus said the kingdom of God was at hand. (These three passages are designated by the Revised Common Lectionary to be read on the first three Sundays of Advent for Year A.)

> In days to come the mountain of the LORD'S house shall be established as the highest of the mountains and shall be raised above the hills; all the nations shall stream to it. Many people shall come and say, "Come, let us go up to the mountain of the LORD, to the house of the God of Jacob, that he may teach us his ways and that we may walk in his paths." For out of Zion will go forth instruction, and the word of the LORD from Jerusalem. He shall judge between the nations, and shall arbitrate for many peoples; they shall beat their swords into plowshares, and their spears into pruning hooks; nation shall not lift up sword against nation, neither shall they learn war any more. (Isa. 2:1-5)

The reference to the height of the LORD'S house doesn't foretell a geological upheaval in the elevation of Mount Zion (where the temple was located); it means a heightened status and veneration will be given to the instruction flowing from it. All nations will seek it, and in obedience to God's word international disputes will not result in war but in the peaceful planting (plows) and harvesting (pruning hooks) of crops.

> A shoot shall come out from the stump of Jesse, and a branch shall grow out of his roots. The spirit of the LORD shall rest on him, the spirit of wisdom and

understanding, the spirit of counsel and might, the spirit of knowledge and the fear of the LORD. His delight shall be in the fear of the LORD.

He shall not judge by what his eyes see, or decide by what his ears hear; but with righteousness he shall judge the poor, and decide with equity for the meek of the earth; he shall strike the earth with the rod of his mouth, and with the breath of his lips he shall kill the wicked. Righteousness shall be the belt around his waist, and faithfulness the belt around his loins.

The wolf shall live with the lamb, the leopard shall lie down with the kid, the calf and the lion and the fatling together, and a little child shall lead them. The cow and the bear shall graze, their young shall lie down together; and the lion shall eat straw like the ox. The nursing child shall play over the hole of the asp, and the weaned child shall put its hand on the adder's den. They shall not hurt or destroy on all my holy mountain; for the earth will be full of the knowledge of the LORD as the waters cover the sea. (Isa. 11:1-9)

The good time coming is now further illuminated by a prophecy that it will in some way be related to a coming child, a shoot from Jesse's stump, whose stunning presence and deeds will bring about a world without threat and filled with the knowledge of God.

The wilderness and the dry land shall be glad, the desert shall rejoice and blossom; Like the crocus it shall blossom abundantly and rejoice with joy and singing. The glory of Lebanon shall be given to it, the majesty of Carmel and Sharon. They shall see the glory of the LORD, the majesty of our God.

Strengthen the weak hands and make firm the feeble knees. Say to those who are of a fearful heart, "Be strong, do not fear! Here is your God. He will come with vengeance, with terrible recompense. He will come and save you."

Then the eyes of the blind shall be opened, and the ears of the deaf unstopped; then the lame shall leap like a deer, and the tongue of the speechless sing for joy. For waters shall break forth in the wilderness, and streams in the desert; the burning sand shall become a pool, and the thirsty ground springs of water; the haunt of jackals shall become a swamp, the grass shall become reeds and rushes.

A highway shall be there, and it shall be called the Holy Way; the unclean shall not travel on it, but it shall be for God's people; no traveler, not even fools, shall go astray. No lion shall be there, nor shall any ravenous beast come up on it; they shall not be found there, but the redeemed of the LORD shall walk there. And the ransomed of the LORD shall return, and come to Zion with singing; everlasting joy shall be upon their heads; they shall obtain joy and gladness, and sorrow and sighing shall flee away. (Isa. 35:1-10)

In this passage the physical world of wilderness and dry land; of flowers, reeds, and rushes; of deer and jackals; of weak, feeble, fearful, blind, and deaf humans—all are blessed by the liberation God will create, even for fools!

Sifting through the imagery of these prophetic poems, certain themes concerning the wanted and promised kingdom are clearer:

- Jewish centrality (Zion, Jerusalem, Torah instruction) will be certain, though all nations, rather than just the people of Israel, will be blessed.
- A "shoot" or "branch" from Jesse's [King David's father] stump is central to its coming.
- God will rule over all in utter righteousness.
- Judgment will be given, and compassion also shown, especially to the poor and weak.
- Creation's dangers will cease, and the earth will blossom in abundant provision for all.
- War and violence will be no more; safety (especially for children), laughter, and joy will be omnipresent.

Other scriptures (and there are many) could be cited, and within them the voice of Jewish triumphalism, vengeful retribution, and other problematic elements are sometimes strong. But these three passages provide a useful snapshot, and from them we glimpse a longed-for kingdom that is this-worldly and material, not a spiritualized other-world utopia; desirable as much for its quality of life as by its place; and a social future; it is a vision of a new community for "us" to share. This public, shared characteristic rules out any attempt to interiorize, individualize, or privatize this kingdom.

A kingdom of one is a misnomer. The very word "kingdom" is a public, political term, not a psychological, spiritual term. The only biblical passage I know of that might suggest otherwise is found in the New Testament, in Luke 17:21, which the King James Version famously mistranslated as: "the kingdom of God is *within* you." However, the Greek text uses the *plural* "you" in this statement, and these words are spoken to the Pharisees—a group not carrying the best New Testament reputation. Although Jesus said and did many shocking things, it strains belief to imagine Jesus speaking such a benediction upon the Pharisees. Also, the word translated as "within" bears the meaning of "among," and hence the phrase may be better translated as "the kingdom of God is among you" (NRSV), or "is already among you,"[2] or "in the midst of you,"[3] or as "it will [suddenly] be in your midst."[4] There is certainly basis for even interpreting this phrase as Jesus' declaration that the kingdom was in their midst at that very moment in the presence of his person! Overall, support for *within* is found mostly among the followers of the often-beautiful but dated King James translation of 1611.

So, the kingdom that Israel wanted was the restoration of this present material world to God's original intention, a setting right of the blight brought about by human failure. The kingdom the Jews sought, in a measure, was this world, right! For them, obviously, this called for their international prominence as God's chosen people. According to Israel's lights, nothing could be right unless its place in this world was set right. Nonetheless, the Hebrew word that comes close to capturing the non-nationalistic factors that Israel longed for is the well-known word *shalom*, meaning a wholeness of all aspects of life in which all the sundered relations within the cosmos are knit together.

Shorn of its nationalism, the substance of Israel's longing for *shalom*, a healing of creation, can still be heard in the song that two twentieth-century Jewish lads, Stephen Sondheim and Leonard Bernstein, wrote for the 1957 Broadway show *West Side Story*. From the broken glass and rubble-filled streets of the violent inner city, bloodied teenagers sing their yearning for a somewhere and a someday when they will "find a new way of living … , a way of forgiving."[5] Or, more recently, there's the song a visionary but destitute father in *The Greatest Showman* sings to his young daughters of the million dreams that keep him awake at night—brightly colored dreams of "what the world could be," the world that he and they are "gonna make."[6]

You can, of course, dismiss all this as little more than a young Judy Garland scanning the skies, singing wistfully about "Somewhere Over the Rainbow"—or a thousand other wishers in every age and place who have pined away in longing for some elusive "heaven on earth." But the truth is, all people in all times have yearned for the kind of world where war and want are no more and justice and peace are the rule. Israel's hoped-for kingdom was simply its way of expressing this universal hope. But that does not make Israel's hope, or the similar hopes of any other people, foolish or wrong.

When I began to come to grips with the primal rightness of this yearning, arising not only from Israel's prophecies and prayers but also from the vacant-eyed stares of thousands in refugee camps as well as from the homeless on my own city's streets, my mind and conscience awakened to the theological importance and missional centrality of Jesus' prayer: "Thy kingdom come, thy will be done *on earth* as it is in heaven." I began to see that the good news Jesus preached was not just about heaven someday. What he sought and what he summoned us to seek with all our hearts was nothing less than Isaiah's vision, a kingdom of God's will being honored on earth. And, need I say it? There is little here that matches easily with the gospel according to The Plan.

"Christians have a long history of trying to squeeze Jesus out of public life and reduce him to a private little savior," wrote Walter Brueggemann, but "Jesus talks a great deal about the kingdom of God—and what he means by that is a public life reorganized toward neighborliness."[7]

Notes

[1] For a helpful introduction, see David B. Levenson, "Messianic Movements" in *The Jewish Annotated New Testament*, 2nd ed., Amy-Jill Levine and Marc Zvi Brettler, eds. (New York: Oxford University Press, 2017), 622-628.

[2] Eugene H. Peterson, *The Message* (Colorado Springs, CO: NavPress, 1995).

[3] *English Standard Version* (Wheaton, IL: Crossway, 2001).

[4] Joachim Jeremias, *New Testament Theology: The Proclamation of Jesus* (New York: Charles Scribner's Sons, 1971), 101.

[5] Leonard Bernstein and Stephen Sondheim, "Somewhere," *West Side Story*, Warner Chappell Music, Inc., Universal Music Publishing Group, 1957.

[6] Benj Pasek and Justin Paul, "A Million Dreams," *The Greatest Showman*, Kobalt Music Publishing, BMG Rights Management, Fox Music, 2017.

[7] Walter Brueggemann, *Deep Memory, Exuberant Hope: Contested Truth in a Post-Christian World*, ed. Patrick Miller (Minneapolis: Fortress Press, 2002), 73.

CHAPTER 6

The Urgency of Now

To me, the most intriguing thing Jesus ever said about the promised kingdom was the first thing: "The time is fulfilled, and the kingdom of God has come near." While others spoke of someday and tomorrow, Jesus spoke of today and now. The days of Israel's waiting and wishing and delay were over; the "day" of God's coming is *this* day. The revolution, the makeover, begins *today!*[1]

Jesus follows the same pattern in his first "sermon," in the synagogue of his hometown of Nazareth. He stands and reads his text from the scroll of Isaiah: "The Spirit of the Lord is upon me, because he has anointed me to bring good news to the poor. He has sent me to proclaim release to the captives and recovery of sight to the blind, to let the oppressed go free, to proclaim the year of the Lord's favor" (61:1-2a). So far, so good. But then things start to unravel.

At this auspicious moment when all eyes and ears are trained upon Mary and Joseph's son and his sermon, all Jesus could come up with was one sentence. Many novice preachers—including yours truly—know the humiliating experience of thinking you have enough material for a full sermon, but when it comes time to speak your piece only a paragraph or two stammers itself out. In Jesus' case, it was only one sentence—one sentence—but what a sentence: "*Today* this scripture has been fulfilled in your hearing" (Luke 4:21). In that one sentence Jesus claimed to be the fulfillment of the pious hopes of all Israel. It was a declaration that "today" a new era of human history has begun. "We just passed Go!"

This "today" emphasis continues as a steady beat in countless gospel parables and events. "This" hour creates an urgent crisis for all who hear him; one is to "sell all you have," to "let the dead bury their dead," to have your lamps trimmed and ready.

More than that, his actions show he wasn't just full of talk, especially tomorrow-talk. Folks who were too sick to get out of bed, he healed long distance. People dismissed by others as lost causes, he welcomed: cripples, whores, lepers, traitorous tax collectors. You name it, and he was on record as having befriended them, broken bread with them, treating them like real people!

When the curious showed up in droves, hungry for hope as much as for food, he fed the whole lot of them with nothing but a sack lunch and a prayer—and had leftovers! Poor folk and children, never powerful constituencies, always had his attention. It was said he could even stop a sea storm with a single word.

In so many ways, wherever he went it looked like "all heaven was busting loose." Even when demon-possessed folks came at him, he didn't flinch. He cast out the demons in a manner that clearly signified there was a "new sheriff" in town; a Higher Power was taking charge. And when his disciples also cast out demons, Jesus said he actually "saw Satan fall like lightning" (Luke 10:18)—the powers of darkness were being kicked off their high and mighty perches!

With only a little imagination, Jesus' listeners could see Isaiah's prophetic word pictures coming to life in him. The longed-for tomorrow of God's renewal of all things was underway. "Turn away from despair and resignation to the status quo," was Jesus' message. "Believe it: the promised kingdom of God is really at hand."

Some students have introduced the term "The New Order" as another way to express the history-shift signaled in Jesus' message of the kingdom of God. The New Order idea offers us "a division of history into two orders. A line is drawn between the order of the prophets, an order of expectation only, and the order of Jesus, an order of realization."[2] This term also helps to unify the message of Jesus with the writings of Paul. In those writings Paul bears witness that "upon us has come the fulfillment of the ages" (1 Cor. 10:11, my translation) and a conviction that "everything old has passed away; see, everything has become new" (2 Cor. 5:17). Thus, the unified message is that the promised "new" is now.

But it is mandatory for us to imagine how this message sounded to those most invested in the perpetuation of the present order. To the fed-up, the beaten-down, and the washed-out, Jesus' message was good news. But "a new world now" sounds very different when you are in the chairman's seat at the head of the table in a mahogany-lined executive board room. The up-ending of everything, today? This is the rhetoric of revolution!

If I were the High Potentate of Religion, Inc., and in charge of all its rituals, political alliances, historic obligations—and its cash needs—would I not be angered by this rabble-rousing preacher from Nowheresville calling for a new order NOW? And if I were the High Sheriff of the Realm [Herod, Pilate, et al], charged to keep the populace in line and the revenues flowing to Rome, would I not be alarmed by the sudden popularity of an agitator raving about a kingdom of justice and compassion taking over, today?

I think Jesus' message of the imminent kingdom was a major cause of his crucifixion. Yes, there were other factors that led to his crucifixion. (For the religious-minded, his critique of Torah, Temple, and Sabbath would have been enough.) But, his "pushiness" about the urgency of now made his challenges to everything else more ominous. In any age or era, so long as religious people restrict their talk to "pie in the sky" somedays, no one in power has need to worry. But when a firebrand from Nazareth began to say repetitiously and with an ever-growing reception that the time of God's kingdom was at hand—now, today—the anxious powers-that-be felt compelled to step in and quash the man and his movement.

On the strictly human level, Jesus' message of the kingdom *now* was certainly a primary cause of his crucifixion. He posed a political, economic, and societal threat to the status quo. And, he still does.

Notes

[1] E.P. Sanders, in *The Historical Figure of Jesus* (London: Allen Lane Penguin Press, 1993), 170, says: "Jesus—or any other first-century Jew who wished to talk about God's rule—[had] the option to combine in various ways here, there, now, and later. The kingdom is either here, in heaven, or both. It is either now, future, or both. The question is what Jesus primarily meant." The position taken here is that all of these apply but that Jesus' primary meaning was here and now. Frederick Dale Bruner, *Matthew: A Commentary, Vol. 1: The Christbook*, rev. ed. (Grand Rapids, MI: Eerdmans, 2004), 300-305, presents the interpretive options as: the Kingdom of Heaven (the second coming of Christ), the Kingdom of the Heart (within you), the Kingdom in History, and the Kingdom through the Homily. My emphasis is upon Bruner's third option.

[2] W.D. Davies, *Invitation to the New Testament: A Guide to Its Main Witnesses* (Garden City, NY: Doubleday & Co., 1966), 142-143.

CHAPTER 7

The Now (but Not Really?) Kingdom

Now, let's take leave of faraway places and times—of Nazareth's synagogue, of high priests and Roman procurators, and all the rest—and re-enter the twenty-first century. Jesus' message of a "new order now" creates problems for us too, doesn't it? At the top of the list is the basic question of its truthfulness.

Did anything in or about the world really change during the days of Jesus' ministry? The brutal fact is that the authorities *did* have their way with this young firebrand. They made a public spectacle of him and his incendiary talk by splattering him on a despicable cross. And, though you hardly need a reminder, today's world doesn't feel very different than when Jesus walked upon it and was killed. Regardless of our pride in evidences of human progress, is anyone ready to say there is an abundance of "heaven on earth" visible anywhere on earth—especially anywhere near the places where Jesus walked?

One good place to begin looking for an answer to this is to investigate the way Jesus' first followers handled the same question. We have no record that when Jesus ascended to heaven the roses immediately looked brighter, the soldiers were kinder, the crime rate declined, or that the lenders forgave all the outstanding debts owed them. There is no evidence that the world took on any New Order look. If anything, for Jesus-people, the road seems to have become rougher—with ostracism and even persecution soon becoming their plight.

So, one of their first responses was in the form of telling themselves Jesus would return soon and finish the job, fully establishing his promised kingdom at that time. They recalled he had said: "There are some standing here who will not taste death until they see that the kingdom of God has come with power" (Mark 9:1). So, they persisted in believing he would soon return. Now, two thousand years later, this is still the way some folks respond to the disappointment of unfulfilled hopes for the kingdom. They wait for the Second Coming.

But for Jesus' first followers, this response was not the only response. As day after day passed, and "same as before" weeks became "same as always" months and then years, easy deferrals wilted.

Some Jesus-people came to believe that the kingdom had actually come "in power" with the descent of the Holy Spirit at Pentecost and that their daily experience of this Spirit was the present-day presence of a kingdom that was still a-borning.

Others found an answer by adjusting the clock. They answered with variations on this theme: "With the Lord one day is like a thousand years, and a thousand years are like one day. The Lord is not slow about his promise, as some think of slowness, but is patient with you, not wanting any to perish, but all to come to repentance. But the day of the Lord *will* come …" (2 Pet. 3:8-10a, emphasis mine).[1]

All of these responses are evident in the New Testament, and all have their value as we deal with our own response to the continuing sameness of human history. One concept, however, seems to unite them all and to provide our best frame for understanding our situation. That concept is in the phrase "already … but not yet." Placed within a sentence, it might read: The kingdom is *already* present and at work in this world by virtue of Jesus' coming, but it is *not yet* what it will be. This concept offers a both/and response to this interim time. It admits that the world continues to be marked by evil and darkness, but it is not an unrelieved darkness. The world, in this estimation, could never be the same again after Jesus. Something had changed—and changed forever. A light was now shining in the darkness, and that light heralded the first rays of dawn on the horizon. Daybreak was sure to come. The promised kingdom was "already" present but "not yet" in full, visible form.

Such were the ways our faith-ancestors addressed the question of the truthfulness of Jesus' central claim. For some of them it appears that the challenge of being people of the dawn, of living at the intersection of two eras, was too great a challenge. The Letter to the Hebrews may be an extended sermonic plea to just such bewildered persons, urging them to persevere and be among those "who through faith and patience inherit the promises" (6:12). Those who persisted in faith, however, unconsciously began to knit together the bits and pieces of what we know today as the church.

Of course, if you are bent toward cynicism, you can conclude that what they in fact did was ditch their kingdom hallucinations and go into the museum business, setting up a gazillion shrines (read churches) around the world to honor the memory of their exciting but misguided Revolutionary. The gist of this cynical response is captured in the statement one of Rachel Held Evans' exasperated readers sent to her: "Jesus went back to heaven and all he left me was this lousy church!"[2]

The problem here is real—and it is deep. As much as we may admire the man we read about in the Gospels, if his main message was this promised kingdom, but it turns out that his so-called kingdom was a one-man, one-time show with no follow-up, there is little reason to pay him much attention—certainly not enough to call him the Lord and Savior of the world! He is just another false messiah, the verdict reached by the yelling crowd before Pontius Pilate on Good Friday.

After all my years of Jesus-fascination, I confess that on any given day, depending on how devastating that day's news has been, I hang my head in wonderment about the presence of God's reign within this sad, bloody world. Even as I write this, the morning news is of two mass shootings, leaving twenty-nine persons dead for no reason other than that they happened to shop at an El Paso Walmart or have a night on the town in Dayton,

The Now (but Not Really?) Kingdom

Ohio—yes, for no other reason than that ... and that hate, fear-mongering, greed, and unlimited access to military-grade weapons now reign in America.

On such days as this, when faith is pushed to the limit, I have sometimes found help for my "already ... but not yet" hope by pondering stories such as the parable of the wheat and the weeds growing together in the field (Matt. 13:24-30). The problem in this parable is the appearance of noxious weeds, sown by "an enemy," where good wheat seed had been sown. Instead of a bumper crop of "thy kingdom come," a disappointing display of "same old stuff" weeds sprouts up next to laboriously sown "thy kingdom come" wheat seeds.

At this point in the parable, my attention easily fixates on the infuriating presence of these weeds. But in doing this I overlook the heartening fact that the good seed has also broken through the soil and is just as stubbornly visible as the weeds. I let myself be overcome by [the continued presence of] evil (Rom. 12:21). It is a mixed harvest, to be sure, and explain it as you will, the master in the parable doesn't seem surprised. Rather, he calmly says: "Wait!! In the end, the weeds will be yanked up, bundled, and burned, but the good wheat will be obvious and will be prized." I want to believe that Jesus gave us this kind of story to assure stragglers like me that good is always present and that there is "more to come."

I also find strength for hopeful believing within the verse I discussed earlier because of its misleading translation in the King James Version: "the kingdom of God is within you." Listen to the full passage: "Once Jesus was asked by the Pharisees when the kingdom of God was coming, and he answered, 'The kingdom of God is not coming with things that can be observed; nor will they say, "Look, here it is!" or "There it is!" For, in fact, the kingdom of God is among you.'" (Luke 17:20-21). Since the scriptures do not come with any underlining or italics, we are left with the responsibility of determining which words are to be emphasized. In this passage, I like to capitalize the word "is" in the last sentence: "The kingdom of God IS among you." What faith longs to hear is some assurance that amid all the hideously observable weeds, the kingdom of God IS at work among us. Jesus says it is—though never in a way we can point to with assured accuracy or that goes unchallenged by the presence of the enemy's weeds. (I will have more to say about this later.)

In the end, however, I suspect we are left just about where John the Baptist was upon receiving Jesus' answer to his question asking if Jesus was really the Messiah. Apparently, Jesus wasn't carrying out John's agenda or wasn't highlighting portions that John considered most important or wasn't operating on John's timetable or in John's style. Jesus replied by reassuring him he was doing "the work" (though surely in his own way and time): "The blind are recovering their sight, cripples are walking again, lepers are being healed, the deaf hearing, dead men are being brought to life again, and the good news is being given to those in need. *And happy is the [person] who never loses [their] faith in me*" (Luke 7:22-23).[3] Walter Brueggemann summarizes Jesus' answer: "Go tell John a new world is being birthed among those who no longer accept dominant notions of the possible."[4] Pondering the exchange between John and Jesus, I must wonder if my frequent problem isn't my criteria rather than my Lord's credibility.

Church historian Jaroslav Pelikan tells us Jesus' earliest followers actually left little material evidence of any continuing disappointment or despair that "heaven on earth" did not ensue immediately. The second- and third-century writings of Christians, he says, reveal a happy both/and conviction. On one hand there is a vivid expectation of a soon-to-come, world-ending second coming of Christ. On the other hand there is a "willingness to live with the prospect of a continuance of human history"[5]—both of these held in place by an increasing emphasis on the centrality of Jesus. These believers reframed their understanding of history so that Jesus was seen as the "turning point of history, a history that, even if it were to continue, had been transformed and overturned by his first coming in the past...." Jesus became for them "the hinge on which history turned."[6]

If for a moment their disillusionment was great (Luke 24:13-21, John 21:2-3), the early Christ-followers did not fold their tents and go home crestfallen and bitter. Miraculously, their numbers swelled with each decade and generation. Whatever may or may not have objectively changed about the observable complexion of history, something had unquestionably changed in and for them. They went about as persons living now in kingdom-come, daily "tasting the powers of the age to come" (Heb. 6:5), and fearlessly confronting the big shots who remained stubbornly unimpressed by the news that their lease was up. For these intrepid souls, the future, whatever it held, belonged to the king who was "throned upon the awful tree."[7]

Notes

[1] This answer is a reworking of Psalm 90:4 that affirms: "For a thousand years in your sight are like yesterday when it is past, or like a watch in the night."

[2] Cited by Rachel Held Evans, *Searching for Sunday: Loving, Leaving, and Finding the Church* (Nashville: Thomas Nelson, 2015), 254.

[3] J.B. Phillips, *The New Testament in Modern English* (New York: The Macmillan Co., 1964). Italics in original.

[4] Walter Brueggemann, "Preaching as Sub-Version," in *Deep Memory, Exuberant Hope* (Minneapolis: Fortress Press, 2000), 16.

[5] Jaroslav Pelikan, *Jesus Through the Centuries: His Place in the History of Culture* (New Haven & London: Yale University Press, 1985), 25.

[6] Ibid., 26.

[7] John Ellerton, "Throned Upon the Awful Tree," *Pilgrim Hymnal* (Boston: Pilgrim Press, 1958), 174. The hymn's coronation image follows the Gospel of John in which Jesus is "lifted up" and being crowned and "glorified" as royalty at Calvary.

Excursus:
One Key Verse and Two Linguistic Worlds

One sentence from the Old Testament seems to inform all the New Testament explanations offered for the delay of the fullness of the kingdom: "The LORD says to my lord, sit at my right hand until I make your enemies your footstool" (Ps. 110:1).

Readers of the New Testament will likely be familiar with this verse since it is the most quoted or alluded to Old Testament verse in the New Testament. (It is quoted or alluded to in Matt. 22:44, 26:64; Mark 12:36, 14:62; Luke 20:42-43, 22:69; Acts 2:34-35; and Heb. 1:13. See also Mark 16:19; Acts 2:33, 5:31, 7:55; Rom. 8:34; 1 Cor. 15:25; Eph. 1:20; Col. 3:1; Heb. 1:3, 8:1, 10:12-13, 12:2; and 1 Pet. 3:22 [and perhaps Rom. 16:20].) All these appearances in so many documents and genres of literature indicate that this verse held great importance to the earliest Christians.

It appears that all these New Testament authors interpreted Psalm 110:1 as a prophecy spoken by King David (the reputed author of this psalm), declaring that the God of Israel (the LORD) told David's lord (the promised Messiah) to sit at his right hand (that is, more literally, to share the LORD'S throne) until the Messiah's enemies were defeated. Interpreted in this manner, Jesus' followers believed their ascended Lord now was enthroned with God as king of the universe, awaiting only God's order for judgment upon all who opposes Jesus' reign—that is, his return in triumph. Thus, for earliest Christians, the present time was a between-time, an indefinite period when Jesus "already" was king, but "not yet" exercising the fullness of his reign.

This understanding gained wide acceptance because it was compatible with ideas that were already circulating in Jewish rabbinic circles of a "temporary messianic kingdom" that would serve as a transition between this present age and the age to come.[1] Blending this "temporary" rabbinic schema with the psalm's "sit at my right hand until ...," the early church found a satisfactory way to explain its claim of an "invisible" king and kingdom.

It is also important to remember several facts about the language and worldview represented in the writings from which we frame our kingdom understandings. First, the prophecies upon which kingdom hopes were based were given in the poetic idiom, a literary genre designed to evoke emotion and action, not to satisfy the engineer's curiosity. We do these texts and ourselves a disservice to expect literal fulfillment of their statements. These prophecies are best understood as Impressionist art offered in literary form, as broad-stroke images and visionary hints rather than precise schedules, logistics, and specifications. Jesus' characteristic phrase, "The kingdom of God is like ..." is in keeping with the prophet's poetic/mysterious reserve.

Also of significance is the apocalyptic, end-of-the-world mindset that saturated the social ethos of Jesus' time. Even our secular era has its occasional eruptions of an apocalyptic mindset, as in the Y2K jitters the Western world experienced preceding the arrival of the year 2000 (and perhaps during the pandemic of 2020). Whereas our experience was brief, the on-edge feeling in Jesus' day was strong and pervasive, generating its own corpus of literature (Revelation is the best extended New Testament example of apocalyptic literature, although "little" apocalypse chapters are found in Mark 13, Matthew 24 and Luke 21) and leaving a lasting impress upon subsequent Christian thought and history. A principal characteristic in all apocalyptic expression is its use of symbolic language; it speaks cryptically of beasts and monsters, of rulers and of angels and demons, of symbolic numbers and signs, of judgment and signs of calamity—that is, it speaks in exclamation points and capital letters, not in footnotes!

The point of this discussion for our present purposes is to wean us from our desire for verifiable, scientific exactitude as we interpret scripture's kingdom texts. These texts emerge from poetic and apocalyptic soil and thus are suggestive, not exhaustive. The language of poetry speaks through *beauty*, whereas the language of apocalyptic speaks through *alarm*. In tandem, these two linguistic worlds whisper to listening hearts the good news of the dawning of alarming beauty.

Note

[1] See Alexander E. Stewart, "The Temporary Messianic Kingdom in Second Temple Judaism and the Delay of the Parousia: Psalm 110:1 and the Development of Early Christian Inaugurated Eschatology," *Journal of Evangelical Theology*, 59/2 (2016), 255-70.

CHAPTER 8

✳

God's Dream: The Kingdom by Another Name

"One day, Jesus told his followers about God's dream of a world where all the children of God are loved and cared for, and no one is left out."[1]

—*Desmond Tutu*

In this chapter and the following four I want to explain more clearly the basis for belief in a gospel of the kingdom. It is one thing for me to say that the good news of the kingdom of God is the better gospel I searched for. It is another to support my conviction that this is, in fact, the Bible's good news. So, in this chapter I offer some clarifying definitions and parameters, and in the following four chapters I provide an overview of where I find this gospel on the pages of the New Testament. If you are disposed to say "Show me," these chapters are my effort to do just that.

Please read again the words just beneath this chapter title. This is the way Archbishop Desmond Tutu introduces the Sermon on the Mount to children. In two separate children's books, Tutu uses the term "God's Dream" as his way of paraphrasing for children's comprehension the meaning of the "kingdom of God."[2] As often happens, when you attempt to state things clearly enough that a child can grasp them, that's when even adults begin to understand. This world of universal, all-inclusive love and care that Tutu envisions is God's kingdom by another name. It is a world that finally works "just right." If you like, stir in a half-dozen other more theological-sounding words such as justice, ecological balance, peace, and holiness to flavor it, but the result is still the end-goal of those who pray: "thy kingdom come, thy will be done on earth."

Do note, however, that the New Testament doesn't speak of this kingdom as something "within" you, like a happy thought. Nor is it up in the sky, tucked away in some distant spiritual heaven and available only upon your last breath. When the Bible refers to the kingdom of heaven or the kingdom of God, it is not referring to such a place or existence "up there"—it is talking about this-worldly reality. From first to last in the Bible, the "dream" is for a display of God's design coming "on earth, as in heaven."

"God's dream" therefore gestures toward an earthly world where daddies don't get blown up by enemy landmines and mamas don't get hooked on drugs prescribed to help her cope with daddy's death. It is talking about a world where …

- Every neighborhood is safe—and where there really are neighborhoods!
- Red and yellow, black and white, gay and straight, old folks on walkers, kids on skateboards, city council members, and soccer moms respect and take care of one another.
- The landfill worker, the black bank president, the schoolteacher, the olive-skinned Walmart cashier, the insurance executive, and the Korean symphony cellist live on the same block—as friends—and everyone's "critters" are respected as God's creatures.
- Tears come from laughing, hands are used to bless, and arms are used to hug.
- Lips do not tremble from fear, and tummies do not ache with hunger.
- Justice is the watchword for all politics.
- Soil, sky, and stream are clean and cared for as life-providing gifts from our generous God.³

This is the kind of world that Jesus' kingdom-talk desires to be our magnificent obsession, promising that as we "strive first for [it] and [God's] righteousness," all we truly need will be given (Matt. 6:33). And this, I believe, is the kingdom that Matthew, Mark, Luke, and John say was inaugurated in Jesus' person and ministry.

I need now, however, to clarify two crucial matters. First, there is a need to be very specific about this term "kingdom of God." I have just attempted to describe its presence in terms of a physical community or society—seeking to vivify its goal in realistic, this-worldly dress. But given all the nuances this term carries in its many New Testament appearances, it is necessary to add that the kingdom of God must also be thought of as a *dynamic* rather than as a *product*, as God's heavenly realm entering earth's fallen realm.

You may want to think of it as a metaphor of God's sovereignty asserting itself in history, or as "a symbol of a dynamic process that moves through history from creation to *eschaton* [conclusion]."⁴ One very respected New Testament scholar, Leander Keck, supplies some verbs that may offer you a helpful angle of vision; he says the kingdom is "the rectifying power of the impinging future."⁵ It is the rule or reign of God making itself known in the present tense. Clarence Jordan, of *Cotton Patch Gospels* fame, used "the God Movement" as his way of expressing its present-tense meaning. A friend of mine speaks of it as God's New Day. Whenever you see Tomorrow's Promised World breaking through the meanness of today, you see the kingdom. My own imagination is still stirred by Walter Rauschenbusch's characterization of God's kingdom as the "energy of God realizing itself in human life."⁶

The kingdom of God, then, is *not* a physical construct of humans—that is, an enclave or municipality or nation that we might build or grow. (The New Testament never speaks of our building or spreading the kingdom!) History's long list of failed utopian communes bears witness to our inability to construct such a place. Though we are to seek it—this world of God's ruling presence—it nonetheless remains a gift from above, not our accomplishment. It is an invincible holy dynamism moving all history toward God's goal. We are graced through Christ to be glad participants of this holy realm as witnesses, embodiments, advocates, and provocateurs, but we are not its administrators or engineers. We strive for the literal enactment of this kingdom, but humbly realize our products are faulty approximations, not the final goal. The kingdom of God remains the creation of the Spirit whose wind blows where it will. The "Dream" is God's to make true.

Said in still another way, the kingdom is Jesus' gift to us of a way of speaking of God's *vision* and of God's *provision*. As vision, it brings before our imagination the prophet's divinely inspired word-pictures of a better world; it paints before our eyes the Dream toward which God is relentlessly moving. But as provision, it is the divine and divinely given animating force pressing toward this goal, sustaining believers in acts of faith and hope and love. In this symbol, we are given the what and the how for our highest God-given aspirations and also the assurance of the Invincible One who stands behind and within these aspirations.

A second characteristic of this kingdom is an extension of the first. The kingdom of God is not a kingdom where soldiers and police or Moral Majorities or "Christian" theocrats impose their will upon others by force.[7] Rather, it is a kingdom practicing a very different kind of power, the kind of power-in-weakness we see described in Matthew's Beatitudes and Sermon on the Mount—which Matthew places in the entrance hall to his gospel as Exhibit One (chs. 5–7) and which he then presents as personified in Jesus the messiah-king.

In this kingdom, the king is meek. When callous, ignorant men slap him in the face, he turns the other cheek. When they strip his garments from him, he gives them his naked body to drape in purple costume-clothing. And when they compel him to "go one mile," he goes two, and more—carrying a splintered cross. The sovereign in the kingdom of God is a "lamb" who astonishingly conquers. Jesus' kingdom is a "peaceable kingdom," shaming all other kingdoms by its humility and shocking them by its unarmed power.[8] His subjects are servants of all, not rulers over any.

To safeguard this distinctive, you might always add the adjective "cruciform" to the kingdom Jesus inaugurated. The word cruciform may be unfamiliar to you, but the idea surely isn't. It means anything that resembles the cross, the crucifix. The interior of many worship spaces is designed in a cruciform pattern—a lengthy, narrow area where worshipers sit (historically called the nave), leading to a wider space (called transepts) representing the arms of the cross, and then the area at the head of the building a shorter, narrower area (the chancel) from which worship leaders guide the service. In non-architectural realms, however, cruciform means deeds or words that remind us of the cross and of Jesus' selflessness. When I use the word with reference to the reign of God, I mean that this kingdom conforms to the standards and way of Jesus' cross. That meaning is always within my assumptions and meaning as I write. In this above all, the kingdom Jesus announced and inaugurated differs from all other kingdoms: it is a cruciform kingdom.

It is essential to state this clearly because Western history has often been pockmarked by a misuse of the idea of the kingdom of God. European rulers of the past used it as a divine endorsement for the so-called "divine right of kings," deeming themselves to be God's appointed earthly rulers. Using the same self-favoring logic, the kingdom of God has been used as the basis for waging "holy war" against Muslims. Thankfully, much of the eventual rejection of war and of the divine right of kings also came from better understandings of the kingdom of God—but not before leaving horrid scars upon history. In the words of Jaroslav Pelikan, "To trace the historical variations and permutations of the kingship of Jesus in its interaction with other political themes and symbols is to understand a large part of what is noble and a large part of what is demonic in the political history of the West."[9]

In a later chapter I discuss the political intersection of church and state and the role of the kingdom of God within the kingdoms of this world, but for the moment it is enough to remember that the cruciform kingdom of God is unlike any other entity we are accustomed to calling a kingdom. It is God's Dream, wondrously working its way toward God's transformation of all creation.

With these clarifications in mind we are ready to look more closely at biblical texts and allusions that tell us of Jesus' work as the bringer and sovereign of God's cruciform realm.

Notes

[1] Desmond Tutu, *Children of God Storybook Bible* (Grand Rapids, MI: Zondervan, 2010), 76.

[2] Ibid. Examples in Jesus' speech: "Everyone who wants to see God's dream come true must see with the eyes of a child" (Mark 10:13-16); rephrasing the Lord's Prayer: "May your dream of love and peace come true, and may the whole world be made new" (Luke 11:2); paraphrasing the Eucharistic instruction: "Whenever you break bead and drink wine like this, remember me and remember that someday God's dream: of everyone caring and sharing, loving and laughing: will come true" (Matt. 26:29); from the cross: "Father, forgive them, for they do not understand your dream" (Luke 23:34). Describing Pentecost: "They became one big, happy family sharing everything together, just like God had always dreamed it could be" (Acts 4:32). The same pattern is followed in an earlier children's board book, Tutu, *God's Dream* (Somerville, MA: Pickwick Press, 2008).

[3] See Terence E. Fretheim, *God and World in the Old Testament: A Relational Theology of Creation* (Nashville: Abingdon Press, 2005). Consider the abundance of botanical references within the prophet's future visions—references that ought not be dismissed as mere symbolism. They are part of the numerous "new heaven and new earth" creation promises of Jer. 31:1-6, 10-14; Ezek. 36:8-12; Isaiah 35 and 30:23-26; Amos 9:11-15; etc.—all in answer to the lament of the abused "land/heritage" of Jeremiah 12, etc. and reversing the "curse" of Gen. 3:17-19.

[4] M. Eugene Boring, *The New Interpreter's Bible*, vol. 8 (Nashville: Abingdon, 1995), 292. See Boring's "Excursus: Kingdom of Heaven in Matthew" from which this phrase comes.

[5] Leander Keck, *Who Is Jesus? History in Perfect Tense* (Minneapolis: Fortress Press, 2001), 71.

[6] Cited by Grant Wacker, "The Social Gospel," in Mark Noll et.al., eds., *Eerdmans' Handbook to Christianity in America* (Grand Rapids, MI: Eerdmans, 1983), 320.

[7] "History shows that when the church uses the tools of the world's kingdoms, it becomes as ineffectual, or as tyrannical, as any other power structure ... Ironically, our respect in the world declines in proportion to how vigorously we attempt to force others to adopt our point of view." Philip Yancey, *The Jesus I Never Knew* (Grand Rapids, MI: Zondervan, 1995), 246.

[8] Reviewing prominent Davidic messianic ideas of Jesus' era, David B. Levenson notes the non-military feature of them: "Notably, this king conquers not by military might; his weapon is 'the rod of his mouth,' based on Isa. 11:4." See "Messianic Movements" in *The Jewish Annotated New Testament*, 2nd ed., Amy-Jill Levine and Marc Zvi Brettler, eds. (New York: Oxford University Press, 2017), 622.

[9] Jaroslav Pelikan, *Jesus Through the Centuries: His Place in the History of Culture* (New Haven & London: Yale University Press, 1985), 447.

CHAPTER 9

One Billboard Outside David's Royal City

In December of 2017, a remarkable movie was released to American theaters: *Three Billboards Outside Ebbing, Missouri*. The plot of this movie revolved around Mildred Hayes' rental of three billboards outside her hometown of Ebbing, Missouri, to protest the dawdling response of local law officers to the rape and murder of her teenage daughter. To publicly shame them into action, Mildred made use of three accusatory billboards.

Two thousand years ago, outside David's royal city of Jerusalem, another "billboard" was used to declare a very different kind of message. That billboard was the sign Pontius Pilate ordered to be nailed to the cross of Jesus of Nazareth: *The King of the Jews*.

This sign, too, was meant to grab attention, to bring traffic to a halt. Modern readers likely speed past it without even slowing down. For years I essentially ignored it as a matter of historical interest but of no gospel significance. When I began to awaken to the theme of the kingdom of God, however, this billboard became more interesting, especially when I realized that this sign is one of the crucifixion details that all four gospels record. Upon closer inspection it became clear to me that this sign was much more than historical trivia.

This is the scene toward which all the gospels' plots have been building. It is a unified exclamation point written into the text by all four writers (Mark 15:26, Matt. 27:37, Luke 23:38, John 19:19). Though they vary in secondary details—one provides our Lord's given name (Jesus), another adds his hometown ("of Nazareth"), and still another uses precise specificity ("this is")—the core message is the same. All are adamant that anyone who looks at the cross of Jesus will get the message: *The King of the Jews*.

If readers have not yet understood the cosmic significance of the story being told, the writers are now going to paint it on a sign—a billboard, if you will—and hammer it across the top of the scene: This crucified Jesus is the promised king of the Jews. The Gospel of John even adds that this billboard was written in the three then-relevant languages: "in Hebrew [the language of religion], in Latin [the language of law], and in Greek [the language of philosophy]" (19:20). This was life-and-death news for everyone of whatever race or language or tradition.

At one level Pilate's sign can, of course, be understood as nothing more than Pilate's official posting of the capital offense of this bloody fool, or perhaps as a final cynical mockery of Jesus and his preposterous preachments or even of the Jews themselves (Here's the "Jewish" king!). But for Matthew, Mark, Luke, and John, this scene and this billboarded message outside David's royal city is the heart of the gospel.

To grasp how this might be so, we must go back to the story of God's call to Abram in Genesis 12. Then those prophecies from Isaiah, included in the chapter "The Kingdom They Wanted," begin to make much greater sense and must be revisited.

The first eleven chapters of Genesis are best understood as the Bible's stage-setting for the drama that will begin in the twelfth chapter, with the calling of Abram and the story of Israel that will be the theme of the rest of the Bible. In these opening chapters we are told of the creation of the entire universe, of its far-flung galaxies and of this earth and all its teeming life-forms, including the human creature, Adam/Eve. Here the ways of these humans are reported: they disobey their creator's commands and suffer because of it, they breed and have children who rise up and kill one another, they scatter into separate camps and build pride-filled cities, they lose their ability to speak to one another. They are a disappointing lot and God, so to speak, washes God's hands of them in a universal flood. It is not a pretty scene that Genesis 1–11 paints. The stage is indeed dark when Genesis 12 begins.

With chapter 12, God begins anew—with the one man, Abram. We are not told why out of all the persons on earth God chose this man. But choose him, God did. And God spoke to him with a command and a promise:

> Go from your country and your kindred and your father's house to the land that I will show you. I will make of you a great nation, and I will bless you, and make your name great, so that you will be a blessing. I will bless those who bless you, and the one who curses you I will curse; and in you all the families of the earth shall be blessed. (vv. 1-3)

In the final phrase of the multiple promises given to Abram, God "spills the beans" of how the rest of this story will develop. Though the lion's share of this story centers around Abram's people, the plot will always wind its way toward *blessing for all the families of the earth*. God will work through this one people for the good of all people. The somber first stories and the deathly world portrayed in Genesis 1–11 are to be healed, re-created, "blessed" by God through the story that begins with Abram. What happens to the Jews doesn't stay in Jewry; what happens to them has downstream effects upon all the world's people.

Now, recall those striking representative paragraphs from Israel's prophets. One of those prophecies said that a "shoot" from Jesse's "stump" would be pivotal in the coming of the longed-for Jewish kingdom. The Jesse referred to was the father of David, the heroic, greatest king in Israel's history. So, the prophecy is saying the ultimate kingdom of *shalom* will also come through another descendant of Jesse. According to the genealogy provided in Matthew's gospel, Jesus of Nazareth was a descendant of David. Jesus was even born in David's hometown of Bethlehem, and on a Friday afternoon just outside the walls of David's royal city of Jerusalem, he was crucified upon a pole that bore a sign declaring him to be *King of the Jews*.

For the gospel writers, this billboard is proclaiming that Abram's story has reached its zenith: the promised king is here! Jesse's royal descendant is right there on that cross. Quite obviously, though, he has become a rejected king, revealed in a stunning, crucified manner that Israel had never expected (though this, too, was foretold in other prophecies such as Isaiah 53).

Here, however, is where this Jewish "coronation" explodes in universal significance. If the omega-point has been reached for Israel, then the long-ago announced intent to bless all people through Israel has also reached its omega-point. In this crucified king all the families of the earth have also been blessed. The healing, the re-creation, the blessing, and the salvation of all people everywhere have now been enacted. The kingdom of God is at hand, for all!

Yes, there are some odd calculations going on here—and the next chapters will shed further light on these reasonings. But as an introduction, I suggest that we imagine the significance of all I have just said is like grains of sand slipping through an hourglass.

At the top of the hourglass, at its widest radius, is the world of Genesis 1–11—all humankind represented in the sorry state and stories told in those chapters. But beneath all this "lost" humanity, in the narrowing portion of the hourglass, there is Israel, Abram's people, through whom all humanity will be blessed. Finally, in the narrowest, lowest portion of the upper cylinder of the hourglass there is one solitary descendant of Abram, Jesse's "shoot," the representative of all Israel: Jesus of Nazareth. All Israel dwindles down to this one Jew. As the leader/king/messiah/anointed one of Israel, Jesus descends into the narrowest passageway, the crucible of Calvary, and through it, out into the spaciousness and blessing of the New Order of existence with all the world in his train. This he does not only for his "own," the people of Israel, but also for all humankind.

That billboard, *The King of the Jews*, therefore, was not just Pilate's sarcastic mockery of the Jews or of Jesus. It was an unwitting announcement of the accomplishment of the world's salvation, its hope. The King of the Jews had led the way into the kingdom of God for all people! And the fact that Pilate, the representative of the world's militaristic superpower, is the one who *insists* (John 19:21-22) that this proclamation be nailed to the cross is also immensely significant. His act constitutes an unconscious confession by the "principalities and rulers and powers" of this world that this crucified Jew is the true king of all! This mangled Jew with his outlandish idealism is the victor, not the victim.

This is why that billboard outside David's royal city is so important. Ebbing, Missouri's billboards contained naught but accusations; Jerusalem's sign proclaims good news for all the world.

The question then becomes this: How in the world did anyone ever come to believe a victory had been won by a dead man with a roughhewn sign over his lifeless, sagging body?

CHAPTER 10

Farewell to Saturday's World

What in this world ever led anyone, particularly the authors of the four gospels, to believe that a crucified rabbi was the king of the Jews? That he was in fact the author of the world's hope, the Lord and Savior of all creation, the inaugurator of the yearned-for kingdom of God on earth?

As impressed as they might have been by his words and his stunning deeds, however taken they might have been with him as a person, all that comes tumbling down when Rome strings him up, doesn't it? Why, after the crucifixion, didn't they write him off as just another of the "all hat but no cattle" disappointments of history?

The answer, in one word, is resurrection. "This Jesus, God raised up" (Acts 2:32).

The most astonishing act of God within the Gospels is the Resurrection. Friday's evil victory was shown by Sunday's first light to be a hollow victory. Women visit Jesus' borrowed tomb at dawn and report it to be empty; disciples run, investigate, and return, verifying the report. Questions consume already ravaged emotions and hopes. Someone says Mary Magdalene has actually seen and even talked to him! Really? A trickle of rumors spreads that Pilate's egregious atrocity has been overturned: God has quietly vetoed Friday's death and raised the dead body of Jesus from its grave. Can this be true? In half-belief and guarded hope his disciples begin to whisper to one another, "He is risen?" In the dizziness of the next days, their questioning whisper becomes a stout declaration. One astonished eyewitness after another insists: "He is risen! He is risen, indeed!"

Those Easter words are now almost cliché worship words for many of us. We typically hear them as part of colorful spring celebrations and sermons assuring us that there is life beyond death. But much more is involved in the fact of Jesus' resurrection than evidence of life beyond death. The larger truth is that with the resurrection of Jesus, history turns a page. The silent Saturday world ruled by death and defeat is left behind on this Sunday when hope is born. The crucified rabbi is shown to be the one who begins the end, for in him the promised tomorrow is unfurled and the era of God's reign is begun.

The idea of resurrection, of life beyond death, was widespread in Jesus' day. Many people believed in such. Within this belief, however, was the assumption that this resurrection would occur only on the "last day" as one of the final "end time" occurrences. When "the day" came, the dead would be raised to life in "the great gettin' up morning" for Israel, and the long-yearned-for kingdom of God would appear in life-restoring power. Mind you, this was to be a resurrection of *all* the dead, not just one man.[1]

But when this one man, Jesus, who had ceaselessly proclaimed the arrival of the promised kingdom, when this one man returned to his followers as alive from a hideous, wrongful death, the conclusion was that the power and power(s) of sin and death had been defeated. God's promised tomorrow had begun! All that Jesus had said was true. The "end time" was already here. God was effecting "God's dream." When Simon Peter tried to interpret for outsiders what had happened, his summary was: "This Jesus, God has raised up ... Therefore let the entire house of Israel know with certainty that God has made him both Lord and Messiah, this Jesus whom you crucified" (Acts 2:36).

So, out of the impenetrable darkness of defeat and death the light of hope emerged, a hope not just for life after death but that a life-restoring God was at work. A world enslaved to the consequences of its past and fearful of its future was set free to reclaim God's intended present-tense joy in the gift of being. That open tomb opened a new era of history for all creation.

That is the wordy essence of the thing; the kind of admittedly elevated verbiage that often fills Easter Sundays with flowery talk but leaves you wishing someone could talk plain English. A story might help.

Not too many years ago I found myself at a very low place in life. The stress I felt was almost unbearable, and such hope as still sustained me was being sucked from me week by week. Deep within me was the desire to press on—if only to save face—but, honestly, I did not think anything I did or could do was going to make any difference. Every day was a journey through desolate, forsaken territory.

One afternoon, while in the darkest portion of that emotional valley I drove past a public garden and, not even knowing why, I pulled into the parking area. I got out and began to walk around the place, eventually finding myself standing in a deeply shaded nook of the garden and staring at one of its many botanical information signs.

Across the top of the sign was the word SUCCESSION. The first sentence told me that "succession is the term used to describe the natural progression of changes that occur over time within an ecosystem." It went on to talk of the changes brought about in ecosystems by storms, wind, drought, insects, diseases, and such. Finally, it mentioned fire and noted that "what was a towering forest one day could be a pile of smoldering ashes the next." That sign had all my attention, for that is how I felt—a burned-out specimen amid a once mighty forest, and now just a smoldering ash heap.

The next sentence came like a lightning bolt: "What appears to be a lifeless landscape is simply an ecosystem on the verge of succession." My eyes glued on just a few words: "lifeless landscape ... on the verge of succession." The sign went on to remind me of the 1980 Mount Saint Helens volcanic eruption that had leveled its pristine forest and covered all its vegetation and wildlife in a thick layer of ash. But two years later, a lone lupine tree grew in the ash, and year by year grasses and wildflowers and small trees began to cover those slopes once again—"a lifeless landscape on the verge of succession."

So it was that this sign "preached" to me the message that the deadness I felt and saw was not all there was; the ecosystem of life would bloom yet again! Here was a heartening new way of picturing my situation, a way that challenged my despair with hope and renewed my will to persevere.

In some persons' understanding, what I wandered into that day was the truth of resurrection. For them, resurrection is the assurance that life always overrules death; that even within the ashes there are seeds that will burst into life; that fallen leaves provide the nutrients and soil for tomorrow's growth; that nothing really and truly dies, but it simply progresses into another continuing life form. To them, resurrection is close to what the naturalist calls succession. My own experience with finding myself "on the verge of succession" testifies to the rescuing power within this idea; it brings comfort and invites patience. But is this what the New Testament means by resurrection?

I don't think so. I think the resurrection of Jesus is something far more astounding than a story of succession, something much greater than a "sacred sample" of the process of nature working itself out. If the resurrection is anything, it is not natural! It is stupendously unnatural! It is unlike anything else we know about—it is that "something new under the sun" that Ecclesiastes says cannot be found. Yet this truly is something confoundingly new and different. It is a second act of creation, and it is just as dumbfounding and impenetrable as the first! It is Genesis, chapter one, revisited, only this time it is the re-creation of life out of stark, unrelieved, total death. Jesus was "crucified, *dead*, and buried" says the Apostles' Creed, meaning precisely what it says.

In Jesus' death the whole tragic story of humankind is put to death. When he cried, "It is finished!" that is part of the meaning. The unrelieved sadness of all the ages comes to an end—full stop!—when the Lord of all dies for it and it dies in him. Thus, when God raises him from the dead, all is begun again. A new creation comes to be in him. The prison of past history swings open to the march of God through history toward the full and final realization of God's Dream for the whole cosmos.

If all we make of the resurrection of Jesus is a demonstration or "proof" of life after death or some form of naturalistic immortality, we are shrinking its significance to a sorry pittance of its majesty. These reductions of meaning come from our individualistic insistence that the gospel be about "me" and, in this case, the prolongation of my life eternally. Most certainly, our Lord's resurrection does assure us of our own resurrection, but more than that, it assures us that all history and creation are headed somewhere good because our God is making all things new.

When our personal story is one of ashes and despair, the encouragement of succession is unquestionably one source of God-given encouragement. But the grander story, the gospel, is that God, through resurrection, has once for all lifted the whole cosmos from death to life and is carrying it to God's own good ends.

That the resurrection of Jesus is indeed a cosmic, world-changing event is underlined by his ascension (Luke 24:50-51, Acts 1:9, Mark 16:19). Though they may appear to be two separate events, it is surely better to see them as two movements within one act.

Finding the Gospel

Admittedly the ascension story can sound more like primitive space flight (the literature of that time had many heroic figures being transported to heavenly realms) than meaningful good news, but Jesus' story is distinctive in that "a cloud took him out of their sight."

Remember, a cloud was the Israelites' ancient symbol of the *shekinah* presence of God that hovered over Mount Sinai at their birth (Ten Commandments/covenant-making) and that then led them through the wilderness to their promised land and finally filled their temple in Jerusalem. Therefore, this odd levitation story is in effect an interpretation of the resurrection, telling us that Jesus conquered death and sin and the power of the devil, and was also received into the very presence and glory of God.

The Apostles' Creed expands it in these words: "he ascended into heaven, and sitteth at the right hand of God the Father Almighty." This is picture language asserting that Jesus now shares the throne of God and that all authority is given to him in heaven and on earth. He already reigns in glory! (Remember the key verse, Psalm 110:1.)

Moreover, because we are said to have been "raised together with him" (Col. 3:1, 2:12) who is our representative, we also can be said to be in some astounding way reigning—already!—with him and being made a kingdom (1 Pet. 2:9; Rev. 1:5, 5:10, 20:6). Whatever one makes of the ascension story it is clear that its intent is to say that when Christ was raised from the dead, a whole new world began.

We do ourselves and our faith a great favor by remembering that all four gospels were written at least thirty years after this event. They emerge from three or more decades of daily living and of theological reflection by persons who lived in the continuing conviction that the resurrected Jesus was still among them as a regal presence. These writers certainly were not ignorant of the continuing horrors within this world. Many of those horrors were aimed at and poured out on them and their friends. Even so, on Sundays they sang hymns with Easter joy to Jesus as the reigning Lord of all, and on weekdays they dared to profess "Jesus is Lord" in point-blank contradiction to all the political and social intimidation of Caesar's lock-down world.

These early Christians were the first in the long procession of those who understood Jesus to be, in Jaroslav Pelikan's term, "the hinge of history." In due time the calendars of the Western world would be recalibrated in recognition of this historical shift. *Anno Domini*, the year of our Lord, became testimony to a new way of seeing history. In and through Jesus, the new age of God had dawned. Saturday's world, though its death spasms would linger, was already doomed.

Note

[1] According to Matthew 27:52-53, resurrection phenomena began occurring moments after Jesus' death, but the other Gospels report only Jesus' singular resurrection on Easter Sunday.

CHAPTER 11

The King Who Saves by His Life

I want now to survey just one portion of the Gospels, the first four chapters of the Gospel of Matthew, to illustrate how the kingdom idea, even if not named, is a dominant and recurring theme. Matthew, more carefully than any of the other three gospels, grounds the story of Jesus in the story of ancient Israel, and, therefore, the kingdom idea can be more easily seen in it. But similar if not as transparent or frequent results could be shown if I turned to another gospel. Therefore, as but a sampling and for brevity and concentration's sake, I survey just the first four chapters of Matthew.

Another desire in this rapid overview is to underline how Matthew presents Jesus as the king who saves us through the words and works of his life, and not just by his death on the cross. My inherited gospel, especially through its hymnody, created the impression that only the cross mattered. (The Apostles' Creed is often scored for the same inattention to the life of Jesus.) Clearly, the death of Jesus is of paramount importance within the Gospels and within Christian experience, but we must not forget that the death we cherish is of the man, Jesus, whose life reveals the magnitude of his death and whose life itself was liberating.

The tendency to focus on only one aspect of Jesus as being the most important is not unique to my tradition, however. William Placher notes that for some Greek Orthodox Christians, the emphasis falls on the moment of his birth—the Incarnation—while for some forms of liberal Protestantism, the all-important issue has been a selection of Jesus' teachings. Placher, however, quotes John Calvin's insistence that we are saved "by the whole course of his [Jesus'] obedience" and then adds this: "In all of Jesus' life, he was obedient to God, and it was the whole course of his life that accomplishes our salvation."[1]

Matthew presents Jesus' life, words, and deeds (chs. 1–25) as much more than just informative background about the man who is crucified at Golgotha (chs. 26–28). He tells us of Jesus whose "whole course" is lived for us and for the world's salvation. On every page the liberating king is at work, freeing the children of God from error, fear, affliction, ignorance, and all other captors so they might live as joyful participants in God's *shalom* kingdom.

Consider how Matthew tells us this good news in the first four chapters of his gospel.

Matthew 1

The first chapter of Matthew uses historical and scriptural allusions, wordplay, and symbolism to present Jesus as the answer to Jewish hopes that have universal consequences.

"An account of the genealogy of Jesus the Messiah, the son of David, the son of Abraham" (v. 1) is how Matthew begins. This genealogy, however, is much more than the tracing of a family tree—it is a kingdom of God sermon. (Matthew uses the Greek word *geneseos* [translated as genealogy] in his first sentence, perhaps suggesting to his original Greek readers that they were about to read another Genesis, a story of re-creation.)

Three groups of ancestors, with fourteen ancestors in each group, are provided in this genealogical line that begins with Abraham (the father of the Jewish people) and ends with Jesus. Jesus is thereby shown to be "the climax and fulfillment of the larger story [of holy scripture] … the definitive denouement of the storyline,"[2] written by God's design. Everything leads, with precision, straight to Jesus, according to this genealogy. Even his angel-decreed name, Jesus (derived from the Hebrew verb "to save"), ties him to this history and people as the one who "will save his people from their sins" (v. 21). Thus, Jesus is introduced as the sin-forgiving Messiah (king) of the Jewish people.

Too, the numerical scheme in Matthew's three groups of fourteen is crafted for effect. Rabbis of that day were fond of giving each (consonant) letter of the Hebrew alphabet a numerical value. This cryptic wordplay yielded the delightful result that the three consonants of the name David, Israel's exemplar king, added up to fourteen [D=4, V=6, D=4]. Since the number seven was thought by Jews to be the perfect number, the number fourteen was perfection doubled! Matthew's genealogy thereby melds this rabbinic practice with Israel's fascination with David as a royal messianic figure.

Also, Matthew makes David's kingship central in his genealogy. His first cluster of fourteen leads to David's reign, his second cluster of fourteen begins with David's accession to the throne (v. 6) and ends with the loss of Davidic kingship (v. 11), and his third cluster leads from David's reign directly to Jesus. Jesus is thus demonstrated to be "the son of David" (v. 1), a legitimate claimant to the title King of the Jews.

There is good reason to suspect that in this schema of sevens Matthew also has in mind the biblical mandate of the Jubilee year. According to Old Testament teaching (Lev. 25, 27; Isa. 61; et. al.), every fiftieth year—the final year of a cycle of seven periods of seven years—was to be a year of Jubilee or of "liberty" within Israel. This Jubilee year was the crown of the sabbatical cycle and was to begin on the Day of Atonement. Though each sabbatical year had its specified liberating mandates, during the Jubilee year all debts were to be forgiven, all human bondage was to be cancelled, and ancestral lands that had been sold to another (usually to settle debts) were to be returned to the seller. In the Jubilee year the calendars were to be reset and a Sabbath rest for the land and people was to be observed. (I crudely liken the concept to a national Monopoly game with a ticking time clock; God, knowing human's greedy propensity, allows forty-nine-year stretches of growing monopoly, but then grants "Get Out of Jail Free" cards to everyone and demands the board be reset for a new roll of the dice.)

Jubilee was a societal recalibration aimed toward justice and continuing opportunity for all. By presenting Jesus as the final person in a perfect set of sevens, doubled, and then repeated three times, Jesus is presented as both the summation of the past and the inaugurator of the supreme Jubilee of Jubilees. Everything is now being rebooted; a sabbath of peace, the *shalom* of God's intent is being restored. Nothing less than a new creation is afoot.[3]

This liberating emphasis is underscored in Matthew's report that "the child conceived in [Mary] is from the Holy Spirit" (v. 20). To Matthew's first readers, contrary to today's (who likely hear only "virgin birth" in these words), this work of the Holy Spirit brought associations with Genesis 1. Just as the Spirit had once hovered over the waters to bring all things into being, so the Spirit was now bringing a new creation to birth in Mary's womb. However, lest anyone should consider this child to be of mere human status, the announcing angel declares that this event fulfills the promise of "Emmanuel, which means 'God is with us'" (v. 23). In this child, the Lord, who had taken leave of Israel four hundred years before (see Ezekiel), consigning the Israelites to exile for their sins, is now returning to them. God is (again) with us! Exile/banishment is now giving way to Presence. The redeeming King of Glory is taking the field!

Matthew 2

Matthew's second chapter begins with a good news item for non-Jewish readers: the appearance of searching Gentile magi who are as eager as any Jew to "pay homage" to the Jews' newborn king. Their followed "star" attests that even the heavens are aware of and signaling the birth of a New Order. Remarkably, these Gentiles (usually dismissed as unworthy of God) are received hospitably by Mary and Joseph and their worshipful gifts dutifully reported for all time. Thereby the descendants of Adam/Eve are as involved in this story as the descendants of Abraham. Of course, careful readers of the genealogy in the previous chapter will already have noticed that Gentiles were astonishingly included in Jesus' lineage in the (female and morally problematic!) persons of Tamar (1:3), Rahab (1:5), and Ruth (1:5).

The encouraging story of the magi is, however, lodged within the horrific story of the slaughter of the innocents. If any reader has imagined that this newborn king of the Jews is simply of harmless religious interest, Matthew destroys that illusion by informing them of King Herod's paranoid response when he is told of his birth (2:3). The savvy powerbrokers of the world clearly understand that this Jesus is a genuine threat to their kingdom and power and glory, and predictably bring all their power to bear to end the threat, even if it means slaughtering innocent babies in Bethlehem or, later, crucifying the Bethlehem-born son of God. This sordid tale is a kingdom-come story, albeit a realistic and sobering one.

Matthew 3

The third chapter of Matthew introduces John the Baptist, preaching repentance "for the kingdom of heaven has come near" (v. 1). Here for the first time in Matthew we encounter the term "kingdom of heaven [God]." Notably, John's announcement is immediately linked to the prophet Isaiah's admonition, "Prepare the way of the Lord" (v. 3b), a prophecy about the return of God, after long exile, to the land and people of Israel. Matthew's meaning is that God is returning to reclaim the land and to restore God's people to their God-given "dream." Jesus' baptism by the prophetic figure of John is in effect a messianic anointing of Jesus, and any doubt the reader may have that Jesus is the one to inaugurate God's dream is answered by God's declaration (v. 17) to the freshly baptized Jesus: "This is my Son, the Beloved, with whom I am well pleased." This is anointing, commissioning, authorizing language spoken to the designated king on the eve of his first major confrontation with the usurping enemy.

Matthew 4

That the conflict between these adversaries will be fierce is clear when Jesus, in the fourth chapter's story of his temptation, does not dispute the devil's bragging claim (v. 9) that "all these [all the kingdoms of the world and their splendor] I will give you." Here is a satanic claim to be the one who is really in charge of "the world" and of all the small fries such as Herod and Caesar who vainly imagine they are in charge. Jesus does not dispute the devil's assertion at this moment, but (to fudge a bit and reveal the end of the story) after his death and resurrection, the resurrected Jesus assures his disciples (28:18) that "all authority in heaven and on earth has been given to *me*!" Obviously, something has happened in the course of Jesus' ministry to alter the balance of power. This world is no longer the devil's toy but is the theater of God's kingdom. The prince of darkness has been toppled!

The "something" that happens in this temptation face-off with Satan is of great importance. On one level, the three temptations Jesus faces and overcomes are unique challenges to his identity and vocation. But on another level, Jesus' forty-day trial in the wilderness revisits the experience of Israel in its forty-year sojourn in the wilderness after its exodus from Egypt. Jesus, too, has "come out of Egypt" (2:15) and now, as Israel of old, he is faced with hunger, testing God, and worshiping a non-God. In this duel with the devil, Jesus is reliving the story of God's people, redeeming it, and also through his own obedience forging the foundation of a new people of God, people of the kingdom. That the reign of God is the goal of all is enshrined in Matthew's note that, with the temptations rebuffed, "Jesus began to proclaim, 'Repent, for the kingdom of heaven has come near'" (4:17). These are his mission-declaring first public words!

Matthew 4 also provides yet another assurance to non-Jewish readers that they are included within this story. Though Jesus confined himself to ministry among the people of Israel, he is here said to emerge from "Galilee of the Gentiles" offering hope for "the people who sat in darkness," because "for those ... light has dawned" (vv. 15-16). The king of the Jews has come for the life of the world, not just the Jews. This is a truth ineradicably embossed upon Matthew's gospel by its repetition in the great commission at the gospel's conclusion. Jesus' followers are to disciple "all nations" (28:19).

With Jesus' call of four of his eventual twelve disciples (4:18-22), the ancient pattern of the twelve tribes of Israel finds a new iteration. A new people of God is being formed: a setting-right of a long-delayed intent is underway. The "Dream" now has a leader and core followers, and thus Jesus begins his campaign of bringing the "gospel" to the people. That message is "the good news of the kingdom," and it is accompanied by his "curing every disease and every sickness among the people" (v. 23, a summary statement repeated in 9:35)—underscoring that Jesus' work is not confined to words and ideas; it includes merciful acts, too. Physical bodies and twisted minds—indeed the created world in toto—feel the force of the arriving, liberating king.

***

Matthew's ensuing account (chs. 5–25) of Jesus' ministry is to be understood as Jesus' campaign waged against the physical, mental, spiritual, and theological bondage of his people—and us. He explained: "If it is by the Spirit of God that I cast out [the] demons, then the kingdom of God has come to you," (12:28). In obedience to the call and will of his Father, Jesus taught a new (kingdom) way of life. As Canon Edward West translated Matthew 7:29, "he taught them as one having the right to."[4] And he unleashes that new life by cleansing the unclean, giving sight to the blind and mobility to the paralyzed, conquering "nature" (calming wind and waves), breaking the power of binding spirits, forgiving sins, rebuking religious error, feeding the hungry, loosing mute tongues, and bringing good news to the poor. In every deed, with every word, Jesus is breaking the bonds that torment humankind and creation. Through his life, he is saving us!

For those who pay attention to the Old Testament prophecies read during the Season of Advent (such as those discussed in Chapter 8), the accounts of Jesus' daily ministry sound like a "promises made/promises kept" checklist. Each deed becomes a Jubilee deed, a setting to rights of injustice/distortion, and a sample of the healing of a broken creation. To put it in the words of a song that itself was inspired by the message of Jesus' kingdom, "He has sounded forth the trumpet that shall never call retreat ... Our God is marching on."[5] Matthew even concludes his gospel with a tympany-pounding affirmation of this good news. In what is now called the Great Commission, the resurrected Jesus says: "I am"—a deliberate use of the ancient name of Israel's Yahweh God—"I am with you always, to the end of the age" (28:20). The Lord reigns!

Notes

[1] William C. Placher, *Jesus the Savior: The Meaning of Jesus Christ for Christian Faith* (Louisville, KY: Westminster John Knox, 2001), 6-7.

[2] M. Eugene Boring, "The Gospel of Matthew," in *The New Interpreter's Bible*, vol. 8, ed. Leander E. Keck, et. al. (Nashville: Abingdon Press, 1995), 356.

[3] See Sharon H. Ringe, "Jubilee, Year of" in *The New Interpreter's Dictionary of the Bible*, I-Ma, vol. 3, ed. Katherine Doob Sakenfeld, et al (Nashville: Abingdon Press, 2008), 418-419.

[4] Edward N. West, *God's Image in Us* (New York: The World, 1960), frontispiece.

[5] Julia Ward Howe, "Mine Eyes Have Seen the Glory."

CHAPTER 12

The King Who Saves by His Death

No one can tally the number of books, songs, poems, sermons, paintings, and plays that have attempted to interpret the crucifixion of Jesus. Surveying this abundance, some people may conclude the world is drunk on his blood. More reverently, it can be said that the death of Jesus is a defining event in world history. Explain it how you will, the execution of this Galilean rabbi two thousand years ago continues to be a source of fascination, horror, devotion, and mystery.

The New Testament itself provides more than twenty interpretations of the meaning of Jesus's death and resurrection. Even the Scriptures find no one way to "explain" this! Across the centuries, numerous Christian thinkers have offered multiple theories concerning the Crucifixion's necessity, accomplishment, and so on. None of their theories has ever gained complete dominance within the minds of worshipers, however. Though we long for clarity, we continue to bow before majestic mystery.

I must now join the long line of unsuccessful "explainers," though nothing anyone can say will answer all our questions or tie a pious knot on any need for further thought. Still, if I am to tell you of my gospel, I must tell you what it has to say about the cross of Jesus. So, here is how I believe Jesus' death can be understood in terms of the kingdom of God.

I begin with the reminder that the faith and life of Jesus, as a first-century Jew, were lived within the rhythms and rituals of Israel. The Exodus, Passover, Covenant, Exile (and apocalyptic mindset) provided the context for his own obedience to God. They were also the backdrop and interpretative keys his followers had for their eventual retelling of their Master's life and death.

Too often in later Christian history this context is forgotten, and Jesus, and certainly his death, have been discussed in terms and categories that are alien to Israel and its traditions. When this happens, the gospel that is excised from the New Testament doesn't fit with the overall story of the scriptures; it becomes an alien "thing" that has been lifted out of its meaning-defining context (a charge I earlier made against The Plan). When, for instance, Jesus' death is presented in a "somebody must pay the penalty" manner, medieval categories of the offended honor of a feudal lord are being introduced, categories that are foreign to the biblical categories that formed the originative matrix of the crucifixion. Moreover, in this particular case, even the character of God is sadly misrepresented: the Holy One is portrayed as a deity demanding his pound of flesh before his offended honor can be moved to show mercy.

So, when seeking proper understanding of the death of Jesus, we must take care that our thinking is "according to the Scriptures" and do our best to take our clues from biblical categories, symbols, and images. Only confusion can come when this indigenous milieu is ignored.

Additionally, it is essential to respect the narrative nature of our scriptures. First-time readers of the Bible are often surprised to discover how much like a storybook it is—the continuous story of a people (Israel) covenanted by and with God and eventually confronted by God in the person of Jesus of Nazareth and what becomes of that encounter. I like to call this long story the Grand Narrative, and in the following explanations I try to take this Grand Narrative and the narrative character of scripture seriously. This story and its stories tell us more than is sometimes heard.

When the story-form of scripture is respected, the Gospels offer their own understanding of Jesus' crowning deed within the story they tell. They tell this story artfully (and theologically) and then leave it to the story-informed reader, with the Holy Spirit's aid, to "get the point." So, to grasp the meaning of the Jesus story, and especially this final story, one must stay within the Grand Narrative and its symbols and nuances and permit this context to inform and shape our understandings of the meaning of Jesus' life and death.

Three features of the story of the final week of Jesus' life offer us significant interpretive clues as to the meaning of his death. Those three are the occasion of the Passover, his going to the Temple, and the meal he shared with his disciples. Let's look at them in turn.

The Passover

Looming over the Grand Narrative of the Bible, there is one preeminent "salvation/freedom" story informing all other Bible stories. That is the story of Moses' confrontation and victory over Pharaoh, leading the children of Israel out of Egyptian slavery through the Red Sea waters and to their promised land. The Jews celebrated this liberating event each year at Passover; this was the greatest festival in Jewish faith, a festival mandating pilgrimage to Jerusalem for all the faithful.

Most significant for our purposes is the fact that Jesus chose—and by all indications, it was solely his choice—to go up to Jerusalem during the Passover. He deliberately chose to face the powers-that-be during Passover, to confront in Moses-like fashion the Pharaoh of his day, Rome, and the entrenched religious establishment of Jerusalem at this precise moment. If you wish to call Jesus' choice of this date "staging," that does not bother me, for I am persuaded Jesus did in fact choose to make his "last stand" during this particular festival because it would provide many of the scriptural precedents and interpretative clues his disciples and later generations would need in order to discern the meaning of his life and of his death.

N.T. Wright, whose historical research and reconstructions inform every aspect of my understandings here, asserts that by the time of Jesus this historic Passover festival had also drawn into its orbit associations with the Day of Atonement—the holy day when the high priest entered the temple's Holy of Holies and offered the stipulated sacrifices for the sins of Israel. And, since the Jubilee years were mandated to begin on the Day of Atonement, even the societal "reset" motifs of Jubilee were arguably emotionally joined to those of Passover/Day of Atonement. If so, three dynamic streams of Jewish faith and practice coalesced in this festival week, filling the occasion and the gathering pilgrims with memories and hopes of oppressors overcome, sacrifices offered, forgiveness granted, promises kept, freedom bestowed, and a just resetting of society.

The sacral/political volatility of this Passover week is attested by the decision of Rome's deputy, Pontius Pilate, to take up watchful residence in Jerusalem for this feast. More importantly, Jesus of Nazareth chose this feast time as his own hour to "go up to Jerusalem." It was the perfect setting for the banners of "God's Dream" to be unfurled. It was to be a clash of kingdoms within the city of David—for the life of the world.

The Temple

Jesus' visit to the Jerusalem temple is the next all-determinative event in his fateful last week.[1] A great deal of devotional material interprets this act as Jesus' cleansing of a temple that had become a commercialized affront to God. There may have been some commercial sleaziness—where money passes hands that temptation always exists—but the literature we have from that period gives scant evidence of such corruption, and thus I doubt that Jesus, the disciples, or the Gospels' first readers understood this as a "cleansing" story in this sense.

The significance of this story is more likely to be found within the longer story of Israel. From Moses' time, the tabernacle, then the Solomonic, and now the Second Temple had been understood as being the dwelling of God, the sacral site of God's presence within Israel. However, the present Second Temple, built after the Jewish people returned to their land after their exile in Babylon (587–538 BCE), lacked one crucial qualifying characteristic shared by its predecessors. There had been no "entrance of God" event, no occasion when God had shown his approving acceptance of this place, no descending *Shekinah* glory appearance within it such as its predecessors had received. Though this temple was an architectural and esthetic marvel, it was a house without an occupant! The people of Israel had returned, but God had not. It is this dilemma of divine absence that creates the post-exilic calls for God to "come" to Israel and also of prophetic promises of God's return to the people and land of his choice—especially to this temple. As but one example, we read in Malachi: "See I am sending my messenger to prepare the way before me, and the Lord whom you seek will suddenly come to his temple" (3:1).[2]

Now, during this Passover, the absent God of Israel, does "suddenly come to his temple" in the person of Jesus, the one named as Emmanuel, but receives no welcome. Within those hallowed precincts it is simply business as usual, religion on automatic pilot. It is not as though he is an unknown. For three years he has been traversing the hills and villages of the land, presenting himself as the Promised One. A parade, as ludicrous as it may have been to critics, has just welcomed him to David's royal city with Hosannas. But when the heavenly "king" enters the grounds of the palace ostensibly built for him, there is nothing but the sound of commerce.

Thus, this story has several layers of meaning. First is the fact that the day of Israel's "salvation" was identified with the appearance of Israel's messiah in the temple. It was believed that when the "king" enters the holy place, Israel will be "saved." So, Jesus' coming to this place is a fulfillment of prophecy, an "end time" sign that the day of salvation had come. God is with us!

Conversely, the "cleansing" aspect of this appearance represents the judgment that had also long been associated with the day of salvation. A review of the several "last straw" parables told by Jesus in this week, along with his cursing of the fig tree (Matt. 21:18ff; Mark 11:12-14, 20-25), are of a cloth with Jesus' purging action in the temple. The king, the son, the Messiah, the Lord came and, finding no faithful response, judgment fell upon the place and people. There is more to be said about judgment within his actual crucifixion, but the stern sound of judgment is audible in the crack of Jesus' rough-hewn whip in the temple's "cleansing."

Third, in this action Jesus assures his death. In doing what he did and by saying what he said about the temple's destruction, he signed his own death warrant. The Gospels are clear that his trial before the Jews focused on his temple affront; false witnesses were even secured to prove his blasphemy on this charge. However, the most essential matter is that in this bold act Jesus knowingly and intentionally lays down his life. He is not to be considered a hapless victim—he is an initiator, a mission-driven volunteer for the fate he surely knows awaits anyone acting so rashly, so obediently. He is saving us through his life.

Finally, as the torn curtain shrouding the Holy of Holies will later attest, the true site of God's presence, the place where God may be sought and found, is shown to be Jesus himself. "One greater than the temple" came and, finding that place inhospitable, the Holy One is no longer ever to be imagined as confined to or by any place.

The Meal

A third "saving" event of the Passover week was the Passover meal, or at least what Jesus' disciples assumed was to be the Passover's historic seder meal. It turned out to be otherwise. The traditional seder ingredients were present, and the ancient rites of Passover meals observed. But there was a noticeable newness present in the upper-room gathering, a newness primarily in the future orientation Jesus gives to it. Rather than focusing only on the seder's remembrance of God's past deliverance from Egypt, Jesus turns the focus to the future by speaking of never again drinking of this fruit of the vine "until that day when I drink it new with you in my Father's kingdom" (Matt. 26:29, Mark 14:25, Luke 22:15-18). A new exodus, a new deliverance of God is at hand.

This announcement is then couched in the language of a new covenant: "This cup that is poured out for you is the new covenant in my blood" (Luke 22:20, Matt. 26:28, Mark 14:24). Jeremiah's prophecy of a new covenant struck by God with God's people is invoked (31:31-34), and through that invocation a new epoch of history is announced—an epoch in which, as the prophecy states, God "will forgive their iniquity, and remember their sin no more!" So, a new deliverance is at hand in which God will relate to God's people in a new covenantal way, a way marked supremely by the forgiveness of sins.

Finally, a newness is stipulated in Jesus' claim that this new covenant is found in "my body" and "my blood, which is poured out for many for the forgiveness of sins" (Matt. 26:28, Mark 14:24, Luke 22:20). He himself will be the sacrifice.

The significance of this meal is not just in the occasion and its actions but also in the hints it provides for the events of the following day. The words and acts from the upper room furnish the commentary and codebook for interpreting the dramatic events that are to follow. Jesus' death is to be a sacrificial offering, given freely by him as our representative, to effect a new covenant between God and humankind through his blood "poured out for many"—not just Abraham's descendants.

All this is in keeping with the story and promises of the Grand Narrative, using its symbols, practices, and thought-world. The promised new covenant, instituting a new relationship with a chosen people, is symbolically established in Thursday night's wine and physically ratified in Friday afternoon's shed blood. There is nothing here to suggest an angry God being placated by the suffering of an innocent victim. What is here is a God of merciful character acting through Jesus to fulfill ancient promises to Israel and, through Israel, to bless all nations. What is here is the dawning of a new order, the bloody labor pains of the birth of the promised kingdom on earth.

The Cross

Finally, there is the grievous execution of our Lord. As I have already said, across the centuries many theories of atonement have been fashioned, each attempting to offer a rational understanding of Jesus' saving death. None has ever won universal support, and certainly none bears the endorsement of any of the early creeds of the Church. The mystery of what happened on that black Good Friday has always defeated our most arduous intellectual endeavors—as befits God's crowning deed. Yet, our love for God yearns to include mental comprehension of what was done on that awe-ful afternoon, to worship with our minds as well as with our hearts. So, we reverently approach this final hour with modest hopes, knowing even our best intellectual efforts fall short.

Finding the Gospel

A first observation must be that the God of the Grand Narrative has always been a God of great forgiving mercies. From Genesis onward, God's compassionate nature was known in Israel, and thus the God whom Jesus served and trusted did not require his bloody execution in order to dispense mercy to wayward sinners. (Consider how early the mercy of God appears within the Grand Narrative: to Adam and to Eve, to murderous Cain, to Abraham, to Jacob). The LORD "who forgives all your iniquity"—who "removes our transgressions from us" even "as far as the east is from the west" (Ps. 103:3, 12)—this God is not a petulant deity, begrudging mercy to sinners. God's forgiving character is affirmed in too many stories and psalms for anyone in Israel to have thought otherwise. One grand example will suffice:

> The LORD is merciful and gracious, slow to anger and abounding in steadfast love. He will not always accuse, nor will he keep his anger forever. He does not deal with us according to our sins, nor repay us according to our iniquities. For as the heavens are high above the earth, so great is his steadfast love toward those who fear him; as far as the east is from the west, so far he removes our transgressions from us. As a father has compassion for his children, so the LORD has compassion for those who fear him. For he knows how we are made; he remembers we are dust. (Ps. 103:8-14)

Above all we must remember that throughout his ministry Jesus himself forgave sins. Yes, his doing so was labeled a blasphemous arrogance, for "God alone forgives sins" (Mark 2:7), but the objection itself bears witness to the common understanding that God was indeed a God of forgiveness, as well as to the fact that Jesus granted forgiveness personally, apart from and prior to his death on the cross. Thus, we must be careful not to portray the cross as being necessary for God's mercy to be shown to sinners. Jesus granted such through his word.

This being noted, scripture is also clear that God gave Israel specific means through which this forgiveness could be ritualized and actualized. The sacrificial system—so foreign to our thought patterns as to stymie truly sympathetic understandings of it—was God's gracious gift to Israel as a means of maintaining its covenant bonds with the LORD. It emphatically was not a device Israel had concocted to appeal to and appease an angry deity. Through the prescribed sacrifices—especially the offering of blood presented by the high priest to God annually within the Holy of Holies—Israel's role as God's covenant partner was maintained and renewed.

Indispensable to this system was the factor of blood. Again, to modern sensibilities this triggers question marks, but this bloody detail must be read within its context. In Jewish context, blood signified life. Thus, what may strike us as pure gore, to Jewish imaginations conjured life. When sacrificial animals were killed, the killing wasn't the point. The point was the releasing of life, and when this blood was offered to God, it signified an offering of life, a symbolic return of life, a gift of life to the One who had first given it. Moreover, the animal that was slain was to be an excellent specimen—no scabrous, sickly creature—so that the life that was presented was of the very best, never a cheap, negligible castaway.[3]

The point here is to say that God, having in ancient times established the rules, so to speak, honors them in the way God went about renewing the whole creation through the final act of Jesus' life, his sacrificial death. God keeps faith with and works within the people of Israel, through their story, their faith, their practices, and their messiah to bless all the world's peoples.

Using the hints given to us from Jesus' words in the upper room as our guide to understanding Jesus' death, we come to this. Jesus fully intended through his death to offer his own life to God for the renewal/salvation of Israel's and humanity's life. This gift of his life (his blood) was to function as forgiveness for sins past and as a covenant of God's compassionate companionship forever. Jesus could effect this renewal of all things because he was human, and thus he offers humankind's life to God as our representative, and, as God's representative, he pledges God's unfailing forgiveness and companionship to humankind.

Central to this, of course, is Jesus' dual role as the representative of humankind and of Israel. In him all the children of Adam and of Abraham find our one true representative. As our representative he dies "for us," and in this death we die also. All of us are within the "many" for whom he died and who, by God's grace, were included within his death. In his death the "fall" of humankind and of Israel is finally judged—all is put to death. Said differently, in the cross and through Jesus' representative capacity, God was "killing off" both Adam and Israel so that God might, through the resurrection of Jesus, raise the whole creation to one new humanity, to live as participants in the kingdom where the divisive barriers of Jew or Gentile, male or female, slave or free no longer apply.[4]

Crowning this fact of representation is the Gospels' conviction that Jesus was not only *our* representative, but he was also *God's* representative. Jesus is God with us, acting for us. Thus, in all that Jesus underwent, we may understand that this is actually God in flesh at work for us. No innocent third party is being gored for us; this is the Author and Creator of all, now re-creating all. It is God who is suffering and sacrificing God's own self for our sakes.

In consequence of this, a fallen creation is given lively hope. Humankind, having been put to death in Jesus' death and raised in Jesus' resurrection, is both forgiven and restored to its God-intended dual vocation of priest and steward. Creaturely purpose, dignity, and mission as agents of the promised future of God are ours, through faith, as gifts of the already and not-yet kingdom and the Spirit.

Even the "cursed" world of nature is released from its bondage so that it might resume the praise attributed to it in the Psalms (148:7-10, 114:4, et. al.). This liberation of the created order is perhaps the meaning of Matthew's note that upon the death of Jesus "the earth shook and the rocks were split" (27:51)—the bonds of death entrapping even this material earth were being shrugged loose.

As I attempt to summarize the meaning of all of this, I can say that this kingdom way of understanding the death of Jesus gives me a God who is worthy of the Jesus I came to love decades ago. This God is a trustworthy keeper of good promises of blessing, not a feudal lord demanding bloody compensation for his offended honor. Jesus forgave sins in the course of his ministry prior to his death, and therefore forgiveness is a matter of God's merciful character, not just of Jesus' bloody death. But in this death Jesus honors all the ancient atoning requirements of his people, and in doing so he once again and once for all displayed and proved the love of God that had been granting forgiveness and renewal to broken and contrite hearts from Eden onward.

Calvary is not so much settling old scores as it is breaking the seal on a new world. The stone we put in place God rolls away! Richard Rohr provocatively summarizes much of this when he says Jesus "did not come to change God's mind about us. It did not need changing." Rather, "Jesus came to change our minds about God—and about ourselves—and about where goodness and evil really lie."[5]

Mysteries and endless questions still linger within the cluster of events we call the death of Christ. What I have written is certainly insufficient for a full-orbed theory of the atonement, but it does represent my best thoughts about Jesus' final week and deed, the culmination of a life poured out for the soul's rebirth and the world's renewal in hope. I hope my thoughts open a way for you to expand your own understanding of this One who lived (and lives) and died to save us.

Notes

[1] The Gospel of John, for its own purposes, reports this event at the beginning of Jesus' ministry, but Matthew (21:12-17), Mark (11:15-19), and Luke (19:45-48) all locate it as a final Passover week event, an event that is part of his obedience unto death for our sake. I choose to discuss it as the Synoptic Gospels present it, as a Holy Week event.

[2] "The whole of what we call the Second Temple period, roughly 538 BC onward, is characterized by this sense of divine absence: God is gone, and he hasn't come back ... the priests are bored and slack in their liturgical duties because, though they've rebuilt the Temple, there's no sense of YHWH [God] having returned.... The story the gospels are telling...is the story of *how YHWH came back to his people at last.*" N.T. Wright, *How God Became King: The Forgotten Story of the Gospels* (New York: HarperOne, 2012), 89-90. The exile and its central role in understanding the New Testament is a prominent feature in Wright's theological project. See his multivolume *Christian Origins and the Question of God.*

[3] The sacrificial system is best understood as akin to our sacraments or God-given means of grace. Its Hebrew vocabulary does not endorse the idea that it appeases God's wrath by the exaction of a

penalty or by imposing it upon a substitute. "The goat in the Day of Atonement ritual in Leviticus 16 is not understood in substitutionary terms; it is a symbolic vehicle for dispatching Israel's sins into the depths of the wilderness," according to Bruce C. Birch, Walter Brueggemann, Terrence E. Fretheim, and David L. Petersen, *A Theological Introduction to the Old Testament*, 2nd ed. (Nashville: Abingdon Press, 2005), 156.

[4]John 11:49-52 offers a key text for this "representative" role of Jesus: "Caiaphas, who was high priest that year, said to them, 'You know nothing at all! You do not understand that it is better for you to have one man die for the people than to have the whole nation destroyed.' He did not say this on his own, but being high priest that year he prophesied that Jesus was about to die for the nation, and not for the nation only, but to gather into one the dispersed children of God."

[5]Richard Rohr, *The Universal Christ: How a Forgotten Reality Can Change Everything We See, Hope For, and Believe* (Convergent Books: 2019), 151.

CHAPTER 13

The Good News of the Reign of God

It is now time to pull together the several threads of the gospel story I have been attempting to tell. Just as The Plan was compressed into four statements, I think we can compress the gospel of the kingdom into five declarative sentences. These five are drawn from the broad sweep of the biblical story, and each one could have abundant biblical references appended to it, but I have chosen to let them stand alone as summaries of the biblical revelation. Here then is the gospel of the kingdom in capsulized form:

1. The God of Abraham and of Israel is the maker and sustainer of all creation, though it be fallen.
2. God, through the people of Israel, has been at work for millennia to redeem and to bless all creation.
3. God, through Jesus, has accomplished this, inaugurating God's cruciform kingdom on earth.
4. God, through the Holy Spirit, now bids all to enter, exemplify, and seek this kingdom for all.
5. God will ultimately accomplish God's dream of all creation flourishing in love-led harmony.

There is nothing novel here; historians of Christian thought can indicate times in the past where this understanding of the gospel was advocated and widely accepted. Even if it has fallen from view in many churches currently, this way of understanding the gospel is neither new nor another gospel. It is a retelling of the story the Bible itself tells, a story that begins with God's creation of the cosmos and concludes with God's final transformation of everything—including you and me.

The Bible's story is a huge, God-sized story of cosmic proportions. Within that stunning story there is the astonishing claim that human creatures are loved, and, by God's amazing grace, fully revealed in Jesus, we are redeemed from futile existence to a godly vocation and a heavenly future. But God's rescue of us is only part of God's greater story of re-creating the entire cosmos, and we err if we reduce God's story to being solely about us and our heavenly destination. The story the Bible tells is of God's love for all created things. It is a story about God and about God's invincible intent to bless all creation—including us. This astonishing story is the good news we are to cherish and to share.

If pressed to cite one passage of scripture that expresses this understanding of the gospel, I would turn to Revelation 21:5-6a: "And the one who was seated on the throne said, 'See, I am making all things new.' Also he said, 'Write this, for these words are trustworthy and true.' Then he said to me, 'It is done! I am the Alpha and the Omega, the beginning and the end....'"

The gospel I have found is about the "the One" seated on the throne. It is good news about this sovereign God, the A to Z of all that is or was or ever shall be. And my gospel is about what this God is doing—making all things new. Do notice the present tense of that statement: God is *making* all things new! There is a sovereign One who is at work *now* drawing all things to God's own ends. We are not alone or without purpose or hope.

God's re-creation of all things is so certain that God can even say, "It is done!" Personally, I cannot hear this divine "It is done!" without recalling another announcement wondrously like it. From the cross, Jesus uttered his last words: "'It is finished!' Then he bowed his head and gave up his spirit" (John 19:30). Jesus' cross and this new creation are of one piece, worked by the same God to be for us just what William Tyndale claimed: "glad and joyfull tydings, that maketh a mannes hert glad, and maketh him synge, daunce, and leepe for joye."

When our eyes are opened to see the immensity of this—and our inclusion within it—our heartfelt response of gratitude and love is no less than those who respond to the gospel of The Plan. This is a good news message that reaches down to each individual, remaking each one of us—if we will receive and participate in its truth. It is a word from God to save "me." Even more, here is a word from God that saves "us." This gospel saves "me" in part by putting me in my proper place and letting me see my place within the big picture, as one beloved facet of God's re-creation of all things, of all of "us." The gospel of the kingdom opens a wider world to me, a wider arena of need and of gratitude for God's grace in making me and all creation new and giving all of us meaningful work to do with one another and for God's glory.

My own personal relationship and devotion to God have been deepened by this wider landscape of God's working. Jesus certainly remains at the center of that faith. In the five bulleted sentences above, the sentence naming him is the middle one, as the hinge and turning point of everything. To say yes to him is to enter into God's refashioning of all things—beginning with myself. At the same time, to say yes to him and to his gospel is to be swept up into God's mind-boggling, steadfast purpose of blessing for the whole creation. It is to be given an ancient and ongoing story to live from and to live within, giving me a heritage and hope, and assigning me a role within the grand saga of God's work throughout millennia. Through the good news of his life and death and resurrection, Jesus saves us *from* the sins of egotism and despair and self-discounting and also saves us *for* joyful, hope-filled partnership in striving toward God's dream. The good news is that God reigns and—surprise—we really matter!

The twentieth-century master preacher and teacher of preaching, George Buttrick, repeatedly told his Union Theological Seminary students that the underlying message in every sermon must be that "the most wonderful thing has happened"—that God has come in mercy to redeem and renew all creation, giving us dignity and hope. "And in all of its words and phrases, paragraphs and 'books,' what the [New] Testament wants above all else to say to us is only this: 'It has happened!'"[1]

If you want a hymn (a doxology) to conclude that sermon, I have a suggestion for that also.

> My life flows on in endless song; above earth's lamentation,
> I hear the sweet, though far-off hymn that hails a new creation.
> Through all the tumult and the strife, I hear the music ringing;
> It finds an echo in my soul—how can I keep from singing?[2]

I am convinced that the church, at least the branch of it I know best, has a better story to tell than it has been uttering lately. That better story is the good news of the reign of God that Jesus preached and inaugurated through his life, death, and resurrection.

Notes

[1] Douglas John Hall, *Why Christian? For Those on the Edge of Faith* (Minneapolis: Fortress Press, 1998), 56.

[2] The poet is unknown, but the tune for *"My Life Flows On"* is most often attributed to Robert Lowry, 1869.

CHAPTER 14

※

Speaking Better Things

Although in Part 1, "Disappointment," I detailed my dissatisfactions with The Plan using H.H. Farmer's warnings about the church's message being too small, too confident, and too easy to be true, my intention has never been to charge The Plan with being wholly untrue. Rather, I believe its way of speaking the gospel truth is inadequate, limited, and limiting. And I believe the gospel of the kingdom of God is better because it is bigger. Its horizon is broader, and its story is richer. To summarize my convictions, consider some areas where I believe the gospel of the kingdom speaks "better" things than The Plan.

Of God and of Creation

A crowning attribute of the gospel of the kingdom is that it is good news about God rather than more boring news about us. All its statements are about God, not about our self-evident tawdry sins and the action steps required if we are to be saved. Our salvation is certainly part of the gospel story, but it is not the whole story. Rather, the gospel is the record of God's patience and tenacity, of God's wisdom, mystery, self-revelation, and self-giving, all coming to white-hot intensity in the person, life, and passion of Jesus of Nazareth. It is a story of cosmic dimension and heart-pounding consummation—a story worthy of God! So, the first commendable attribute of this gospel is that it calls us to lose ourselves in "wonder, love, and praise" of this unfathomably purposeful, indomitable God.

Implicit within this theocentric gospel is the surprising notion that God is still at work. Far too much church life is smothered in yesterday-stories, in sermons and lessons about what the late, great God did once upon a time, creating the impression that God was fascinating in the days of chariots and sandals, but like all the elderly, God has now slowed considerably and doesn't get out and about much anymore.

The gospel of the reign of God insists that the intriguing God of yesteryear is still dynamically, vigorously engaged with this world. The God of Israel "does not faint or grow weary" (Isa. 40:28). The Holy One is "in the midst" and God's dream of a "right" world has not been abandoned. It is in process, a goal, an already within a not-yet, and therefore God is not just "on a hill far away." God is in last night's city council vote for fair housing and in next Sunday's children's choir singing "Fairest Lord Jesus," in the grandeur of the symphony's performance of Mahler's *Ninth Symphony* and in the medical mission team's Honduran tent and a mother's quiet care. Such kingdom signs are sometimes too few and infrequent and even when glimpsed are open to dispute—but so were the works of Jesus! Nonetheless, it is part of the excitement and duty of kingdom believers to point to and celebrate those occasions when the rumor of a present-tense God can be thankfully confirmed.

Also, while the gospel of the kingdom does not eliminate the truth of the severity of God, it surely magnifies the steadfast love of God. It speaks of God's fidelity and patience more than of God's wrath—a wrath fully justified but mercifully restrained by compassion. The God of the kingdom may therefore be loved profoundly, not from cringing fear of damnation, but from deep astonishment and gratitude for the longsuffering enactment of the Grand Narrative, for the sheer grace of our inclusion within God's dream, and for God's hope-giving promised consummation.

This does not mean, however, that the love of God is trivialized into nothing more than grandfatherly indulgence. God's love is revered as a fiercely holy, redeeming force incarnate in Jesus and still at work in this created order, crafting a new world of justice and joy. God maintains a righteous anger toward all that stifles God's intent, and in some way God will reveal this in the final judgment. But in the interim, the astonishment is that even amid a fallen, flawed world, God's loving power every second is actively upholding and restoring us and the entire cosmos.

Above all, the gospel of the kingdom does not misrepresent God by saying: *God sent Jesus into this world to die for the punishment of my sins in order that I might be forgiven and go to heaven when I die.* This sentence, which I first stated in the opening pages of this book, has been spoken by many, including me, as good news, but it actually speaks bad news about God. Here the unity of God as Trinity is severed. The Father and Son are depicted as "good cop/bad cop" deities, Jesus being sent as the "good cop" who dies in order to placate the anger of the "bad cop," God the Father. Here the mind of God is misinterpreted. Jesus is said to suffer God's punishment—a concept that finds scant scriptural basis—to make it okay for God to forgive our sins. This, in spite of all the biblical assurances of God's mercies apart from anyone having to "pay" for them! That forgiveness always involves suffering, no one can deny—but to suggest that God inflicts pain/punishment on an innocent third party before God's mercies can be given is not good news about the God of the Bible. There is little to admire in such a god; this god is a bookkeeper and Calvary a bloody, book-balancing transaction to fit us for residence with the Almighty. Indeed, such an Almighty would seem to have very narrow interests—really, only one: to protect his home from infestations of unworthy mortals. Gone from view is a God who is love, and who "so *loved the world* that he gave his only begotten Son" to be a friend of "sinners."

In contrast, the gospel of the reign of God assures us that God, without prompting or placating, does indeed care about all aspects of this created, populated world. This One takes this world's history, its health, its planets and nations and politics and peoples very seriously. This means that all we see and feel and deal with every day of our lives is not a throwaway, irrelevant theatrical prop. It is the real thing; the materials God is already fashioning and re-fashioning into a new creation. God is at work in its history, with this planet and this universe—within every little quirk and quark and subatomic bundle of energy—working for its everlasting good, and ours.

And if this be true of God, then the world and all that is within it are intrinsically involved in the meaning of God's gospel. The message to be proclaimed is not only the grace of God appearing in Jesus for our salvation, but also the grace and purpose of God encircling art, commerce, healthcare, government, and all other aspects of creation. No subject is outside God's concern or rule, and therefore no subject is off-limits for Christian engagement. Of this gospel we can say, as of Ezekiel's vision of the river flowing from the throne of God, that "wherever [this] river goes, every living creature will live ... everything will live where the river goes" (47:9).

This understanding of creation also introduces us to better things about our "feel" for this world. A frequent strain running through my inherited gospel is that "this world is not my home, I'm just a' passin' through" and that "some glad morning, I'll fly away." While these sentiments support the worthy concept of life as pilgrimage, they also can leave us with the feeling that this world is a doomed wasteland of little worth. If, however, this world has a nobler role than this, if it is in fact included within God's redemptive intention, then it would be far better for us to sing "We're marching through Immanuel's ground" as claimants to turf already under new management and redevelopment by God's vice-regent, Jesus. Such an altered landscape revolutionizes the "feel" of the spiritual pilgrimage before us.

And certainly, given the ecological crisis that is ours, such an understanding of creation means it is a grievous dereliction of duty not to engage vigorously and forthrightly with creation care. The very stuff of matter and human flourishing is at stake. Our planetary home, given us as a stewardship by the Creator, demands our protective care. This is not an ethical implication of the gospel; it is inherent within the gospel itself!

Finally, consider a fascinating possibility that emerges when we imagine God's finished new creation through the lens of a gospel of the kingdom. For many of us, heaven has been portrayed only in such gaudy (streets of gold, gates of pearl) or lethargic (eternal rest) terms as not to be that appealing. For some of us, the best thing that can be said for heaven is that it is not hell. But the gospel of the kingdom gives us another way of thinking about our eternal home.

That better way begins with recalling our first earthly assignment to be stewards of creation, caretakers of God's "garden," and it proposes that this vocation just might continue into the world to come. John Stackhouse Jr. explores this prospect by recalling the multiple promises that God's people will "reign with Christ" (2 Tim. 2:12, Rev. 5:10, 20:6, 22:5) and wonders if what we will reign over with him is a renewed earth, finally "having dominion" over it correctly, as the "image of God." If so, heaven will be more than nonstop choral performances or blissful contemplation of the geometric mysteries of the Triune God. As Dallas Willard put it: "Our faithfulness over a 'few things' in the present … develops the kind of character that can be entrusted with 'many things' … [God's] plan is for us to develop, as apprentices to Jesus, to the point, where we can take our place in the ongoing creativity of the universe."[1] It is folly quadrupled to pretend we know very much about heaven, but the future envisioned in this scene certainly complements the biblical theme of God's reign—and has a lot more attractiveness to me than many other scenes of heaven I have been given.

Of the Bible and of Jesus

The gospel Jesus is and preached through his life and in his death requires both biblical testaments to be sensical. The Hebrew scriptures were his Bible, and through its words he learned his role within the purposes of God and drew the strength to fill that role. His church cannot fulfill its mission apart from those same scriptures. When, however, 70 percent of the Bible (the Old Testament) is seen as foreign territory, mostly to be raided for stories, types, phrases, psalms, and concepts that suggest or supplement a plan of salvation, Jesus' church is put on short rations.

This evisceration of the book is corrected in the gospel of the reign of God. Here the long story of Israel's flawed attempts to govern its life apart from God becomes a major plotline rather than archaic detritus. Here the yearnings for a divine ruler claim stage center. Here the intrigues of power, politics, privilege, race, sex, national interest, militarism, and economic disparity—that is, all the matters that fill today's headlines—here, the communal, corporate dimension of life, and God's relevance and working within it, is laid bare for our guidance. The gospel of the kingdom returns this vast store of social wisdom to us as part of God's word to us as saving gospel. This gospel gives us an entire Bible, restoring the vacuum created when the gospel is misperceived as about "just Jesus and me."

Moreover, the gospel of the kingdom gives us a unifying thread along with a useful evaluative criterion by which to interpret the Bible and our ethical choices. The idea of 1) a people of God, 2) called to live under God's rule, and 3) a parallel hope of a coming kingdom of God's *shalom*—this cluster of ideas finds voice in virtually every stratum and era of the Old Testament. In the message of Jesus these come together in powerful fusion, becoming the focal theme of the New Testament. Thus, though seldom in a direct line, these ideas propel the Grand Narrative of scripture, providing a theme that unifies both testaments into one record of God's self-revelation through the ages. Correspondingly, the kingdom theme may serve as a criterion by which readers can discern the pertinence of any passage or portion of scripture. Asking how a biblical text (or ethical choice in life) exemplifies or corresponds to the character of the realm of God's *shalom* ("Does this square with the cruciform kingdom of Jesus?") gives a helpful criterion for fruitful interpretation.[2]

Now, both The Plan and the kingdom believe Jesus is the One toward whom the Bible's story leads, that he is its apex. I believe, however, that there are two ways in which better things are spoken of him by the gospel of the kingdom.

In its hymnody and devotional thought, my inherited gospel says in effect that Jesus' only purpose in coming was to die. He is viewed predominantly as the suffering servant, the sin-bearer, the fount of forgiveness. While these images have essential truth, there are other images of Jesus—king, door, bread of life, first-born of all creation, lord, vine, the way, the truth, the life, head, bright and morning star—that give us other windows for seeing and cherishing him. Rather than locating Jesus' significance in just the final chapters of the Gospels (the passion narratives), the gospel of the kingdom seeks to enlarge our understanding of Jesus by pointing to every chapter of the Gospels (and the long Old Testament story leading to him).

In the gospel of the kingdom, every gospel page holds revelatory gospel significance. Here Jesus strides through the days of his flesh as a victor more than as a victim, a compassionate Champion, in each encounter releasing captives from the tight fist of sin and restoring them to their lofty vocation as stewards and priests within God's world.

The insightful mind of second-century bishop Irenaeus of Lyons (130–c. 202 AD) saw this truth in a most encouraging light. Irenaeus taught believers to think of Jesus' physical journey through life as a *recapitulation* of the progressive stages of our life, from infancy through death, each stage lived by him in faithful obedience to God. Therefore, even in Jesus' emotional, spiritual, and physical pilgrimage through human existence, he redeems and liberates us from bondage to our failed ancestry. His exemplary life corrects and restores the botched history of humankind's life. We are saved by his faithful obedience! As much as his death accomplished, it is of a piece with his life, and it is shortsighted to minimize the accomplishments of the fact and deeds of that daily life. British theologian P.T. Forsyth, two thousand years later, gave his amen to Irenaeus' insight, writing: "The death of Christ ... was a function of His total life ... His blood was shed in Gethsemane as truly as on Calvary."³

The gospel of the reign of God also speaks better things of Jesus by virtue of its cosmic note. While not discounting the value of the intimacy of The Plan's personal Lord and Savior, the gospel of the kingdom accents that before all and above all Jesus is the Lord and Savior of the entire cosmos. In kingdom thought, the resurrected Jesus is the magisterial Lord of the universe whose Lordship extends to the farthest galaxies, the lowest hell, and the tic-toc of every hour of history. He is the agent of creation who also holds the keys of death and Hades, the one who alone is worthy to open the scroll of eternity (Rev. 1:8, 5:1-14). Thus, "he was before there was a was," and he will be when time shall be no more, and in the here and now of history "he is [present tense!] ruler of the kings of the earth" (Rev. 1:5).

A "too small Christ" is therefore the great danger a kingdom gospel avoids. "When Christians hold to a too-small Christ," that is, to a Christ whose lordship is construed chiefly in terms of personal intimacy and religious matters, "they lose the ability to resist false sovereignties and make an idol out of family, race, or nation."[4] The Christ who strides through the epochs of history just as purposefully as through the pages of the New Testament is the antidote for this ever-present and currently virulent error.

I think the New Testament expects us to say exalted things of Jesus. And it expects us to render obedience to him as the cosmic Lord over our families, our race, our pocketbooks, our nation, our politics, our speech, our churches, our everything. The gospel of the reign of God highlights this expectation.

Of Faith and of History and Hope

Scripture says we are saved by grace "through faith" (Eph. 2:8). Faith is then the essential requisite in the Christian's life. Yet there is a difference in the character of the faith my inherited gospel requires and the character of the faith the gospel of God's reign calls for. That difference can be expressed in the words propositional and interpersonal.

The faith required by my inherited gospel is problematically propositional. This characteristic appears in the creedal nature of The Plan that constitutes its heart. I noted this creedal nature earlier, but now I add that according to The Plan, if you believe that Jesus died for your sins and that he was raised from the dead by God, the result will be that "you will be saved" (see Rom. 10:9, The Plan's "action step"). Thus, the faith that is being solicited is your agreement to claims about two events that happened two thousand years ago, and upon believing these propositions, you are promised "you will be saved." I will concede that in actual practice users of The Plan know that there is more to it than this, but I still believe this summary fairly presents the nature and kernel of what is asked of those who are saved according to The Plan.

For the gospel of the kingdom, however, the faith that is sought is interpersonal. It invites you to believe Jesus—not statements *about* him, nor a doctrine, but to believe *him*, to trust his word. It asks you to believe he was telling the truth when he said, "The time is fulfilled, and the kingdom of God has come near" (Mark 1:15). It challenges you to believe him when he says, "I am the way, the truth, and the life" (John 14:6), and "obey him when he says "take up your cross daily and follow me" (Luke 9:23).[5] Where my inherited gospel puts two-thousand-years' distance between you and Jesus so that you can talk *about* him, the gospel of the kingdom places you within the experience-field of those who first had to answer the face-to-face question: "Who do you say that I am?" (Matt. 16:15).

The faith-crux for the gospel of the kingdom is: Do you find Jesus credible? Is he trustworthy? It is enough to turn over the keys to *your* kingdom and become a participant in his? What any of us do with the propositions comes later. The Latin words *solvitur ambulando*, drawn from John 7:17, meaning "the thing will solve itself as you go on" is the way earlier generations expressed this evolving faith life. In the beginning, though, there is just this disturbing, fascinating man, and the question is whether he has "hooked" you, causing you to want to follow him, trusting him and his way as the right, the saving way. Thus, the gospel of God's reign says we are saved by the Savior, not by doctrines affirmed about him. In this way, faith is seen as relational and interpersonal, not ideological or propositional. Faith relates you to a person, not to a body of doctrine—and this is infinitely better.

I have two reasons for saying the interpersonal is infinitely better. The first is that this kind of faith provides room for growth. Indeed, it assumes and expects that one's life and experiences will lead to changes of mind about doctrines or belief statements. When faith is tied to a person, rather than to propositions of belief, the life of faith does not crumble when these changes come because faith is understood as heart-loyalty to a friend rather than head-agreement with a creed. The relationship with this friend survives changes as all true friendships do. This dynamic is precisely what I seek to demonstrate in this book: that when one's faith is in Jesus, all manner of changes in how one interprets subsidiary doctrines need not sever loyalty to your saving friend—or his to you.

A second reason interpersonal faith is better is because life inevitably reaches rock bottom. When tragedy strikes, the strength to stand does not come from propositions affirmed. In fact, my experience is that tragedy may actually demolish your faith in some propositions. In such times it is not what one believes, but who one believes. It is the friend who sticks closer than a brother, who sustains even "when all around my soul gives way."

This assurance provides a segue to a parallel concern, the better things said about history and hope by the gospel of the kingdom. I begin with a question posed to me by a twenty-something fellow who had recently accepted Christ according to the propositional faith of The Plan. His question was this: "Why doesn't God just take us on to heaven once we've been saved?"

As this young man saw it, God's purpose for the rest of his life was for him to behave, win others to Jesus, and wait for heaven's gates to open. While he wasn't questioning these goals, he did feel he was facing a span of spiritually unexciting years now that the "big" issue had been settled. In effect, this young man represented my earlier character "Arnold," voicing what faith-vacuum feels like, when faith has most to do with things that happened long ago in Palestine and will happen "once upon a time" in heaven. Here was "Arnold" at a teachable moment before an underlived life was spent.

The depth issues for him are history—a meaningful present-tense history—and the vitalizing power of a this-worldly hope to accompany his assurance of heaven. These are the issues that form the backbone of the gospel of the kingdom, but, as the young man's question reveals, they are too often veiled in the leapfrogging of life that lurks in my inherited gospel. The gospel of the reign of God would tell young "Arnold" that God's purposes for the life before him are for him, in loyal friendship with Jesus his Lord, to enjoy the fullness of God's creation and to discover within it some corner to tend. Yes, he is to "behave," and yes, he is to reflect and to point others to Christ, but he is also to bring beauty, order, justice, laughter, and love ever more prominently into view each day in whatever ways he can, preparing the way for God's ultimate victory. A life of holy purpose, losing himself in the richness of the hope-giving dream of God, is the meaning of the salvation God is giving to him. There are countless, astonishing ports of call for young "Arnold" to enjoy before his final harbor is reached.

In this regard, I fear that when scripture tells us of spiritual gifts for the church's ministry (Eph. 4), we too narrowly define the church and its ministry. The church is called to be a servant of the coming kingdom, and if that be so, no more than we are resourceless in the internal ministries of the church are we empty-handed or alone in worldly ministries of seeking justice, disseminating knowledge and beauty, reclaiming ravaged lands, or any other kingdom-come task. Spiritual gifts for these ministries are surely ours as well, if we are open to receive them. How can it be otherwise if each day and every place is valued as an arena of God's presence and yearning? How can it be otherwise if the entire cosmos is groaning in labor pains for the new creation? Astonishingly, God calls mortals such as young "Arnold" and you and me to be midwives of this new creation, living and working in "the confidence and the pride that belong to hope" (Heb. 3:6).

Hope is an endangered species on Planet Earth today. Weariness and fear-fed cynicism have settled upon our spirits like a smothering, suffocating blanket. Even church folk speak of hope mostly in the sweet-by-and-by sense, or in world-ending scenarios drawn more from science fiction than scripture. Far too few entertain lively hope that we might be able to sit down together, rationally address our problems, marshal the needed resources, and with God's help actually accomplish something redemptive. The church of Jesus can give no greater gift to this fearful world than the good news of the God of hope. Its other name is the gospel of the kingdom.

Of Salvation and of Vocation

Ultimately, a gospel that centers upon the reign of God gives us a different and a better understanding of salvation itself. Two theological terms, justification and vocation, are useful in explaining the difference I see.

Since the Reformation, the heart of Western Christianity's idea of what the Bible is all about, and specifically what salvation is all about, is found in the concept of justification. Credit Martin Luther for this dominance due to his joyful discovery that the Apostle Paul's writings about justification (see Romans 2–5 and Galatians) tell us of God's "righting" of sinners through the ministry of Jesus rather than by our pious strivings. The importance of this justification has often been popularly presented in the statement that because Jesus died for our sins it is "just as if I'd" never sinned. Our indicting record has been wiped clean. God has "righted" us because Jesus took our punishment for us. Thus, what we need to do to be saved is to believe that this is what God did.

I have earlier stated my dissatisfaction with this way of putting it, so there is no reason at this point to repeat those objections. What I now want to add is that this way of understanding what the Bible is all about is a misreading of the Scripture. The Bible is not just about God "righting" us so that we can go to heaven when we die. The observation of Ellen Davis, quoted in the first chapter, that salvation is best thought of as a derivative of revelation now may be augmented by stating that what the Bible reveals is the nature and purpose of God. More specifically, the Bible is about a gracious God's purpose and relentless actions to bless all creation. "Righting" us, therefore, is most certainly one key portion of God's work, but it is not the sum of it, nor is justification the Bible's great passion. A holistic view of scripture reveals that the theme of vocation is even more prominent than justification.

Vocation is the theological term for God's "calling." At least in its churchly dress, vocation has little to do with whether you are a butcher, a baker, or a candlestick maker, that is, with what you do to pay your bills. Rather, it goes back to the old Latin verb *vocare* that meant "to call," and when Protestants speak of vocation, we most often are pointing to God's intent, God's will, God's "calling" and claim upon us as human creatures made in God's image.

The Bible is supremely a book about the *callings* of God. The first of these is heard when God *calls* creation itself into being (God "speaks" and it appears) and gives this created world fruitful potentiality and purpose. Next, there is the appearance of the human creature who is *called* to be a reflector (image) of God and a caretaker (steward) of God's creation. Thus, in the Bible's opening pages, a cosmic theater and human actors, both having specific *callings*, are placed before us. The phenomenon of *calling*, however, continues to drive the plot.

The overarching storyline of scripture, from Abram, to Moses, to Samuel, to David, to Amos and Isaiah and Jeremiah and other reluctant prophets, to Jesus of Nazareth and his apostle Paul—presents us with a cavalcade of persons, all *called* of God to interpret and advance the dream, the intent and purpose, the goal of God. Finally, the focus falls upon those whom the Spirit of God *calls* into the fellowship of the forgiven, the church (Rev. 1:5-6, 5:9-10). We, too, are part of God's relentless march toward the consummation that Jesus audaciously claimed was already "busting loose" in and through him.

This story of callings is what the Bible is all about. Its revelation is of an ages-old divine plot that is still afoot and whose Author is still recruiting (calling) provocateurs for a world beyond imagination, a world of God's own dream. The salvation the Bible speaks of is a call to become co-laborers with no less than God in the care and remaking of creation; it is rescue from pathetically squandered little lives and tragically underlived ignorant lives. It is to see life in IMAX and to play our grateful cameo role within it. All this, and heaven too! This is Scripture's larger, more profound depiction of salvation; a panorama that surely includes liberation from anxiety and guilt over our sinfulness and assurance of being right with God—that is, justification—but that by no means is solely about this one entrance-gate truth. Justification is but one aspect, the releasing dimension, of the greater salvation of knowing oneself to be called, sinful though we be, to holy and eternal deployment. The gospel is that our brief, tiny lives (can) have deep meaning.

To say this yet another way, justification is a work of God within God's own self. It tells us of astounding mercy and generosity acted out within the Triune God for our benefit. It is the work of God that is done *for* us. Vocation, however, is the work of God that is done *with* us; it is the facet of salvation that coaxes us into experienced salvation that includes justification and so much more.

In my youth revival days, we often sang an invitation hymn titled "Softly and Tenderly." Its words told us that Jesus was calling softly and tenderly to you and to me, "Come home." This hymn, for all its emotive impact, called us only to heaven, or, to use the distinctions I've drawn here, only to justification, not to vocation. In doing so, it filled church membership rolls with persons who were "saved," but who often never learned the meaning of their saved lives. We are in urgent need of new songs that call us to lose ourselves in the grandness of what God is doing, and in that rescuing lostness discover our salvation.

The good news of the reign of God speaks better things of salvation. It calls us to more than walking an aisle; it calls us to a life with God, loving what God loves and caring for the world Christ died for. It calls us to be so transformed by the way we handle this life that heaven won't seem such a foreign place after all; it will feel like "home."

Of Us and of Evangelism

The priority of "us" over "me" is central to biblical thought, and I believe it is another way the gospel of the kingdom speaks better things.

To review, God's "dream" has always been of "us," not of a gaggle of unrelated individuals. Abram's calling was to be the father of a great people who would in turn be a blessing to all people. Moses' work was to free this people and to give them God's covenant guidance in being a holy people. The prophets' task was to call this people back to their covenant, communal responsibilities to one another under God. Jesus' ministry gave great attention to the re-forming of this people through the calling and training of twelve disciples, that through them a "body of Christ" might be present for all people. The balance of the New Testament is addressed to churches or to leaders of churches, giving them counsel on leading this people, the body of Christ, in ministry to "the ends of the earth." Throughout all these phases of God's dealings, the goal is "us," not "me."

So thoroughly did this mindset permeate the thinking of the early church that St. Augustine (354–430 AD) titled his most mature theological work *City of God*, choosing a social image, not an individualistic one, to speak of the goal of our spiritual striving. "His controlling metaphor for the new life that God creates is not, for example, being born again, but becoming part of a city, entering into its communal life." The dominance of this "us" perspective is seen also, says historian Robert Louis Wilken, when Augustine meditated upon a verse you and I likely know best from Fourth of July religious services: "Blessed is the people whose God is the LORD" (Ps. 144:15). Augustine, however, heard its emphasis in a word most of us don't even notice. For him the verse read this way: "Blessed is the *people* whose God is the LORD." Wilkins adds that for Augustine, "when the scriptures speak of peace they do not have in mind simply a relation between the individual believer and God; in the Bible peace is a gift that human beings share in communion with God."[6] Our present-day loss of any sense of "us" as a valued essential in church or society is telling.

The gravity of this loss can be seen in two books written in the last decade by David Brooks, the insightful political commentator for NPR (National Public Radio) and conservative columnist for the *New York Times*. The first of these books, *The Road to Character*, deals with the importance of personal character. Its pages describe crucial, important character traits and how they might be developed; its pages could be described as a secular plan of salvation.

Four years later, Brooks published its sequel, *The Second Mountain*, in which he says *The Road to Character* was written when he "was still enclosed in the prison of individualism." At that time, character formation was, in his mind, an individual's task, the product of discipline and solo grit. But America's political meltdown and the end of his twenty-seven-year marriage taught him the emptiness of this individualistic approach. In brokenness he learned the necessity of community and the strength of relational life. "I now think good character is a by-product of giving yourself away," he says. "You love things that are worthy of love. You surrender to a community or a cause, make promises to other people, build a thick jungle of loving attachments, lose yourself in the daily act of serving others as they lose themselves in the daily acts of serving you." Because of his reorientation, Brooks is persuaded that our "whole cultural paradigm has to shift from the mindset of hyper-individualism to the relational mindset...."[7] I hear that as a plea for the church to claim and incarnate a gospel of "us" that is central to the kingdom idea.

This brings me to the better evangelism that is inherent within the gospel of the kingdom. Rather than beginning evangelistic efforts by telling others what damned sinners they are (as Point 1 of The Plan requires), this gospel suggests evangelism begins by demonstrations of community. Surely this must include a church that is inclusive, authentic, and open to strangers.[8] A gospel of "us" will also mandatorily display as much interest and involvement in hearing others' plans and hopes as it does in telling its own story.

Listening ears are grand kingdom equipment, especially when followed by ongoing thoughtful responses to what our ears are told. Sometimes a workplace or lunch conversation during Christmas, Lent, and Easter seasons offers opportunities to talk about the Grand Narrative and of Jesus in informative, non-pushy ways.[9] Especially by joining others in the "secular" work of striving for "the beloved community" (good schools, racial justice, voter registration, neighborliness, for example), others may note and value our presence and participation. In such situations, opportunities arise to say why we are there, in effect, to give "an accounting for the hope that is in you" (1 Pet. 3:15). Every time our interest in and involvement alongside the dreams and hopes of others draw us into conversation, the door is open to speak of God's dream and our belief in God drawing us all toward that dream's fruition.

I no longer can evangelize in the tongue of The Plan. For all the reasons I have reviewed, that way of speaking the gospel is no longer mine. But this does not mean I have no good news to speak. I have better news than ever before!

—The Plan presented propositions to be accepted; the kingdom introduces a transforming relationship to enter.
—The Plan built upon guilt for sin and fear of damnation; the kingdom rises from a story of hope and faith.
—The Plan spoke of a scales-balancing God; the kingdom speaks of a promise-keeping God.
—The Plan settled something; the kingdom starts something.
—The Plan promised heaven; the kingdom opens the door to life today as well as hope for tomorrow.

Especially in this hour when the fabric of public trust and respect has been slashed by the knives of power-hungry littleness, we need the story of God's unwavering pursuit of a "right" world—and of God's call for us to seek it! You can sense the absence of this message in the rawness of the rage in our society, in our not-so-quiet desperation, and in the frothy escapes we seek in stadiums, theaters, bars, and yes, even in many churches. Though political nostrums and self-help regimens are hawked nonstop, durable hope remains rare. The good news of a quiet God, working through centuries to "bless all the families of the earth" (Gen. 12:3) has no equal.

Evangelism is therefore as urgent now as ever before—*if* the good news of the reign of God is its message. As Jim Wallis writes, "Without the central focus of the gospel of the kingdom, the Christian message loses its core and integrating center."[10] The gospel of the kingdom is the only message worthy to be called a gospel, especially in this hour.

It is neither *too small*, nor is it *too confident*, nor is it *too easy* to be true. It brings personal healing through the mercies of God *and* social hope through the promises of God. People need to hear this gospel!

Within it there is a call to "be saved" that is just as true and urgent as any ever issued by a passionate evangelist. But it calls us to be saved from sins more destructive and damning than yesterday's list of moralistic no-nos. It promises to save us from one-dimensional, shallow existence; from slothful boredom, moral indifference, idolatry, selfishness, and loneliness by transforming our little lives into purposeful lives, reintroducing us to our God-given role as co-laborers with God, striving for God's dream for the cosmos.

This gospel also calls for a repentance as searching as anything The Plan ever asked. The "turning" it calls for is a turning away from sin—that is, from lives lived without reference to the reign of God, from values and practices that thwart its full presence within ourselves and our world. The radical nature of this repentance, this change of mind, must be heard. When Jesus opened his ministry with his announcement of the "nearness" of the kingdom and a call to "repent," the very first response to his message came from two grown men, Simon and Andrew, who promptly "changed their mind" about the supremacy of family and career. Shockingly, both involvements are demoted in order to follow Jesus! This astonishing change of mind and life must not be overlooked, for it sets a proper high bar as we consider our own responses to Jesus' good news. The radical "turning" Jesus calls for is a turning to God's future—and to live from and toward that future, following Jesus, the Lord of all. As we invest our lives in daily work and personal attitudes and economic and political vision that incarnates God's tomorrow, we are assured our labors will not be in vain nor without a divine companion—right up until our work is done, and then, when the curtain falls, a welcoming presence waiting in the wings.

In sum, this gospel calls us to live out of and in loyalty to the most absurdly preposterous assertion anyone can dare make. That assertion proclaims: There is a God who cares, a God who has been and is always at work in all our chaos for the good of all creation, whose liberating power may be found in the deeds and words of Jesus of Nazareth, and whose summoning kingdom is more certain than sunrise! This is no new gospel. I firmly believe it is only a "better" way of understanding the good news the Gospels themselves declare. Best of all, standing at the door of this gospel is the same Jesus I met so long ago, and the same rescuing cross. But both look different now, in the light of the kingdom. And the salvation they offer is richer, deeper, broader—and more costly. This is my gospel.

Notes

[1] Dallas Willard, *The Divine Conspiracy: Rediscovering Our Hidden Life in God* (San Francisco: Harper, 1998), 378. See Stackhouse's discussion in his *Why You're Here: Ethics for the Real World* (New York: Oxford University Press, 2018), 13-21.

[2] The provocative triad (community, cross, new creation) for ethical discernment proposed by Richard B. Hays, though far more exacting than my simple "kingdom" proposal, is a thoughtful and more thorough expansion of it. See Hays, *The Moral Vision of the New Testament: Community, Cross, New Creation: A Contemporary Introduction to New Testament Ethics* (San Francisco: HarperSanFrancisco, 1996).

[3] P.T. Forsyth, *The Cruciality of the Cross* (Wake Forest, NC: Chanticleer Publishing, 1983), 101.

[4] Ernest T. Campbell, "Lord of What?" in *Christian Manifesto* (New York: Harper & Row, 1970), 18.

[5] In speaking of Jesus' words in this manner, I do not mean to imply that I am quoting the historical Jesus word for word. I do believe the Gospels give us the Spirit-preserved message we need from Jesus. See the later chapter regarding the Bible and also "A Question of Authority" in my book, *If Jesus Isn't the Answer, He Sure Asks the Right Questions* (Macon, GA: Smyth & Helwys, 2015).

[6] Robert Louis Wilken, *The Spirit of Early Christian Thought: Seeking the Face of God* (New Haven: Yale University Press, 2003), 195. Fairness demands acknowledgement that Augustine's corporate emphasis also bore an individualistic strain that bore unfortunate fruit in Western Christianity, beginning with Anselm's classic work *Cur Deos Homo?* (*Why Did God Become Human?*). Anselm answered that God became human to save human souls, "not the reconciliation of the universe but the redemption of the soul stands in the center" in both otherworldly and individualistic manner. This established "the tendency to regard salvation as a private matter and to ignore the world…. The hope of the kingdom of God was transformed into a hope of 'heaven.'" David J. Bosch, *Transforming Mission: Paradigm Shifts in Theology of Mission* (Maryknoll, NY: Orbis Books, 1991), 216.

[7] David Brooks, *The Second Mountain* (Random House, 2019), xix-xx. This book amounts to a testimony of "conversion" to a lifestyle mirroring the kingdom of God—in secular idiom. The concluding chapter, "The Relationist Manifesto," ought to be required reading in every seminary and Bible college classroom.

[8] A seminal text calling for the church's common life of service and worship to be understood as evangelism is George Sweazey, *The Church as Evangelist* (New York: Harper & Row, 1978).

[9] For an excellent guide to such conversations, I recommend the useful guidance found in David M. Stratton, *Talking About Jesus* (Eugene, OR: Wipf & Stock, 2019).

[10] Jim Wallis, *Agenda for Biblical People* (New York: Harper & Row, 1976), 29.

PART 3

※

Discernment

"We have but faith: we cannot know ... A beam in darkness: let it grow."

For the better part of an hour I watched a father and daughter playing Giant Jenga on a picnic table in a public park. Their tower of wooden blocks reached ever higher, with the two of them in turn tapping the structure here and there to find a wooden block whose removal might not send the whole tower crashing ... and then pulling that block loose with surgical precision and placing it on top. Their stack became so high, the girl could no longer place her block on top. So, her dad did it for her. The drama of their deconstruction/reconstruction game was delightfully fascinating! All three of us were crestfallen when a wicked gust of wind unfairly sent their grand project tumbling.

There is a reason Jenga has remained so long as a fun-time staple. Relocating just one small block can become a high-stakes gamble, exposing your clumsiness or miscalculation as well as demolishing others' work. If nothing more, Jenga reminds you that tinkering with the existing has consequences. That is certainly true with one's beliefs. Tamper with one belief, and you discover another one now needs attention. No wonder many believers are tinker- and tamper-averse.

In this section I offer a selection of some of the consequences, for me, of tinkering with my inherited gospel. I do not suppose the consequences for you would or must be the same. Each person must discern where the gospel leads. But the good news of the reign of God does direct our feet to a different path, and in the following you can read where that path has and is leading me.

Let me stress that last point. The gospel of the kingdom will not permit you to leave everything else in place, and it certainly will not let you compartmentalize your faith. Weekly newsmagazines (for example, *Time*) have the editorial license to divide their content by subject headings such as politics, art, business, and religion. But life, especially when lived within the kingdom, disallows such neat compartmentalizing. For us, all things are related to the God who is making all things new, and thus any idea, say, of separating religion from "social issues" or any other issue no longer works.

So, in this section there are six chapters of consequences, as I see them, of following a gospel of the kingdom of God. You might think of them as exercises in living simultaneously in two time zones: the "already" and the "not yet" of the kingdom. Three chapters speak of how my mind has changed about "theological" matters: the church, its worship, and the Bible. Three chapters speak of how my mind has changed about "ethical" matters: race, sex, and politics. A final chapter is a plea to claim the gospel in all its fullness.

CHAPTER 15

✦

Church: Premature Ambassador of the Now and Future King

"Strictly speaking, one ought to say that the Church is always in a state of crisis and that its greatest shortcoming is that it is only occasionally aware of it."[1]
—*Hendrik Kraemer, 1938*

The first real church I remember was the people who assembled in a county-seat, blonde-brick First Baptist Church building. Across the street was an equally impressive Assembly of God church. They were allegedly experts in the "Holy Ghost," and, since we Baptists were self-professed experts in "Jesus," we felt it our Christian duty to maintain a watchful eye on our Pentecostal neighbors. Call it Christian mindfulness, if you will, but it was a skill I early developed and polished, particularly noting that they were always still in session as we headed to Baker's Cafeteria for lunch.

My little-boy tummy was always grateful that my parents had enrolled me in the Baptist Sunday School. There I became familiar with fascinating Bible stories told by ladies with flannel-graph storyboards and was taught to "Be ye kind one to another." There I soaked up more life-shaping concepts than I yet fully realize as I nuzzled up against my momma's side during the long sermons and listened to her gentle alto voice singing Sunday songs from the *Broadman Hymnal*. There I learned, in order, the books of the Bible, and there I—though I remember it not—walked an aisle and made a profession of my faith in Jesus and, upon my baptism (in very cold water—that part I do remember), became a member of the church. Or so said the preacher and my parents.

In truth, my name was entered on that church's membership list. It would be years later before I actually "joined the church." That decision came when, as a young pastor, I had to decide if this brick-and-mortar thing, this frustrating, exhilarating, blood-sucking, mystery-rich, thankless, wonderful monstrosity was really what I wanted to hitch my life to.

Only in that sorting-out period of my life did I come to see how inescapably central to Christian existence is the church. That's when I began to understand that before there was a Bible, there was the church; that it was the church that had assembled the many apostolic writings and through her worship determined which would become our Bible. Also, it was the church whose conversations and councils set the parameters of Christian theology and worship. And it was the church who put shoes on the gospel and walked it across continents and sailed it across seas to make of it a global faith. In sum, without the church the Christian faith would not be. She really is the mother of it all, and even if at times I didn't like her very much, I had to admit that her blood had given me birth and her presence sustained my life and hope. (I use the feminine pronoun for the church, honoring Paul's metaphor of the Bride of Christ.)

The Catholic biblical scholar Alfred Loisy (1857–1940) is remembered mostly for his now-famous statement: "Jesus came preaching the kingdom of God, but what emerged was the church."[2] His words remain known because they express the struggle many people have with this disappointing remnant of higher hopes, a make-do improvisation from her birth, yet tolerated as Jesus' only child. In its institutional expression, the church invites all the rage and rejection she has received across the ages—the understandable disgust received by anyone who speaks the loftiest sentiments but then proves to be mundanely human. Whatever else must be said favorably on her behalf, the church is undeniably human, and she remains as weak and susceptible to error as any other human institution. A folksy saying declares that the farther up the pole a monkey climbs, the more his bare bottom is visible. Well, the church is perched high on history's pole. Believing as I do that God put it up there, I suspect God did so with a bit of humor, knowing its bare bottom would always be embarrassingly visible and unwiped. You cannot miss it.

The scandal is only slightly reduced if you change the image and dub the church, as the New Testament does, the bride of Christ. Even so, who hasn't wondered if the groom was in his right mind when he proposed, since this bride is neither beautiful nor young, and is often silly, sometimes gaudy, and always speaks with more than a hint of halitosis. Some have even accused her of being more whore than bride. Theologians have sought to soften the scandal, offering distinctions between the church militant, expectant, and triumphant; the church as concept and as institution; the church visible and invisible; and so on. But the only church you or I really know anything about is still the congregation down the road that meets in a bricks-and-sticks building and that has its "issues." This all-too-human group—this and all its predecessors and counterparts throughout the world—this clumsy, bruised beauty is the bride of Christ, the embarrassing mother of our faith.

Growing Beyond Embarrassment

The question for this chapter is how, if we change our minds about our gospel, our thoughts and feelings about this messy church might also change. For my own response, I borrow an image from Richard John Neuhaus. In a discussion of "authority for ministry," he once suggested for pastors an identity and an authority more energizing than being the forever apologetic representatives of this besmirched institution. He proposed:

> We are the ambassadors of a sovereign who is to come: who, until he comes, is enthroned on a cross, exhibiting his majesty in love that suffers with a world that suffers.... We are premature ambassadors, having arrived at court before the sovereignty of our king has been recognized.[3]

Church: Premature Ambassador of the Now and Future King

This quote from Neuhaus strikes me as a fitting image for the church itself. She is an ambassador. She stands before and in this world as one of many voices seeking an audience, but she does so from the awkward posture of one who speaks on behalf of a Sovereign whose rule is not yet recognized. Her life is anchored in an authority that has always been and is now present, even though his rule is contested, denied, or ignored by many, and she lives toward and lobbies for this (almost) here authority. The church is therefore an oddball entity, living in a time-warp, a representative of the Eternal in time, advocating and practicing tomorrow-life today. Or, tweaking Neuhaus' wording, we are the premature ambassador of the now and future king, and our announcement is the arrival of this king and kingdom.

How might this image help us? To begin with, it makes a clear distinction between the kingdom of God and the church. Timothy Dwight's well-known hymn, "I Love Thy Kingdom, Lord," cannot get beyond the second line before equating this kingdom with "the church our blest Redeemer saved with his own precious blood." And so it goes for four more stanzas. I'm sorry, but no. The kingdom is not the church, nor is the church the kingdom. There are many connections between them, but these two are not the same. The church is the servant of the kingdom, not the kingdom in disguise, not even the kingdom's look-alike stand-in. The kingdom is higher.

Especially when I become most upset with the church's pettiness or pokey-ness or flagrant hypocrisy, this is a rescuing truth. It reminds me that this church is only the emissary, and therefore is always less impressive than the realm represented. A measure of disappointment, if not occasional large doses of embarrassment, is unavoidable. I must not expect all the excellencies of the king and kingdom to be resident in the ambassador. To expect more of a servant is unfair. This in no way excuses the church from its responsibility to be a worthy servant, but it does dismiss the legitimacy of any shocked response when the servant proves to be just a servant. If there is any good news within this sobering reminder, it may be within Martin Luther's encouraging observation that God can still shoot with the warped bow and ride the lame horse.

A parallel admonition that comes with this distinction is the error of denigrating or rejecting the church for its obvious impurities. This fallible servant is still the king's ambassador. I know of no other organization that bears this frightful designation. Consequently, she is due my respect. Putting this idea in more biblical language, the church is the body of Christ and is to be respected as such. This body metaphor is a principal New Testament metaphor for the church, and it is far more than just holy talk.

I find it helpful to think of this body as the fruit of the resurrection of Jesus. When Joseph of Arimathea buried the body of Jesus late on that black Friday afternoon, the body of Jesus was just that—the body of Jesus. But when God raised up that body on Sunday morning, more than just a resurrected physical body came to life: it was the body of Christ that came forth from that tomb. The church, this flawed ambassador of Christ, is the child of the resurrection, and now exists as the body of Christ in this world. She now physically represents before the world the unacknowledged Sovereign of all.

Therefore, those who imagine that they can now have access to Jesus while disdaining his body must deal with the absurdity of their tactic. Would they "disembody" him and commune with a wholly spiritual Jesus, or in some manner so sever him from his body as to have communion with just the holy, pure essence of Jesus? Either way, this tactic concocts a truly gross image, reflecting the impossibility within it. Shirley Guthrie puts it this way: "Whoever tries to do without the church tries to do without Christ. Whoever is too good or too 'spiritual' for the church ... is too good or too spiritual for Christ himself, the God who sent him, and the Holy Spirit who continues his work."[4] A spirituality of "just Jesus and me" is a dead end.

This does not mean, however, that Jesus is trapped in the church. It does mean that the church, according to Guthrie, "is where the Christ who is at work in loving and liberating power everywhere is specifically known, thankfully trusted, and voluntarily served" and, therefore, "although God is not bound to the church, we Christians are bound to it."[5]

The celebrated lay Roman Catholic theologian Hans Kung, who was a significant contributor to the theological agenda of the historic Second Vatican Council, left a deeply personal testimony about his love-hate relationship with the Roman Catholic Church:

> I have always had the feeling that to get out of the church boat—which for many people is an act of honesty and protest—would for me personally be an act of failure and capitulation. No—despite everything, I have received too much in the community of faith in which I grew up to be able to get out of it so simply ... I have no time for an elitist Christianity that wants to be better than the many who are there, and no time for church utopias aimed at an ideal community of pure, like-minded people. Despite all my sorry experiences with my church, I believe that critical loyalty is worthwhile, that resistance is meaningful and renewal is possible, and that another positive turn in church history cannot be ruled out.[6]

So, this distinction between the church and the kingdom gives me a helpful way to frame both my embarrassment and my participation within the church. Just as "Christ loved the church and gave himself up for her" (Eph. 5:25) and also speaks judgment upon her (Revelation 2–3), so may I. Sometimes even Christ seems to be outside, knocking on her door like a stranger seeking entrance (Rev. 2:1–3:20). But he has not given up or walked away. "I am with you always," he said. So be it.

Church: Premature Ambassador of the Now and Future King

Engaging in Mission

Yet another benefit of the distinction between the ambassador (church) and the kingdom is that it clarifies the church's mission. The church, as servant, exists to be of service to the King and the kingdom, to be an advocate for and representative of the "yet to be fully seen" reign of God. Her assignment is to keep the *vision* clear and lively and to cherish and access the *provision* within it. Said in the reverse, the church is not present in and before the world to engage in self-promotion or self-preservation. No more than the United States' ambassador to France is commissioned to build a fan club for him- or herself among the French is the church to be self-seeking in her ministry. The church is in the employ of Another and is obliged to further the interests, the cause of that Other.

Unfortunately, this is a distinction and an assignment the church has often ignored. The church in my lifetime is no exception. When the "everything's coming up roses" days of Billy Graham revivalism began to recede in the 1970s, the next trend in religious circles was the "church growth" movement.

Ostensibly based upon global missiological data, proponents of the "church growth" movement told church leaders that "effective" (most of us read that to mean "big") churches could still be built by putting into place several growth-enabling practices (one popular book advocated "twelve keys"). The salesmen for this movement knew their stuff; they knew how to build organizations that hummed, and many of the churches who drank their Kool-Aid and were strategically located in populous areas experienced remarkable numerical growth. And at the same time, a number of professional fund-raising companies helped churches raise impressive sums for the construction of even more impressive church buildings to house the fruits of all this "church growth."

It was a heady time; mega-churches and their smorgasbord of seven-days-a-week activities became headline news—and countless wannabe congregations followed their lead. Easily lost in all this exhilarating swirl of onward and upward, however, was a vital sense of why these churches were in business. Outreach was typically based upon what the church can do for you and what Jesus can do for you—only minimally was it a call to serve or to be changed or become a change-agent.

Easily obscured from vision was the purpose of being a community called of God's Spirit to be advocates of God's rule, servants of God's dream of a world re-wrought in justice and peace. For many people, the mission of the church had become church growth, not kingdom witness.[7]

But in time, church no longer was the place where Americans sought their social or religious fulfillment, let alone any disciplining of their lives. "Just Jesus and me" individualism revealed its fickle anti-institutional face. Attendance began to decline, imperceptibly at first, but then in a noticeable lack of volunteers to staff all the activities housed in our impressive buildings—and then the greatest blow of all: offerings began to tumble.

The day of reckoning had come, with buildings mothballed, programs dropped, and budgets slashed. Survival anxiety mushroomed.

Failure or Fidelity?

It would be cheap and inaccurate to say the plight of the American church today is attributable to a loss of kingdom mission. Many other factors have also been at work: sociological, economic, demographic, political, and cultural. But it would be just as inaccurate to deny that the absence of a kingdom gospel and mission did play a role in the present dilemmas of many churches.

The fact is, very few churches in America today can claim the numerical benchmarks of success they could boast just a few decades ago. Pastors and church leaders are bending over backwards trying to keep their ship afloat, walking on eggshells trying not to offend anyone for fear of losing even one more member or family or donor, while many are also delicately leading congregations to downsize prudently without pointing blaming fingers or feeling like failures.

Rather than churches and church leaders smothering themselves in the sadness of guilt for institutional failure, however, how about donning the glad rags of ambassadorial mission? Church leaders can muddle through the current straits by wise downsizing, hoping for a rosier day—trying to soften the crash landing. Or, better, we can risk all by enhancing our prudence with a gutsy turn to being premature ambassadors of the now and future king and kingdom. We can "repent" of our past idolatry of success as the world defines success; we can quit trying to preserve yesterday (as good as it was) and pivot toward full fidelity to the king and kingdom at history's horizon. We can dare to be the salty, prophetic minority pointing to the promised kingdom where "thy will be done on earth" is not just a memorized Sunday phrase. We can elevate beauty in all its rescuing forms and advocate boldly for this-world justice, gesturing all the while toward the Christ who died for us and lives for our hope. We can be people of the kingdom.

On the endpapers of one of my favorite books I long ago copied the now disturbingly relevant words of one whose name I unfortunately failed to note. That author said: "It is not only of individuals dear to them, but about ways and institutions dear to them, that Christians must be prepared to say: 'The Lord gave, and the Lord hath taken away. Blessed be the name of the Lord.'" There is wisdom in these words—and hope.

I do not say this easily. God knows I love a handsome big church building, a full parking lot, a packed sanctuary, a thriving children's and youth ministry, thrilling music, community esteem—I love it all and have given my life to building just such churches. I have lost count of how many capital campaigns I have led—and led with a "pace-setting sacrificial pledge"—to build or renovate buildings for such use. I am as much an addict of this ecclesiastical model of success as any clergy person I know, and I grieve, yes, grieve, when I see it dwindling.

But if our addictions are being taken from us, if societal shifts are spelling our demise, if God's own self is pronouncing judgment upon our infatuation with "our" churches, then I must deem this convergence of factors to be a call to claim a new and better identity—" premature ambassador of the now and future king and kingdom"—and trust that our Sovereign will raise up new forms and fresh expressions of church that will be faithful and fitting for the next chapter of God's intent. I must do more than grieve; I must rejoice in the God who is making all thing new.

A Suffering Church

This risky response is more than simply painting a halo around inevitability. Rather, it is a call to shift our focus from seeking success to accepting suffering as our way of life. For centuries the church has utilized four criteria, gleaned from the Nicene Creed, to describe herself: One, Holy, Catholic (universal), and Apostolic. However, Canadian theologian Douglas John Hall, noting that these four actually "are all latecomers on the scene" of Christian thinking about the church, urges us to reclaim suffering as our great characteristic. "There is more in the New Testament about the suffering of the church than about any other single theme or issue of ecclesiology."[8]

To establish a basis for his assertion, Hall notes Jesus' statement concerning his followers: "If any would follow me, let them take up their cross and follow." Though all of us have likely squirmed under the sound of that requirement, I have always heard it as a word to individuals, not the church. And indeed, it is a word to us individually, but if it is true of us one by one, it must also be applicable to all of us in the aggregate, that is, to the church. (*We are the church*, a fact that all our fuming about the church tends to forget.) Thus, the persons and the people who would be followers of Jesus are told from the very start that their life—and life together—is to be one of suffering. What else could it be if we truly are premature ambassadors of a rectifying kingdom impinging upon the present powers that be?

Jesus was born of the chosen people Israel, for whom suffering was a hallmark. We see this, among other places, in the "suffering servant" passages of Isaiah (ch. 53 et. al.), in the writings of Jeremiah and Lamentations, and in the experience of Job. Hall confirms: "The theme is fixed in Hebraic faith that the people chosen by God to represent God's way and will among the inhabitants of the earth will suffer in their pursuit of this vocation."[9] We should expect nothing less.

Hall points to this same experience and expectation within the writings of the Apostle Paul and by the writer of 2 Peter.

Therefore, since we are justified by faith, we have peace with God through our Lord Jesus Christ, through whom we have access to this grace in which we stand; and we boast in our hope of sharing the glory of God. And not only that, but we also boast in our sufferings, knowing that suffering produces endurance, and endurance produces character, and character produces hope, and hope does not disappoint us, because God's love has been poured into our hearts through the Holy Spirit that has been given to us. (Rom. 5:1-5)

For we do not proclaim ourselves; we proclaim Jesus Christ as Lord and ourselves as your slaves for Jesus' sake. For it is the God who said, "Let light shine out of darkness," who has shone in our hearts to give the light of the knowledge of the glory of God in the face of Jesus Christ.

But we have this treasure in clay jars, so that it may be made clear that this extraordinary power belongs to God and does not come from us. We are afflicted in every way, but not crushed; perplexed, but not driven to despair; persecuted, but not forsaken; struck down, but not destroyed; always carrying in the body the death of Jesus, so that the life of Jesus also may be visible in our bodies. For while we live, we are always being given up to death for Jesus' sake, so that the life of Jesus may be made visible in our mortal flesh. (2 Cor. 4:5-11)

Beloved, do not be surprised at the fiery ordeal that is taking place among you to test you, as though something strange were happening to you. But rejoice insofar as you are sharing Christ's sufferings, so that you may also be glad and shout for joy when his glory is revealed. If you are reviled for the name of Christ, you are blessed, because the spirit of glory, which is the Spirit of God, is resting on you. But let none of you suffer as a murderer, a thief, a criminal, or even as a mischief maker. Yet if any of you suffers as a Christian, do not consider it a disgrace, but glorify God because you bear his name. (1 Pet. 4:12-16)

I confess I have always heard these and similar passages as referring to the early missionaries of the faith or to hard-pressed churches in Christendom's infant days. Theologian Hall forcefully challenges this reading and, I think, rightly insists these texts are talking about the *essence* of the true church in every age. "If you claim to be a disciple of the crucified one, you must expect to participate in his sufferings; if you preach a *theology* of the cross, you will have to become a *community* of the cross. Anything else would represent a kind of hypocrisy."[10] Until the resurrected, living Lord comes in kingdom fullness, he is present in his "body," this *community* of the cross, as a despised, rejected, crucified Lord who suffers with and for all who are victims of evil.

This would mean church is not a societally approved Christian club featuring inspiring Sunday morning talks and sing-alongs and offering free classes in middle-class niceness for children. This would mean church is more than attending quiet vespers and cultivating a fondness for candlelight and holy water. Rather, church is Jesus' ambassadorial presence "exhibiting his majesty in love that suffers with a world that suffers." Leonard Hodgson reminds us that "neither truth, beauty nor goodness can be established on earth without suffering" and "the Church is a body of men and women asking that they may be allowed to bear that suffering, because by the Spirit of the living Christ it can be treated as the raw material for the output of love."[11]

For some churches this may mean suffering the loss of social prestige and of no longer being the place to be seen. For others this may mean suffering the humiliation of selling buildings we no longer can afford, or the embarrassment of apologizing to black and brown neighbors for our practices of racism and struggling to find new ways to be neighbors and sisters and brothers. For still others it may mean taking lonely stands against the community's opinions on race, immigrants, sex, war, politics, poverty, and more. In a society increasingly unimpressed by all organized religion and especially by a discredited Christianity, it will mean suffering as a minority who continue to honor Jesus as Lord of all.

He, who was strung up by the rulers of this age, calls and empowers us to follow in his footsteps—to feel the lash of public scorn and the nails of the establishment's wrath. We are called to be upstream swimmers, fellow sufferers for a world reborn, ambassadors of tomorrow today.

And, let it be clear, this church—because she understands herself as an ambassador and not the kingdom—is free of self-concern and protective anxieties over self-preservation. She is free to say and do whatever her Sovereign instructs her to say and do. Even if those instructions seem suicidal and lead to institutions and ways dear to us being taken away, she will trust in the God of resurrection to raise up other forms of "church" for tomorrow.

A legendary pastor of New York City's Fifth Avenue Presbyterian Church, J.H. Jowett (1864–1923), once preached about avoiding suffering. Noting that suffering seems to be built into life, he said we can avoid much of it simply by cultivating "an insignificant life." If all we desire is to avoid suffering, said Jowett, then all we need do is to "cut the wings of every soaring purpose, and assiduously cultivate a little life with the fewest … relations. Reduce yourself to the smallest compass." The sorrows of the world never disturb those who acknowledge no ties to others. But if we open ourselves to others, pain will enter. "Enthrone a world-purpose, the Christ-purpose, and [your] sufferings will be increased on every side." But he went on to say that a big, holy purpose does more than introduce us to suffering; it "also makes us more sensitive toward God." "If we suffer with Christ, Christ himself becomes a great reality" promised Jowett. "There is no surer way of becoming sure of Christ than to follow the way of sacrificial life and service. It may bring us into a fiery furnace of suffering, but 'in the midst of the fire' there shall be one 'like unto the Son of God.'"[12]

Who is Sufficient for These Things?

Now for a closing confession: I know how to do "church." That is, I know how to do church in its past forms. I know how to draw up a church constitution and bylaws, to organize committees, to elect officers. I know how to interview and hire staff, to set goals, to lead growth and building campaigns. I know how to write pastor's columns and make hospital visits and conduct funerals. I know how to baptize and preside at the table, how to structure worship services, and how to prepare and preach sermons—I've even taught this stuff to seminarians. I know how to do church!

But I don't know how to do "kingdom." I don't know how to "suffer." I don't know how to "lament" or "protest" or "die." Nobody ever taught me how to do these things. I certainly don't know how to teach others to do these things. About them I am as clueless as the disciples on the eve of Pentecost, the day when the Spirit of God descended upon that ignorant-though-Jesus-taught handful and began to make them representatives of God's new thing.

With this said, I am back to where I began this chapter, with my haughty comment about the experts in "the Holy Ghost" being the Assembly of God folks across the street. I don't have a clue how much those AG folks knew about the things I've been talking about. But I do know they had a lively sense that it was the Spirit of God, and not their know-how, that was in charge. This is not to elevate them to angelic stature, because I am sure they had their "issues" just like everyone else. But it is to admit that in great measure, the folks on my side of the street knew and know how to do "church"—and we don't necessarily need the Spirit to do it. We've got this! And it is to admit, with sorrow, my deep suspicion that the "church" as I have known it is as much a product of managerial/entrepreneurial smarts as it is the work of the Holy Spirit.[13]

So, if the next chapter of the church's life is to be as a premature ambassador of the now and future king, we must be taught how to do this new thing. We know too little about it to pretend otherwise. We must become more the children of Pentecost than the church of my past, for only the Spirit is sufficient to show us and to help us now. At the very least, our new environment of dependence upon God is a saving reminder of one pertinent phrase: "For *thine* is the kingdom …"

Notes

¹Hendrick Kraemer, *The Christian Message in a Non-Christian World* (London: Edinburgh House Press, 1938), 24.

²Alfred Loisy, *The Gospel and the Church*, trans. Christopher Home (New York: Charles Scribners' Sons, 1912), 166.

³Richard John Neuhaus, *Freedom for Ministry* (New York: Harper & Row, 1979), 61, 62.

⁴Shirley C. Guthrie, *Christian Doctrine*, rev. ed. (Louisville, KY: Westminster/John Knox Press, 1994), 355.

⁵Ibid., 356.

⁶Hans Kung, *Credo: The Apostles' Creed Explained for Today* (New York: Doubleday, 1993), 131.

⁷A stout rebuke to the "church growth" movement came in Robert K. Hudnut's *Church Growth Is Not the Point* (New York: Harper & Row, 1975) in which Hudnut argued that most churches could be two-thirds smaller and lose no power. The point of the church, he said, was, among other things, to be reduced, to preach, to create, to pray, to be forgiven, to be humbled, to suffer. This last action will be developed in this chapter.

⁸Douglas John Hall, *The Cross in Our Context: Jesus and the Suffering World* (Minneapolis: Fortress Press, 2003), 140, 138.

⁹Ibid., 141.

¹⁰Ibid., 140, italics in original. Douglas Hall presents this theme more fully in *Confessing the Faith: Christian Theology in a North American Context* (Minneapolis: Fortress Press, 1996).

¹¹Leonard Hodgson, *Christian Faith and Practice* (Grand Rapids, MI: Eerdmans, 1965), 90.

¹²J.H. Jowett, "The Sufferings of Christ" in Clyde Fant and William Pinson, *20 Centuries of Great Preaching*, vol. 8 (Waco, TX: Word Books, 1971), 73-77. Italics added to original.

¹³I do not place these two in opposition; surely, they can work in tandem. But I do believe prayer will be more crucial than professionalism, to *receive* will be more essential than to continue giving from a barren cupboard.

CHAPTER 16

✱

Worship: Painful Party of the Woke

"Worship is the supreme and only indispensable activity of the Christian Church. It alone will endure, like the love for God that it expresses, into heaven, when all other activities of the Church will have passed away. It must, therefore, even more strictly than any of the less essential doings of the Church, come under the criticism and control of the revelation on which the Church is founded."[1]

—*William Nicholls*

For the first three decades of my life I attended churches that used a personal tracking system called the Six Point Record System. Every Sunday School attender received a dollar-bill size envelope for each Sunday. The envelope contained blank spaces to enter your name, Sunday School class, date, and amount of the offering enclosed and also six rectangular boxes to be checked, one for each of six points having a percentage value assigned. You could earn 10 percent just for Attendance (Point One), and another 10 for a Brought Bible (Point Two), and 15 percent for Lesson Studied (Point Three), and so on. The last of the six points, Attending Preaching, was worth a bunch of points!

I draw attention to "Attending Preaching" because that is how I was taught to speak and think about what the greater Christian tradition would call worship. But in my tradition, the underlined emphasis was upon the weekly sermon; it was the venerated means of evangelistic outreach, and hearing the sermon was the paramount reason for our assembling. Thus, all of us Sunday School pupils were handsomely rewarded for "Attending Preaching." We were not alone, however, in this way of thinking.

Untold thousands of Protestant churches in America have a heritage of the Sunday morning gathering as being primarily a preaching service—concluded with an opportunity to accept Jesus as one's Savior, traditionally during the congregational singing of an invitation hymn. These services typically give the first part of the service to songs preparing the congregation for that sermon, which always consumes the lion's share of the rest of the time and is followed by the invitation hymn. The assembly spaces themselves were built to accommodate these practices: for example, clear sight lines to a central "stage" and pulpit for the preacher (and risers for the choir), conveniently spaced aisles and "slip" pews to facilitate movement to the "altar" or "mourner's bench" (front pew).

In these ways, architecturally and liturgically, these churches display their rootage in a nineteenth-century American revivalistic pattern in which for the first time in Christian history Sunday worship was centered around sermon and appeal. For the preceding eighteen hundred years, the sermon (if one had been given) had been followed by prayers or, especially, by a communion observance. Within revivalism, however, this pattern lost favor. The Sunday gathering became devoted to enacting the gospel as expressed in The Plan, which meant that communion services became infrequent or conducted at other times, prayers were fewer in number, scripture readings were shortened and selected for evangelistic impact, and the content of hymnody shifted from theology to testimony. All things must support and move toward an evangelistic appeal, to registering public decisions to accept Jesus.

To their credit, my Six-Point ancestors spoke honestly of Attending Preaching, not of worship. Nevertheless, the word "worship" was often used to refer to these gatherings, even if the word was, and mostly remains, an unexamined term. Had it been more carefully studied, my predecessors would have realized that "worship" refers to actions offered to God in praise and thanks—not to meetings geared for evangelistic results. They might have understood that their Sunday meetings were not in a biblical, historical sense "worship." Possibly they might also have realized, as many of us have, that it was possible to attend preaching faithfully for a lifetime, yet seldom, if ever, worship God in those moments.

If we are to have a church that functions as a servant of the reign of God, I am convinced a better understanding and practice of worship is essential. The question this poses can be stated simply: How might worship be different if the gospel of the reign of God, rather than The Plan, is the foundational theology for that worship?

"The Woke" as Worshipers

This question has led me to conceive of worship as being "The Painful Party of the Woke." By using the term "the woke," I am obviously employing a term recently introduced to our vocabularies to indicate someone who has fully awakened to new social configurations now in play, especially regarding race and gender. In some circles, the term is unfortunately seen negatively as a synonym for being "politically correct." But I am using it to refer to a spiritual, theological awakening, and though I recognize that "the woke" is an awkward term, perhaps that is what is needed to refer to something as odd as the kingdom of God.

Once you have awakened to the centrality of the kingdom concept in the scriptures, have heard the ringing bell of justice, and have in any measure tasted the Christ-released presence of the reign of God, you are "woke" to a distinctly expanded way of valuing and living. Your mind has been "messed with," and you can no more flick it away than you can live up to it fully. Your eyes have seen something strikingly different, and if you are truly blessed, you "get" the concept of living simultaneously in two worlds (the present one and the kingdom-come one). You see yourself as a tomorrow child today. You have stumbled into a new self-understanding. You are among "the woke."

Worship: Painful Party of the Woke

However, this "woke" double-life of ours means an existence that is inescapably both joyful and painful. It is joyful because it is grounded in the good news of God's present-tense and promised deeds in this world and the world to come. The reign of our God has begun! But this rescuing victory also brings pain because God's work is not yet complete, and the suffering of this waiting world now becomes our burden as well as God's. The cosmic struggle is not yet ended, injustice has not been banished, children are still starving, cardboard and tent cities of refugees still exist, bullies still stalk the world—God's anguish continues, and if we are God's children, participants in God's reign, that anguish is known to us too.

Paul expresses the both-and character of this way of life by celebrating that "we are children of God, and if children, then heirs, heirs of God and joint heirs with Christ"—and pairing this with the painful reminder that we also "suffer with him so that we may also be glorified with him." Paul concludes by saying: "The whole creation has been groaning in labor pains until now; and not only the creation, but we ourselves, who have the first fruit of the Spirit, groan inwardly while we wait for the adoption, the redemption of our bodies" (Rom. 8:16-17, 22-23).

To be among the "woke" is to be among the being-redeemed guests at God's painful party, a party that like the church itself is somewhat premature. The party and the pain, the noun and the adjective are equally true and always joined. How we conduct ourselves in this in-between time, during the unfinished work of God's remaking of all things is the essence of our worship.

In some ways this premature party is like Handel's great oratorio, *Messiah*.[2] This oratorio, telling the story of Jesus from prophecies of his birth to his resurrection, is recognized worldwide, and its "Hallelujah" Chorus has become so popular that it is even played by marching bands at half-times as entertainment for uncaring, half-drunk football fans. But I learned to sing the bass lines of the "Hallelujah" chorus as great sacred music while a teenager. I was surprised when years later I learned that this majestic "Hallelujah" is not the finale of the oratorio. To me, Handel's words were so final and his music so triumphant, I was certain they had to be the very last words and notes! "The kingdom of this world has become the kingdom of our Lord and of his Christ, and He shall reign forever and ever. Hallelujah! Hallelujah!" Can anything be more climactic than that?

Well, obviously Handel thought something could be more climactic. His "Hallelujah" is placed approximately three-quarters of the way through the oratorio, upon the eve of the resurrection of the Messiah. There are twenty more minutes of music before Handel is finished. A lot more remains to be said and sung before this show is over! Handel's "Hallelujah" outburst of victory is, therefore, an illustration of the worship of the "woke." Our song breaks forth now, too, before the show is over, in the midst of waiting and laboring for the promised culmination. Ours is a party, to be sure. But it is also a painful party. Sometimes we even groan our hallelujahs.

"The Woke" in Their Earthly Temple

I now understand worship as a matter of liturgy and of *lifestyle*, as opposed to the common view that worship is only a Sunday morning affair. I believe scripture teaches us that presenting our bodies, that is, our daily living, for the service of God is also a form of worship (Rom. 12:1). The Apostle Paul, who wrote these Romans words, goes on to say this worship consists of acts such as sober self-assessment, devotion to the other's good, generosity, hospitality, and even loving one's enemies (Rom. 12:3-21). These are the weekday liturgies of Christian worship. They echo the counsel of the prophet Isaiah (ch. 58) who, weary of Israel's "religious" worship, called for the "daily" worship of loosening the bonds of injustice, letting the oppressed go free, sharing bread with the hungry, clothing the naked, bringing the homeless into your home, and caring for your family. Not a one of these is a temple task.

I am, in fact, struck by the fact that in the creation accounts of Genesis 1 and 2 God creates everything—except a temple. Amid all the reports of the flora and fauna, the terrestrial and celestial wonders, and the human caretaker, there is not one hint of "religion" per se within this garden world of God's creation. No temple, no altar, no sacred shrine is specified. Might the reason for this omission be that the creation itself is understood to be the temple of God, a holy place of God's residence where "God might walk about in the coolness of the day"? If this way of understanding our world is remembered, it means the largest frame of reference for worship is in the world—not inside a temple, a shrine, or a church building.

Worship pertains to all that transpires in this place called the world. Christian worship that is informed by the universal kingdom of God must talk about worship in terms of our daily work, not just our Sunday devotions. It sees worship as how we spend our days and nights, not solely with where we spend an hour or so each week. On Sundays our worship is expressed in the forms of praise and prayer; on weekdays it is expressed in the form of ministry and service. Both are essential.

The Tic-Toc of Worship

In true worship a spiritual tic-toc is present; God's revelation (the tic), when answered by human obedience (toc), constitutes worship that is pleasing to God, accomplishing a mutually attentive conversation between heaven and earth. Thus, wherever God's word finds a Yes response, there God is worshiped. Whenever God's will is done on earth as in heaven, God is worshiped. The concept of the kingdom of God tells us that the worship of God arises whenever and wherever acts of care and healing and fidelity and growth are being offered. Worship arises when:

… a mother cares for a child
… a lawyer seeks justice
… a teacher helps a student "get it"
… a polluted river is cleaned
… a cop protects and defends citizens
… politicians seek the good of all
… a musician masters the notes
… a forest is saved
… a patient is kind to a hospital aide
… a wrong is righted.

Wherever and whenever the well-being of God's world, its health and wholeness, is being sought and the brokenness of human life is being mended, there divine worship is being conducted. Some of us, "the woke," may offer this worship knowingly, while others may offer it unknowingly, but whenever and however God's dream of this-worldly *shalom* is being enacted, God is being worshiped. Celebration of the "already" is visible even as the yearning for the "not yet" is audible. The painful party is in process.

Meanwhile, Back at the Church-House …

What transpires in sanctuaries and cathedrals and crossroads church-houses is therefore done to nurture the painful party's flourishing in the world. It is this or it is worthless religiosity, a devilish deceit. Sunday's meetings are to keep this life-posture of groaning and rejoicing in view and in balance, refusing to let worship become a tragic ignoring of the world's anguish or a doleful abandonment of kingdom joy. Both lament and celebration, both "remembering the world to God"[3] and rejoicing in the presence and promise of God, are essential Sunday tasks. Walter Brueggemann says it is the preacher's (and by extension, all worship leaders') "primal responsibility to invite and empower and equip the community to reimagine the world as though God were a key and decisive player."[4] Indeed, to place God at the center of our worship, and to receive from God fresh energies to be counter-cultural seekers of God's reign—this is our shared assignment when the community gathers to worship.

As people of the dawn, who live on the border of now and forever, our liturgy is to say and to help us live this saving truth: "The day of God's triumph is at hand!" Therefore,

> Shuffling through rituals empty of grief or joy,
> Doing Sunday's duty,
> Mumbling pious ditties, set to deader tunes,
> Enduring well-meant wads of preacher talk

Crawling toward an exit called Benediction
This I cannot and will not call worship!
It is poorly disguised death on a seventh-day platter.
And it need not ever happen—or be suffered.

The God of Hope

How might Sunday's worship be more helpful, more of a painful party of the woke?[5] One place we might begin is in a consideration of the images of God floating within the thoughts of worshipers. Of course, it is anyone's guess what is going on in the minds of worshipers, but I suspect that if they are thinking of God at all, it is a God with certain features. Two images come easily to mind. One is of a grumpy, seated old man you'd be wise not to mess with, and the other is of a solid rock you can depend on in every storm. For some worshipers these two may be crazily blended. Both certainly have their merits. The old man can be talked to, cajoled, and related to even if ever so gingerly. The solid rock is an anchor and a landmark even if somewhat lacking in personality. But, above all, both understand God to be fixed and immovable, settled in the sky.

My supposition is that both of these images are homely spin-offs of some facet of our dense, classic understanding of God as the Eternal, Unchanging Three in One: Father, Son, and Holy Spirit. To be sure, they are sadly disappointing spin-offs, but nonetheless I think they likely stem from some facet of the richness of the Trinitarian concept. Noticeably, both have latched upon the fixed, immovable, Great I Am dimension of this doctrine. What may not be as noticeable is that this dimension fits well with a theology of salvation by The Plan. There is a fixedness and a settled permanence, a certainty to both. This God and this salvation are a match.

I would suggest that by turning the prism of the Trinity to another angle we might garner other and much more promising images of God. As an example, how about God as "The Now and Future Sovereign over All Things Seen and Unseen"? Such an image is obviously not as graphic as the old man or the solid rock, and, if you are worried, I am not seriously proposing we trot it out for liturgical use next Sunday.

But I am seriously asserting that the way in which we think of God shapes and is shaped by all else in our faith. And I am seriously proposing that our worship and worldview, if they are to be shaped by the dynamism of the reign of God, must find more dynamic, purposeful, present and future tense images of God such as the awkward one I have just suggested—but better!

Our images of God must be refreshed, pulled out of their chairs, and made to move again. Our ways of speaking of God must say the Old Man is a lot younger than you thought and The Rock is a rock that moves.

Who is God? God is one who is making all things new! Who is God? God is one who was before there was a was and who will be when the last tic-toc of time heralds the trumpets of God's forever party! Who is God? God is the now and future sovereign over all things seen and unseen! Who is God? God is the mystery who has much to explain and one day will.

I trust that you see I am still talking about the eternal Triune God, but with certain facets turned to refract the prism most needed for our day. In this I am once again following H.H. Farmer's counsel to bring from the biblical treasury the vessels best suited to present need. And in doing so, I am saying that the traditional Triune Majesty lens for "seeing" God has led many to an imagining of God as a static, Immovable One, solid if not even sedentary, and that this image shapes their worldview, faith, and even the God-sense of the Sunday gathering. Without doubt, the Unmoved, "Great I Am" image of the God who is and was and will be everlastingly always the same, is most rescuing at times. A solid rock who is dependably there is essential, and I am not discounting this. However, a theology of the reign of God asks us to adjust the spotlight occasionally so that other dimensions of God can be seen, specifically a dimension that in its very wording gestures toward a lively, dynamic, purposeful God.

Recalling our Ancient Roots

A case can be made that lively, beckoning images of God animated the earliest Christians. It would be centuries before the dense permanence of the doctrine of the Trinity would begin to enter the life of the church. Theirs was an era of unsettledness in doctrine as well as in practice, yet from those chaotic days we have drawn our guidance for two thousand years.

The God to whom they prayed certainly was nowhere close to the seated, senile old man that now beclouds our church culture. Rather, an eager "Maranatha"—Come, Lord—was on their lips. Theirs was a world that had been gloriously reborn and yet was also agonizingly unfinished; it was a creation waiting for its redeemed completion, and theirs was a Lord who was "making all things new." Even their chosen worship day, Sunday, bears witness to this.

Jesus had been raised from the dead on a Sunday, the very day scripture also said God created the world. To Christian minds this was no coincidence. Sunday would be their worship day, for on this day God had created and now re-created the world. One second-century document even speaks of Sunday as "the eighth day, that is, the beginning of another world."[6] So, every Sunday was the Lord's Day, a day to mark their belief that tomorrow would not be simply a copy of yesterday because the now and future sovereign of all things seen and unseen was on the march!

The same vibrancy continues to sparkle in the descriptions the early Christians wrote of those Sunday meetings. One of the earliest of them tells us that, gathering in homes, they read scriptures "as long as time permitted"—they were eager to listen and to discern what God was up to—and they listened to sermonic encouragement to heed what had been read; they entered into a period of group prayer that led to a concluding sharing of bread and wine with one another. They called it a "communion," a communion with one another, obviously, but also with the Lord whose presence was still with them. He was in fact the host for this "meal," a meal that was nothing less than a dress rehearsal of the final messianic banquet.

Thus, their meetings moved with unvarying step toward this climactic moment when they communed every Sunday with their Lord and one another, until the day when they would eat and drink with him in glory. (They typically called this meal the *eucharist*—the good gift, the thankful, "happy" meal!) Through bread and wine, his body and life given for them, they received nourishment for life in this new world "until he comes." And to be certain that there were no stragglers, no drop-outs from this cadre of the new creation, they carried portions of the bread and wine to any who were absent. This act put flesh to their belief that theirs was a life-together existence and that they were a kingdom-of-God people among whom no one was left out—especially the poor, for whom an offering was received.[7]

Here is the painful party of the woke—in its earliest Sunday dress. Even in those robust, "make it up as you go" days of development, there is evidence that the early Christians' image of God was not one of a sedentary senior citizen or an immovable rock (or a three in one Trinity). Their image of God was the out-front yet ever-present, guiding re-creator of this world.

Because God had opened their eyes to see that the promised unimaginable had actually happened, and was now afoot, they gathered in open defiance of the ever-visible reign of wrong before them, to be a people shaped by God's story, by its long history, and its promised culmination. They departed with gifts for the poor and a prayer of longing: "Maranatha—Lord, come!" These were meetings that sculpted our ancestors in a worldview and manner of life that made them the people who "turned the world upside down" (Acts 17:6). Their concept of God had everything to do with that tribute being given to them.

A Better World to Live In

The first five books of our Old Testament, the Jewish Torah, received their final and present form in Israel's darkest hour. This was the period (539–333 B.C.E.) when Persia dominated the Jewish nation. Israel's land, heritage, customs, autonomy were all lost and its life was lived under Persia's thumb in a foreign land. This demoralizing context had an all-determinative influence upon what Sam Balentine calls "The Torah's Vision of Worship."[8] His meticulous study of the worship materials within the Torah led him to conclude that the dynamic of hope is the overwhelming factor driving every word and deed of the worship patterns laid out in these first books of our Bible. The worship festivals of Israel were meant, by their structure, location, and conduct, to awaken worshipers' imaginations to the world of God's creational intent—to the world as God planned it, to a world that works "right."

When, for Israel, nothing visible seemed holy or hopeful, these worship forms were prescribed so that Israel might by faith and through the power of its ritual and liturgy remember and revitalize its hope in "a better world to live in." When the "presumed world" of evil's unending reign seemed to be the only world, the Torah's vision of worship gave to Israel a "counterimagined" or "proposed" world—a world where God's reign was near.[9]

Not by any measure is our day as grim as Israel's Persian period, but ours is a day when the red-blooded hope that throbs through every page of the New Testament seems to have been sucked from the church's life. A new vision of worship worthy of the reign of God is needed. All suggestions are welcome.

Notes

[1] William Nicholls, *Jacob's Ladder: The Meaning of Worship*, Ecumenical Studies in Worship No. 4 (London: Lutterworth, 1958), 9.

[2] I am indebted to N.T. Wright for this *Messiah* analogy.

[3] See Don Saliers, "Interceding: Remembering the World to God," ch. 8 of Saliers, *Worship as Theology: Foretaste of Glory Divine* (Nashville: Abingdon Press, 1994).

[4] Walter Brueggemann, *Deep Memory, Exuberant Hope: Contested Truth in a Post-Christian World* (Minneapolis: Fortress Press, 2000), 2.

[5] See additional ideas in my book, *Seeking the Face of God: Evangelical Worship Reconceived* (Macon, GA: Nurturing Faith, 2013).

[6] Epistle of Barnabas, 15:8-9, in Edgar J. Goodspeed, *The Apostolic Fathers: An American Translation* (New York: Harper & Brothers, 1950).

[7] This description follows one of Christian worship in Rome written around 150 AD by Justin for the Roman emperor Antonius. Justin's account and other early Christian worship patterns are discussed more fully in *Seeking the Face of God*, 109-190.

[8] Sam Balentine, *The Torah's Vision of Worship* (Minneapolis: Fortress Press, 1999).

[9] The terms "presumed," "proposed," and "counterimagined" worlds are from Walter Brueggemann, *Texts Under Negotiation* (Minneapolis: Fortress Press, 1993), 12-18. Neither he nor Balentine are suggesting other-worldly escapism in such terms. These terms are a summons to reorientation and hopeful engagement in this world.

CHAPTER 17

✣

Bible: Archives of the Kingdom

"I pledge allegiance to the Bible, God's holy word, and will make it a lamp unto my feet, a guide unto my path, and hide its words in my heart that I might not sin against God."

There you have it—the "Pledge of Allegiance to the Bible" that I memorized as a first grader and recited each morning during the opening exercises of my church's two-week Daily Vacation Bible School. In retrospect, I don't know whether to be more impressed with the 1950s mothers and grandmothers who staffed those two-week marathons or with the genius who came up with the idea of beginning each day with a stately children's march into the church with flags flying and ceremonially solemn oaths sworn by all the children to the Bible, to the Christian flag, and to the Stars and Stripes. Obviously, I still remember those weeks. And I most certainly remember that pledge to the Bible, verbatim. It was my introduction to words *about* the Bible. In the following years I would hear many more words *about* the Bible. Most of them, unfortunately, were arguing words.

When I was in college there was a big flap in our denomination about a book a seminary professor had written about Genesis. Our denominational press had published it, so you'd think somebody at headquarters had read it before it hit the bookstores. But some pastors were much displeased that the professor had left the door open to belief that creation took more than six twenty-four-hour days and to the possibility that Adam and Eve weren't the sole biological ancestors of the human race. The angry clerics got their way; the professor moved on to another job, and the book was withdrawn. The Bible was saved—for the moment.

When I was in seminary the same crowd again became angry that the denominational press had published yet another book about Genesis that opened the same doors. Since the author was British, the unhappy crowd couldn't fire him, but they did get his book withdrawn and rewritten by a more agreeable professor. Words *about* the Bible were becoming all-important to a lot of people.

A few years later, offspring of these error-sniffers began a successful years-long purge of professors, administrators, and pastors who would not affirm "the plenary verbal inspiration and infallibility of the inerrant word of God." There, in one smelly pile, are all the words *about* the Bible that had become the litmus test for my tribe. Notably, only the words "inspiration" and "word of God" are Bible words. The rest were words fashioned centuries later, divisive, angry words *about* the Bible, that typically support a literalism that both misrepresents the Bible's message and gives the world one more reason to ridicule the faith of those who cherish this book.[1]

Throughout the years while all this blood-letting was transpiring, I was preparing and delivering sermons, often two or three a week, to persons who, for the most part, could not have cared less about all the preacher-fights. They, too, had gone to daily Vacation Bible School and were happy enough to affirm that the Bible was God's holy word, a lamp and a light to show us the way and keep us from harm. For myself, my seminary studies had led me to the conclusion there was no way I could accept the idea that God had dictated every word in the Bible (plenary verbal inspiration). Nor could I say that everything in the Bible had to be historically, scientifically accurate (infallible, inerrant) for this book still to be just what I had been taught in Vacation Bible School: God's holy word. As Roman Catholic scholar Raymond Brown says, "Measuring fish gullets in order to prove the historicity of the Book of Jonah" was and is, indeed, a sad waste of time.[2]

For me the Bible was a book about God and not science; it spoke wisdom about life, not archaeological or geological data. If I wanted the latter, I'd seek a textbook dealing with those subjects. If I wanted a trustworthy word from or about God, I'd seek it from the Bible, for I increasingly realized that the Bible offered Godly life-truth even if some of its ways of speaking that truth were whimsical or even fabricated. As Methodist pastor D.L. Dykes once put it: "The Bible is made up of true stories and truth stories, but either way it's telling it like it is." Above all, as I prepared and delivered my sermons, I realized that the best sermons were always rooted, not in my thoughts about a subject, but in biblical texts I had really tried to listen to. The book had an uncanny ability to "deliver" when it was honored. Thus, I resonated wholeheartedly when I came across P.T. Forsyth's 1905 statement that he did "not believe in verbal inspiration" but he did believe that "the true minister ought to find the words and phrases of the Bible so full of spiritual food and felicity that he [sic] has some difficulty in not believing in verbal inspiration."[3]

So it is that I continue to be astonished by the wisdom, the insight, the aha! that grabs me time and again through a phrase, a story, a psalm, even the use of a specific word or the placement of a single word within a verse of the Bible. I cannot and need not explain this phenomenon, but I must report it as a fact experienced too many times for me to doubt or deny it. Of course, there are other times when I run across a statement in the Bible that is outrageous, offensive, and begging to be struck through with a fat, black-ink marker! This, too, must be reported. But perhaps, like a long-appreciated friend whose flaws you learn to live with and around, I find it easier in the fourth quarter of my life to "read around" the Bible's ugly verses because this old friend has served me so well for so long.

Even so, reflecting upon those Bible-battles of yesteryear, I am impressed today with what a cocky bunch we were. So many were so sure they knew exactly what was in the Bible! If only we had given more attention to attentively listening *to* the Bible rather than fighting *about* the Bible, perhaps we might have learned that our generally shared, blind loyalty to the gospel according to The Plan had led us into the theological swamp this book attempts to drain.

My own exit from this dismal swamp began in part when, in exhaustion, I gave up on the debates over infallibility and inerrancy and even biblical authority and gave myself permission to begin reading the Bible, searching for a better gospel. That relinquishment and that search led to my discovery of the gospel of the kingdom and to a new way of viewing the Bible that I call "archives of the kingdom."

When I call the scriptures "archives of the kingdom" I mean that the Bible is where the Grand Narrative is to be heard. Here I can hear "the old, old story" in its rich, many-layered, baffling, heartening, contradictory, instructive original form and, because I understand the Grand Narrative to be a narration of the saga of the unfolding kingdom of God, the Bible's sixty-six documents may justifiably be called archives of this kingdom. Here are the tall tales, the love poems, the sermons, the dissenters' testimonies, the moral reasonings, the songs, the court records, the mini-biographies, the war stories, the statutes, the memorabilia that can introduce us to, and form us in, a kingdom-of-God way of thinking and living and hoping.[4]

Of course, the archives of the kingdom include more than just these sixty-six documents. The better part of twenty centuries of history have been lived since these sixty-six books were designated as holy scripture for Christians. God did not retire upon publication of the Good Book. Therefore, the story these centuries have to tell is also a part of the archives. So, I must listen to the ensuing centuries' records as well as to the biblical documents if I am to profit from God's ongoing story. The primal, originating documents are, however, most important.

Building and Using an Interpreter's Bridge

The larger idea within my characterization of the Bible (and subsequent Christian history) as archives of the kingdom is this: *no one lives in the archives*. We visit the archives; we don't live there. We study the archival materials, but then we return home, to a very different world. We wander in that strange world of yesterday, seeking landmarks that may help us chart wise paths in the present that are true to the best of our past. We do this hoping that our studies within the archives' stored wisdom will form and inform us and our ways of assessing present-day matters. Several factors are involved here.

First, there is the assumption that archival materials from a distant time and culture can help us find our way forward—if we interpret them rightly. Interpretation is the key word here since there is no one-to-one correspondence between today and the culture and situations we read about in the Bible. There are similarities, surely, but not repetitions. This means we are forever walking back and forth across a bridge between a shadowy *then* and a pressing *now*. And, as the saying goes, "The past is a foreign country: they do things differently there." Even when the Hebrew and English languages have a word that refers to the same thing, that does not mean that this word held the same meanings to an ancient Hebrew author as it does to you and me today. As an example, the word "marriage" carries quite different meanings in our romanticized day than it did in Abraham's day.

We can observe these cultural-linguistic challenges even in translating modern languages today. Witness these examples of dialogue appearing as subtitles in films from Hong Kong:

"I am darn unsatisfied to be killed in this way."
"Gun wounds again?"
"A normal person wouldn't steal pituitaries."
"Darn, I'll burn you into a BBQ chicken."
"Take my advice, or I'll spank you a lot."
"Who gave you the nerve to get killed here?"
"I'll fire aimlessly if you don't come out!"
"Beat him out of recognizable shape!"
"I have been scared silly too much lately."
"Beware! Your bones are going to be disconnected."
"How can you use my intestines as a gift?"[5]

If such laughable results can come when we are working with two modern languages, how much greater is the need, when working with an ancient language/culture, to do our bridge-walking with great care and modesty, trying not to misrepresent what the archives are saying.

A second complicating factor is that we approach this interpretive bridge from different communities. My community of origin greatly influences what I see and am able to hear when I visit the archives. I am a white, male, Baptist clergyman from the American southland. Those are the eyes and ears I inescapably use when I read the Bible or when I watch a film or process life. My friend who is a black, female, Ivy-League-trained lawyer raised as an Episcopalian has received a different set of eyes and ears to process what she reads, watches, or experiences. Neither of us can escape those vantage points; they are inherent in who we are, and they largely determine what we immediately perceive in any situation. This is demonstrably so in our reading and interpreting the Bible.

Cleophus LaRue, among many other black preachers, has noted that the story of the exodus of Israel from Egypt's slave-state, and its revelation of a God of compassionate power, provides "the heart of black preaching."[6] That story, with all its liberation motifs, is the central well-traveled bridge for African-American interpreters to move from *then* to *now*. An example of this is Gardner C. Taylor's sermon "His Own Clothes" based upon these words: "And when they had mocked him, they took off the purple from him, and put his own clothes on him, and led him out to crucify him" (Mark 15:20 KJV). From this text, Taylor, a prince among America's black preachers, launched a powerful sermon contrasting the unworthy, false "clothes" humans have placed upon Jesus and the majestic clothing that is appropriate for the King of Kings. But in his introduction to this sermon, Taylor speaks of the humiliation Jesus and the black race have endured—sometimes by having their clothes stripped from them. Born in 1918, Taylor was still within easy recall of those who suffered this treatment in his native Louisiana.

I do not believe a white preacher could or would ever have seen in this text what Gardner Taylor saw. My white, privileged community certainly did not give me eyes to see what the eyes of this child of oppression saw without a second glance. Just as Cleophus LaRue and Gardner Taylor come to the archives across bridges built by their community, so do I. Everyone begins somewhere.

My point here is that our archival work is complicated not only by "the strange world within the Bible" but also by the specific, lived world the interpreter brings to these documents. We see what our eyes are prepared and have been conditioned to see. This book is in effect a report of my attempt to gain a more holistic understanding of what the archives have to say, to visit the archives with the eyes of other communities who bring other life experiences and expectations to the same documents. Mine has been an attempt to see the gospel whole, to hear it as good news for all earth's communities today. And, at this juncture in my life, the concept of the kingdom or reign of God offers me the most inclusive set of eyes and ears I can find to overcome my inherited gospel and my community's limited perspective.

But I must confess that this way of viewing scripture and its interpretation results in a more modest estimate of my own correctness. I am now uncomfortable when someone attempts to end debate by saying, "The Bible says…." Yes, that kind of answer and even those words have been much a part of my past. I still resonate with it, as these pages document repeatedly. But the Bible says many things, and some of them don't agree with what is said at another place in the Bible. "It is a mistake to look to the Bible to close a discussion; the Bible seeks to open one," was the verdict of William Sloane Coffin, adding that "the Bible is a signpost not a hitching post. It points beyond itself, saying 'Pay attention to God, not me.'"[7]

Sabbath and Circumcision

A final consequence of viewing the Bible as archives of the kingdom is that it calls upon us to go forward sometimes by faith rather than by quotations—it removes the security blanket of a Bible verse to back up our every move. Sometimes we must move into the future with something less than dead certainty (there may be something important to be learned from that coupling: "*dead* certainty") that we are on God's side. We act, trusting that our archive-aware, best instincts are in the stream of God's always-coming kingdom. In effect, this is the practical importance of archives that include post-biblical history. If a kingdom-of-God theology means anything, it means that God is not dead nor without a continuing and present-day activity within this creation. We must, then, pay attention to and learn from both the present and the past if we are rightly to discern the will, the footsteps of God.

Two instances of this from within the New Testament itself are instructive. One of these is the early church's choice of Sunday as its day of worship. As indicated in the chapter on worship, there is no record of any directive from God or an apostle to do so. Indeed, that decision slips by without any fanfare within the archives; the Acts of the Apostles just matter-of-factly begins to report Jesus' followers meeting on Sundays. But all of these followers were Jews and from the time of Moses the hallowed day of worship for Jews was designated as Saturday, the Sabbath. Sabbath-keeping finds a place within the ten foundational covenant "words" from God's own hand. So, for these Christians to select another day for their worship amounted to disobedience of one of the Ten Commandments. We can, of course, assume they also continued to observe the Sabbath in addition to their worship of the risen Jesus on Sundays. But if so, that practice died out and only Sunday remained. Hence, these earliest Christians in good faith actually set aside clear commands of the Bible; they dared to disregard the archival, "the Bible says," because they believed God was doing a new thing in their time and place.

A second case study is the church's rejection of circumcision's necessity. From earliest times, the rite of circumcision had been a sign of inclusion within the covenant people of Israel; its institution dated to the time of Abraham, Israel's founding father. But in Acts 15 there is the story of the council in which the early church dismisses the necessity of this marker for Gentile converts to the gospel of Jesus. Apparently by majority vote this council deleted the ancient requirement, boldly deciding that the God of Israel, the God and Father of Jesus Christ, had no interest in perpetuating an ancient marker of the faithful. This too is a remarkable putting aside of the archive's precedent, and it is explained only in the phrase "it seemed good to the Holy Spirit and to us" (v. 28) to make this decision. The members of that council knew their Bible, but they also knew the wind of the Spirit of God was blowing in new ways—kingdom of God ways. They voted to go with the wind of the Spirit, not the letter of the texts.

I am fully aware that my words may be taken as an encouragement to pay no attention to the Bible. That, however, is not my intention. Rather, I wish only to be honest about how the Bible itself shows us how it is to be used.

At the least, these two biblical examples demonstrate how devilishly difficult it is to implement the notion of biblical authority. Not everyone working on the interpretation bridge sees the same thing! Nonetheless, some Christians insist that any disagreement or departure from any word within the Bible is absolutely forbidden. Such deification of the text is idolatrous. At the same time, it is stupidity of the highest order to dismiss the value of these texts to our life. The archives are not God, but they are essential to our life. They are our archives. But, to repeat, we do not live in the archives. We must live and offer our witness in these times, doing so, we hope, in the lineage of the best that has gone before and in response to where we sense God moving into the future.

The dilemmas we wrestle with today are often dilemmas that in biblical times had not yet surfaced. I do not, for example, believe there is a simple one-size-fits-all archival answer for abortion, gun control, national borders, sexual orientation, and so on. On many public and personal matters, we simply cannot establish an archival chapter-and-verse resolution. Therefore, like the early church, we must listen to the biblical and more recent past and then be faithful enough to follow the ancient paths or to push beyond the walls of the archives when we sense that is what the Spirit of God desires.

A helpful illustration of our situation in these in-between times has been sketched by N.T. Wright, who imagines the discovery of an unfinished play begun by William Shakespeare.[8] The literary world comes awake with interest, as well as with speculation about how the great Shakespeare might have concluded the play. To resolve the question, a team of Shakespearean scholars is enlisted to complete the play. Their first concern is with a review of all the other plays and sonnets of Shakespeare, studying his methods and plots and resolutions. In light of the past, they dare to write the balance of the unfinished play of Shakespeare. In a measure, this is the church's perennial task: to continue and complete the great Author's intentions by careful Spirit-sensitive study of the archives and by daring decisions consistent with the spirit of the Author.

Hiding in the Archives

Our ever-present temptation is to content ourselves with being knowledgeable archivists rather than becoming brave activists for the reign of God, to know our way around in the Bible but be ignorant of the way of the cross. I can attest too personally that the archives are wonderful hiding places, for they are quiet, "dead," and safe. Discipleship, on the other hand, puts us into noisy, conflicted spaces that are anything but safe.

A *Jeopardy* show once posed a Final Jeopardy question asking for the homeplace of a biblical giant who was killed with a stone from a slingshot. From my archival study I knew that the giant was Goliath and that David's was the sling-shot responsible for Goliath's "downfall." But neither I nor any of the contestants could come up with the homeplace of said giant. (It was Gath.) The question before us today, though, is not our mastery of the names of biblical birthplaces but whether we can name today's Goliaths— a sometimes tricky assignment since few of them strut around in discernible Philistine armor or even wear black hats as bad guys are supposed to do. Nor are their deeds as universally agreed upon as evil. So, we risk our best opinions and opposition, rooted in the wisdom gained from the archives of the kingdom, trusting that we are on target—but choosing to be wrong, perhaps, rather than to hide in the archives.

Apart from the archives we have no history, we are a non-people without an identity. Shackled within the archives we have no relevance; we are a pointless-people without a place. But, when we live in teachable conversation with the archives, we have a vocation, and we are a needed people with a witness to bear.

This is all I have to say *about* the Bible. But I will add this: To listen *to* it is better than to talk *about* it.

Notes

[1] See Karen Armstrong, *The Lost Art of Scripture: Rescuing the Sacred Texts* (New York: Alfred Knopf; 2019).

[2] Raymond E. Brown, *Responses to 101 Questions on the Bible* (New York: Paulist Press, 1990), 31. Brown goes on to say that the Book of Jonah's truth is about God's merciful desire for all nations to live within God's will, and that we do not have to believe that a historical figure named Jonah was swallowed by a large fish to receive that truth.

[3] P.T. Forsyth, *Positive Preaching and the Modern Mind*, 3rd ed. (London: Paternoster Press, 1998), 24.

[4] If this way of seeing the Bible is adopted, there is no room for fights over infallibility and inerrancy, as though our faith rests on individual words; rather, our faith arises from the worldview gained from the many words and the cumulative witness of the entire collection of writings of holy scripture. It is a way of life we seek, an orientation to time and eternity—not a codebook or error-free encyclopedia of religious information.

[5] *Raleigh* (N.C.) *News & Observer*, Nov. 4, 1998.

[6] See Cleophus J. LaRue, *The Heart of Black Preaching* (Louisville, KY: Westminster John Knox Press, 2000).

[7] William Sloane Coffin, *The Courage to Love* (New York: Harper & Row, 1982), 7, 8.

[8] N.T. Wright, *The New Testament and the People of God* (Minneapolis: Fortress Press, 1992), 140.

CHAPTER 18

Race: *One* Nation ... with Liberty and Justice for *All*?

"It is time for Americans to wake up and realize that black Americans are not going to tolerate what we've had to put up with in the past ... Sometimes it seems like to tell the truth today is to run the risk of being killed. But if I fall, I'll fall five feet four inches forward in the fight for freedom ... and until I'm free in Mississippi, you're not free anywhere else. The future for black people in America is the same as the future for white people in America ... If you survive, we will too. If we crumble, you are going to crumble too."[1]

—*Fannie Lou Hamer, 1968*

Dunbar High School in my hometown was located somewhere over in "Niggertown." Yes, that's what we called it. (Actually, in my home "we" never ever called it that; my parents would not permit the use of that name or the use of the N-word.) It sounds so ugly to me now I can barely type it or confess it. But that was the way things were in the 1950s in Oklahoma—which is quite a distance from the maligned Deep South where *they* had a problem.

As far as Dunbar High School was concerned, I was ignorant about who or what the name "Dunbar" represented, nor can I now tell you what condition the school was in; I never saw it, nor did I ever venture into that area of town. The message was clear for white kids like me: Don't go over there! My counterparts "over there" probably received the same message, since I don't remember many of them walking around downtown or attending city events.

(An irony of this is that my hometown had been established in the late 1860s by one strand of the Creek Indians as a governmental center for their portion of the Trail of Tears "Indian Territory." By the time of my boyhood, though, whites ran the place or were so intermarried with the Indians that no one noticed or cared much who was of Scottish-Irish and who was of Indian descent—and, yes, "Indian" was acceptable in those days; we had not yet heard of "Native American.")

I was told that a town nearby had a law that forbade the presence of Negroes within its city limits after sundown. I've since learned this was so common that there's a term for it: "sundown towns." My hometown obviously had no such rule, but we probably had other rules that were equally as discriminatory. Had I known about them I would not have thought them wrong, though. I just would not have thought about them. People at my church certainly never brought up the subject, or if they did, it was done so delicately that I missed it.

I was well into my fifties before I learned one reason why the black-white divide had been such a not-talked-about issue in my childhood. It was then that I first heard from the elegant black historian John Hope Franklin (who was a child there at the time) that in 1921 a race riot in nearby Tulsa left thirty-six African Americans dead (many estimate it was at least five times that number) and burned down the Greenwood District of the city, known then as America's "Black Wall Street" because of its nationally noted economic vitality. Though all this had taken place only twenty-one years before my birth—and in a city only forty miles away, where I had relatives living—that chapter of our recent, regional history was a secret well-hidden from youngsters like me.

In my college years my Oklahoma classmates made quite a to-do over a Nigerian fellow enrolled in our Baptist university. To their credit, some of the leaders of the student body befriended him and almost made a celebrity of him. He was a product of our Baptist mission work in Nigeria, so there may have been some trophy mentality going on there, but I always gave them credit for trying to display hospitality to a stranger—especially in those days when reports of a Negro Baptist pastor named Martin Luther King Jr. were beginning to filter into our world. I do not recall the presence of any "home-grown" blacks in our ranks, though. Nor do I remember any enrolled in the seminary I attended.

For that matter, I do not recall the first time I ever touched black skin. I do remember wondering if it felt the same as white skin and my pleasant surprise and relief when a handshake—probably at some interracial religious event—established that the black hand I had just grasped felt like all the white hands I had shaken in my life. Even into the Sixties—when I stood to sing "We Shall Overcome" with black ministers, all of us holding hands—I was as sensitive to the feel and touch of "colored" skin as I was to the anguish and hope of the words we were singing. There was something about the closeness, the skin-on-skin touching, that made me uncomfortably aware that these so-called brothers and sisters truly were a race apart, an alien factor in my all-white world.

Color Becomes Status

Since those early days I've often asked why I felt this way. Why were persons of dark brown skin so discarded and discounted by us? They certainly posed no numerical threat to our 1950s dominance of Indian Territory, aka Oklahoma. The integration of whites and American Indians was, even in my own family's history, so normalized that race-mixing, or in that horrid expression "miscegenation," surely couldn't have been logically construed as a degradation of my white race. Yet it is clear that there was a deep divide, an ugly abyss, between the Negro and us.

Race: *One* Nation with Liberty and Justice for *All*

My question, of course, reaches far beyond my hometown to the soul of every person and place in this nation. My white ancestors have, at least in American society, a tragic trait of fearing and devaluing the "different," regardless of the specific difference perceived. For illustration of this, look no farther than to one of America's Founding Fathers, Benjamin Franklin. In Franklin's *Observations Concerning the Increase of Mankind* (1755), he demanded to know why the "Palatine *Boors*" should be allowed "to swarm into our settlements and, by herding together, establish their Language and Manners to the Exclusion of ours? Why should *Pennsylvania*, founded by the *English*, become a colony of *Aliens* who will shortly be so numerous as to Germanize us instead of our Anglifying them, and will never adopt our Language or Customs any more than they can adopt our Complexion?"[2] For all the largeness of his thought in other areas, Franklin was playing an early form of the "race card" with his final complaint of a different "Complexion."

The equation of "color" and "inferiority" was, in fact, a mental fiction cooked up in Franklin's era by white Europeans and then used to justify their enslavement of blacks. In the late 1600s the idea of sorting peoples by skin color (four were identified: white, yellow, brown, and black) emerged in French literature. By the early 1700s, white skin had been identified as the most excellent by Jean Baptiste-Chardin, who was struck by the lovely, naked, white-skinned ladies he saw in the Caucasus Mountains (hence, the term Caucasian). His assessment quickly became Europe's opinion, though there was not one whit of scientific evidence then or now to support it. The ranking of whiteness as "best" was the self-elevating invention of white people—white people with social, economic, and political power.[3]

So, in Franklin's mind, and in the minds of his fellow white Founding Fathers, the association of color and inferiority was already at work. Small wonder, then, that America's first Africans, brought to our shores in chains in 1619 to be the white man's labor device, would be valued as only three-fifths of a person in the nation's 1787 Constitution. Small wonder, too, that even though the Fourteenth Amendment of 1868 finally accorded full personhood (citizenship) to the nation's slaves, the toll for this devaluing of the "different" was not resolved simply by a change in the laws. When Booker T. Washington responded to an 1881 invitation from residents of Tuskegee, Alabama, to establish a school for blacks there, one of his first acts was to assess the needs of the people in the surrounding Macon County area. Washington later wrote:

> I remember I asked one coloured man, who was about sixty years old, to tell me something of his history. He said that he had been born in Virginia, and sold into Alabama in 1845. I asked him how many were sold at the same time. He said, "There were five of us, myself and brother and three mules."[4]

The dehumanized self-perception revealed in that former slave's statement, a perception instilled by power-holding whites, and the subsequent resentment, resistance, and gulf it has created, remains as a poison still coursing through our national bloodstream.

The Nourishing Corpse

In 1995 the previously mentioned Harvard-trained black historian John Hope Franklin was selected to receive a Presidential Medal of Freedom from President Bill Clinton. On the night before the ceremony, Franklin hosted a dinner for a small group of friends in Washington's Cosmos Club, of which he was a member. As he strolled through the lobby of the club that evening a white woman called out to him, presented him with her coat check, and ordered him to bring her coat. This woman's nonsensical color-based act was a sad contemporary echo of an incident retold the following day by President Clinton as he honored Franklin. Clinton recalled that John Hope Franklin, along with other black passengers on a train from Greensboro to Durham, North Carolina, in 1945, were removed by the train's conductor to a half coach for blacks while six white passengers were left to occupy a full coach—and those six were all German prisoners of war![5] Only a culture saturated in color bias could instance such treatment.

Bring the story of oppression nearer. When a black lady of great professional accomplishment tells me in 2017 that she always "dresses up" to go to the mall and never lingers long at any counter lest she soon feel the monitoring presence of a store detective suspecting her of shoplifting, I cannot find any reasonable explanation for that treatment other than that her skin is black. When she tells me she raised her child to avoid as much as possible any contact with police officers, she reveals the deep historic taproot of today's Black Lives Matter movement. And, just to keep things in balanced perspective, I must embarrassingly confess that, when I find myself in unknown surroundings and note that the big man walking toward me is black, my body goes into "Beware" mode.

With deep disappointment in myself, I admit that an unwarranted predisposition of fear and threat is not that far from me, regardless of my intellectual rejection of color bias. Though I write these pages to advocate a kingdom that supersedes skin color, come Sunday I still worship in churches whose color-division contradicts my words. For all our flag-waving, we are not "one nation … with liberty and justice for all." We are a nation tragically divided, staring at each other across a ghastly racial divide—a divide that is exploited again and again in our politics and that damns all our best efforts to rise as one.

Social activist and author of numerous books, Jim Wallis, says the most controversial sentence he has ever written was this lead sentence in a 1987 article in his *Sojourners* magazine: "The United States of America was established as a white society, founded upon the near genocide of another race and then the enslavement of yet another."

Some of Wallis' readers called this statement courageous; others called it outrageous. Wallis himself judged it "simply a historical statement of the facts."[6]

I must agree with Wallis if for no other reason than that his summary is corroborated in my boyhood experience of growing up white in Oklahoma. The "near genocide" of Native Americans was demonstrable by the presence of the historic Creek Indian Council House at my city's geographic center, though the Creeks themselves were no longer visible as a distinct people or in any politically significant manner. And the "enslavement" of African Americans (geographically and culturally) was demonstrable by an isolated "black" section of town given a pejorative name by the dominant whites. Hence, though I was born and reared hundreds of years and thousands of miles away from my nation's founding scenes, the America I grew up in was indeed a "white society." And it still is.

African-American writer Ralph Ellison, author of *The Invisible Man*, has given us a graphic summary of our racialized nation in his proposal that "we view the whole of American life as a drama enacted on the body of a Negro giant who, lying trussed up like Gulliver, forms the stage and the scene upon which and within which the action unfolds."[7] Fifty years after Ellison offered his grotesque image, Edward Baptist, a white Cornell University historian, used it as the organizing paradigm for his painful-to-read 450-page historical documentation that it was indeed "the commodification and suffering and forced labor of African Americans [that] made the United States powerful and rich."[8] The image of a trussed-up Negro giant, stretched out like a nourishing corpse on the torture rack of America's rise to international power, must not be dismissed as revisionist history—even if it offends white sensibilities.

Racism: More Than Attitudes

Here is where so many white persons stumble in our understanding of racism. We see racism as a personal problem of prejudice against persons of color, as a rejecting attitude toward blacks or browns or anyone whose skin isn't white like ours. And as we examine our own hearts many of us can quite honestly say we don't harbor—at least consciously—any of those feelings. We greet these people cordially in the grocery store, smile at their children, sit next to them at ballgames, and sometimes even share a meal with them. "See, I am not a racist," we say, and perhaps by our individualized, attitudinal definition, we aren't racists. For some of us this is a giant step forward, and it is indeed a step forward and for it I give thanks. Civil coexistence is a baseline.

The problem, however, is that racism goes deeper and is more complex than just our individual attitudes toward non-whites—attitudes that sometimes can be only a form of tolerance or obligatory political correctness. In a more profound understanding, racism is a structure of favoritism built into our society. It builds upon our historically demonstrable but unconfessed belief that whiteness is the norm, is the best, and that other skin colors are not as pure nor as good. This assumption then shows itself in policies and practices that, consciously or not, favor whites. The upshot is that an admitted or unrecognized belief in *white supremacy* accepts and even endorses historic patterns of *white preference.*

When we read the statistics regarding today's appalling gap between our white and black populations in education, housing, health, incarceration, and income, raw racism might conclude that these data only statistically document and confirm the inferiority of blacks. However, what this situation more truly reveals is the horrific result of four centuries of practices of white preference rooted in the myth of white supremacy. That story begins with America's original sin of condoning the enslavement of blacks and its subsequent repression of them in Reconstruction-era policies and Jim Crow statutes. But the story does not end there.

For instance, when America's soldiers, black and white, returned from World War II, the nation realized it owed a great debt to them. Many had placed their lives at risk for the country, but all of them had also forfeited several years of potential earnings and educational opportunities due to their time in military service. So a grateful nation enacted a GI Bill that provided grand educational and financial benefits for these veterans. When the original GI Bill expired on July 23, 1956, 7.8 million of 16 million veterans (1 million of whom were black) had participated in this government-paid college or vocational training program. But only 4 percent of black GIs participated in these opportunities. Why?

The program had been set up to be administered by local banks and college officials who were often determined to maintain the racial status quo. Applicants to white universities encountered black enrollment quotas (only x number of seats had been allotted to persons of color) or were directed to vocational training programs in lower-paying jobs. Even historically black colleges were unable to accommodate the flood of applicants. In 1947, for example, these schools did not have space for an estimated 70,000 black veterans. Too, many of the black veterans were returning to families still suffering from the effects of the Great Depression—their families needed an immediate wage-earner, not a college student. (Curiously, the Social Security Act of 1935 excluded agricultural and domestic workers, most of whom were African Americans.) The upshot is that a remarkably generous Federal program of "affirmative action" paid off handsomely for white veterans, granting them economic and vocational advantages that black veterans did not receive because the system itself favored white veterans.

The same discrepancy can be detected in the financial loans that were made under the auspices of the same program. As but one example, in New York and northern New Jersey, fewer than 100 of the 67,000 mortgages insured by the GI Bill were for home purchases by nonwhites. The primary investment opportunity—owning one's own home—that offered pride and economic betterment for millions of white Americans following World War II, was missed by most blacks. Instead, cunning real estate practices of "redlining" certain neighborhoods as less desirable were introduced. These practices drove down the value of the homes that were black-owned, and thus whole sections of cities became blighted or were razed for new interstate highways built for people with automobiles. Home ownership then was replaced by resettlement into rented Federal housing "projects" where pride of ownership and accruing equity were *de facto* impossible.[9]

Carol Anderson, a professor of African-American studies at Emory University, has meticulously documented a steady stream of countless instances (from the Black Codes of the Reconstruction Era, to the relentless assault upon voting rights and suppression of the black vote via gerrymandering, to a phony war on drugs, to the abandonment and vilification of public education) where racism, usually cleverly concealed, has denied black advancement. It is a story of "White Rage," as she terms it, against the threat of blacks with ambition and aspirations, a sickening story of white supremacists no longer wearing sheets and burning crosses but working the halls of government to their racist advantage.[10]

White persons have sometimes responded to this history of discrimination by saying that this situation is not their fault. The vast majority of all of this, they say, was done by others, and sometimes long ago, and it is unfair to lay it at the feet of this generation. I find this to be an unworthy response, for I fear it reveals that objectors are unaware of their personal profiting from this history (and likely continuing belief in white supremacy?)—and I know it dooms us to an even grimmer future, needlessly alienated from one another. As Abraham Joshua Heschel has famously said, "Some are guilty, but all are responsible"[11] for the injustice we see and for addressing the wrongs of the past and present.

To say, "Let bygones be bygone" is easy enough to say, particularly if you were not wounded by the past, but it cannot be the response of followers of Jesus. He who made a despised Samaritan the hero of his "good" Samaritan parable, and who noted that another despised Samaritan ("this foreigner"—Luke 17:18) was conspicuously the only leper who showed gratitude for his healing, and who commissioned his followers to "go ... and make disciples of all nations"—was and is not a friend of racism in any form, ever. Ella Wheeler Wilcox voiced it well, more than a century ago:

> I slept. I seemed to climb a hard, ascending track;
> And just behind me labored one whose patient face was black.
> I pitied him; but hour by hour he gained upon the path;
> He stood beside me, stood upright—and then I turned in wrath.
> "Go back!" I cried. "What right have you to walk beside me here?
> For you are black and I am white." I paused struck dumb with fear.
> For lo! the black man was not there, but Christ stood in his place;
> And oh! the pain, the pain, the pain that looked from his dear face.[12]

Dying to Whiteness

In the early days of my ministry I naïvely thought racism was just an educational flaw and that we could topple it by Bible studies exposing the fallacy of the "Hamitic Curse"—a then-prevalent notion that Noah had pronounced a God-ordained curse on his son Ham (Gen. 9:18-29), dooming Ham's descendants to a "black" life of slavery. (An amazing number of folks at that time incorrectly thought Negroes were descendants of Ham, and thus their subservient status was God-decreed.) And, when I wasn't telling myself that correct biblical interpretation would solve the problem, I busied myself by preparing and preaching sermons saying, "Love one another!" or planning joint worship services with a local black church to demonstrate collegial relationships.

Those were not wrong efforts. They were just short of the mark, well-intended band-aids for a metastasizing cancer. Now, fifty years later, I am much more aware of the intractable, diabolical embeddedness of the sin of racism in our society and within my own soul. Bible studies about drunken Noah, a few "love" sermons, and an annual choir- or preacher-swap with the black church down the street just won't do!

Black theologian James Cone has made a good case for what will do—and what must be done if we are to be one nation, and what must be done if so-called Christians are to be people of God's kingdom. In a shocking phrase, he says we who are white must *die to our whiteness*.[13] As things stand today, we are dying *from* our whiteness! Our refusal to own our own practices of white privilege, past and present, forecloses our future. Entire realms of possibility are walled off from us because we are walled off from one another. Consenting to the belittlement of others, we are less than whole ourselves. This is true not only for this nation, but even more so for a church whose charter says that "as many of you as were baptized into Christ have clothed yourselves with Christ. There is no longer Jew or Greek, there is no longer slave or free, there is no longer male and female; for all of you are one in Christ Jesus" (Gal. 3:27-28).

Cone is right. We who are white must die to our whiteness. (I dare not say what my black neighbors ought do; mine is only to speak to my own race.) But what does this actually mean? It means we who are white will bury our assumptions that our white ways are the best and correct ways, that we are the standard. It means we will forsake our expectations that white people will be in charge. It means we will become acutely aware of what Peggy McIntosh calls the "invisible package of unearned assets which [we who are white] can count on cashing in each day; but about which we are 'meant' to remain oblivious."[14] It means we will accept our place in line and, expecting no favors, respect as equals those in front and behind us. It means we will never proceed without the voices of everyone being heard and honored. It means we refuse to think in terms of us and "them," but only of "us"—for in Christ there is no "them."

Jemar Tisby, in a recent book that should be required reading for all white Christians (*The Color of Compromise: The Truth about the American Church's Complicity in Racism*), gets provocatively and helpfully specific by offering a list of reconciliatory actions that signal a death to whiteness: reparations, take down Confederate monuments, learn from the black church, start a new seminary, host freedom schools and pilgrimages, make Juneteenth a national holiday, participate in the modern-day civil rights movement, publicly denounce racism, start a civil rights movement … toward the church.[15] Actions such as these offer hope through deeds that speak louder than words.

To die to our whiteness will mean we renounce our idolatrous investment in whiteness in order to be reborn in humanness. A death to our prideful white self must occur and be given a truly Christian funeral that a resurrection to a grander, larger family might be found. That death, which is a form of true repentance or "turning," has an enduring musical expression and promise in the Shaker song, "Simple Gifts."

> 'Tis the gift to be simple, 'tis the gift to be free,
> 'tis the gift to come down where we ought to be;
> And when we find ourselves in the place just right
> 'twill be in the valley of love and delight.
>
> When true simplicity is gained
> to bow and bend we shan't be ashamed;
> To turn, turn, will be our delight
> till by turning, turning we come round right.

In the first section of this book I included three lengthy passages from Isaiah as examples of the Hebrew peoples' vision of what God's world would look like when set right. In one of those passages, Isaiah 11:6-9, that vision is of a world where "the wolf shall live with the lamb, the leopard shall lie down with the kid … the cow and the bear shall graze, their young shall lie down together."

A pertinent feature of this vision is that these creatures do not cease to be themselves, they still are wolves and lambs and leopards and cows and bears. Their identity is still intact, but their antagonism and threat to one another is gone. They no longer "hurt or destroy" one another because "the earth shall be full of the knowledge of the Lord as the waters cover the sea."

I do not believe this Isaiah passage is speaking only of animals; its reference extends to peoples, nations, races, and skin colors. This prophesy concerns a world wherein these outward identity markers remain, yet are taken up in a greater identity that changes their antagonistic relationships. This vision is not of a melting pot, but of a mosaic of many tribes and nations and languages, living not as enemies or wary neighbors but as fellow participants in the knowledge of the Lord that removes from them the compulsion to hurt or destroy one another. Or, to put it in the language of this discussion, whiteness remains, but it is no longer an indication of dominance or of subservience; it is but one color within the many colors within God's multicolored human family.

Best of all, in the heart of this scripture there is that marvelous, mysterious line: "and a little child shall lead them" (11:6). I believe that marvelous, mysterious child is the "Star Child born to set us free" from the sin of racism and to transfer us into his own kingdom of mutual respect and kinship. When the vision of that kingdom fascinates and animates us more than defending our shabby, little, lily-white kingdoms, then there is credible hope for "one nation, *under God*, with liberty and justice for all."

***

A place to begin is to cultivate friendships with persons of color—honest to God friendships!

A place to begin is to ask yourself how you might react to the day's news if you were black.

A place to begin is to consider the "invisible package of unearned assets that you can count on cashing in each day; but about which you are 'meant' to remain oblivious."

A place to begin is to note who is not present in your club, church, school—and to ask why.

A place to begin is to contribute to those entities enhancing the status of persons of color.

A place to begin is to refuse to laugh at any racist joke or to let any racist speech go unprotested.

Notes

[1] "Sick and Tired of Being Sick and Tired" in *The Failure and the Hope: Essays of Southern Churchmen*, Will D. Campbell and James Y. Holloway, eds. (Grand Rapids, MI: Eerdmans, 1972), 166-167.

[2] Cited in Robert Hughes, *American Visions: The Epic History of Art in America* (New York: Alfred A. Knopf, 1997), 41. Capitalization and italics appear in the original.

[3] In their discussion of "Race and History," Will and Ariel Durant, authors of the eleven-volume *The Story of Civilization*, cite Comte Joseph-Arthur de Gobineau's 1853 dictum: "History shows that all civilization derives from the white race" but their retort is: "History is color-blind, and can develop a civilization (in any favorable environment) under almost any skin." See *The Lessons of History* (New York: Simon and Schuster, 1968), 29. An introduction to racial categories and whiteness in particular is found in Nell Irvin Painter, *The History of White People* (New York: Norton, 2010).

[4] Booker T. Washington, *Up from Slavery* (New York: Dover Publications, Inc., 1995), 56.

[5] John Hope Franklin, *Mirror to America: The Autobiography of John Hope Franklin* (New York: Farrar, Straus & Giroux, 2005), 340-341.

⁶Jim Wallis, *America's Original Sin: Racism, White Privilege, and the Bridge to a New America* (Grand Rapids, MI: Brazos Press, 2016), 33.

⁷Ralph Ellison, "Twentieth-Century Fiction and the Black Mask of Humanity," *Shadow and Act* (New York: 1964).

⁸Edward E. Baptist, *The Half Has Never Been Told: Slavery and the Making of American Capitalism* (New York: Basic Books, 2014), xxi.

⁹The statistics cited in these paragraphs are drawn from Debby Irving, *Waking Up White and Finding Myself in the Story of Race* (Cambridge, MA: Elephant Room Press, 2014) 32-37, and Jim Wallis, *America's Original Sin*, 88-90.

¹⁰See Carol Anderson, *White Rage: The Unspoken Truth of Our Racial Divide* (New York: Bloomsbury Publishing, 2017).

¹¹Abraham Heschel offered this helpful distinction several times in varying contexts. In a 1969 presentation titled "The Reasons for My Involvement in the Peace Movement," he said: "It became clear to me that in regard to cruelties committed in the name of a free society, some are guilty, while all are responsible. I did not feel guilty as an individual American for the bloodshed in Vietnam, but I felt deeply responsible." *Moral Grandeur and Spiritual Audacity*, Susannah Heschel, ed. (New York: Farrar, Straus and Giroux, 1996), 225.

¹²Excerpt from "Christ Crucified" by Ella Wheeler Wilcox, *Poems of Experience* (London: Gay and Hancock, 1910). This poem was included in the courageous sermon preached in 1947 by the white Methodist pastor in Pickens, South Carolina, Hawley Lynn, following the murder of a young black man by thirty whites who had forcibly taken him from that city's jail. Will Willimon reports this event and his own ruminations upon it in *Who Killed Willie Earle? Preaching to Confront Racism* (Nashville: Abingdon Press, 2017).

¹³James Cone, *God of the Oppressed* (Maryknoll, NY: Orbis, 1997), 222.

¹⁴This is Peggy McIntosh's definition of white privilege in *White Privilege: Essential Readings on the Other Side of Racism*, ed. Paula S. Rothenberg, 3ʳᵈ ed. (New York: Worth Publishers, 2008), 123.

¹⁵Jemar Tisby, *The Color of Compromise* (Grand Rapids, MI: Zondervan, 2019), ch. 11 "The Fierce Urgency of Now."

CHAPTER 19

*

Sex/Gender: Below the Belt, Between the Sheets, and Beyond Reason

"When a scientific answer ... is sought to the questions, 'What is a man?' 'What is a woman?', increasingly we are aware of how misleading a purely biological approach can be. Our anatomy is not our destiny."[1]
—*Paul K. Jewett, 1975*

Sex remains one of the most difficult subjects for Christians to discuss. From the nakedness of Adam and Eve in the garden of Eden, to "the talk" with our children, to the "choice v. orientation" arguments within our society, to today's #MeToo Movement, sex continues to be rough terrain for us. It lives in its own realm as a visceral twilight zone, beyond reason.

I was rudely reminded of this recently as I attempted to read a book whose subtitle is *A Gender-Friendly Primer on What to Know, What to Say, and What to Do in the New Gender Culture.*[2] It is a well-written work by a transgender educator who is trying to help us with the tasks that subtitle specifies. The book was given to me by a frightfully bright young adult, honoring me by her belief that an old man might learn new ways of speaking in this era of "identifying" as this or that or the other. However, page by page I realized I was proving to be a very poor student. The glossary itself was a steep hill to climb, and too soon my old legs craved yesterday's flat land of simple, binary male-female distinctions. It just got so terribly unfamiliar and complicated!

So I can understand why so many people want, when it comes to matters of gender and sex, for us to just hush—and freeze all the change. But, like it or not, we cannot freeze all the change—that train left the station years ago. And, like it or not, we cannot even evaluate the merits and demerits of those changes if we cannot talk about gender and sexual matters rationally. So, in this chapter I want to speak rationally of how my mind has changed with regard to one aspect of gender (the role of women) and one dimension of sexuality (homosexuality). My hope, of course, is that my changes of mind have been in the direction of the kingdom announced by and brought to us in the person of Jesus.

The Daughters of Eve

Let us begin with Jesus' treatment of women. It is well known that the Bible is not always the friend of women, some of its passages and even its assumptive world often being offensively dismissive of women. That was the culture, the world in which the Bible's story is cast. And, without excusing the male dominance thus reflected within the Bible, this cultural context allows me the wiggle-room to understand all of this as the dark background against which Jesus' treatment of women stands in sharp, liberating contrast. That is, *if* Jesus treated women differently than did his peers.

Significantly, Jesus didn't issue any emancipation proclamation for women. Rather, he let his actions do the talking, and there his record is clear. His respect for his mother is unquestionable. (The Roman Catholic veneration of Mary would hardly have been possible if there were any hint of less coming from Jesus, the fruit of her womb.) Though he was clearly his own person and not guilty of letting her dictate his actions, he shows concern for Mary's welfare even in the final moments of his own life, nailed to the cross.

The Jesus portrayed in the Gospels befriends women, whether a woman of five former husbands or the admiring sisters of Lazarus, Mary and Martha. He defends women, be it the woman taken in adultery or the woman who anoints his feet and kisses them. In a very unorthodox gesture for his time, he teaches women such as Mary and Martha. He makes women the admirable model in his parables of the lost coin and importunate widow. He notes their pain and grief and restores their children to health and life. He heals women and girls from everything from a chronic issue of blood to a crippled body. He praises a woman's great faith. Women, in turn, display a greater loyalty to him than do the men in his life.

Though the disciples flee in the final hours of his life, women remain to the end and on the dawning of the third day, it is some still-caring women who are the first to discover the Resurrection, to recognize Jesus as alive, and to tell the story. Never is there a disparaging word or act from Jesus regarding women. In light of the devaluation of women that was common in his time—and throughout the centuries since—Jesus' thoughtful, caring interactions with the women in his life is stunning.

The Daughters with the Gift of Prophecy

But, of course, there remains the sticky issue of his choice of twelve men—no women—for the inner circle of his disciples. Too, there are some prohibitive words concerning women in leadership written later by these disciples or, more likely, by their descendants. This record of discrimination, rather than the lived practice of Jesus, continues to thwart the efforts of countless women who long to respond to God's call to Christian leadership.

This is not the place to provide a full response to this dilemma, but in brief I can say that I believe Jesus' choice of twelve men rather than a mixed-gender group was in response to two concerns. One of them is the concern of public perception of propriety. My impression of Jesus' ministry is of an extended camping trip, the kind of arrangement that would surely have elicited accusations of improper sexual conduct had Jesus been leading a band of six men and six women around the countryside. Given that there seems to have been some women who followed Jesus' all-male circle around anyhow, this charge may already have been possible. But to invite this criticism by calling women into his inner circle would have been imprudent to the extreme. Considering his otherwise positive actions concerning women, it is reasonable to assume his omission of them from the Twelve was from concern for their reputation as much as for his own.

A second, and arguably more telling reason for the choice of twelve men, suggests that his choice had more to do with history than with gender. In all I have written in this book regarding the reign of God, there has been great concern that our ideas be guided by the story of God's self-revelation through Israel. And fundamental to Israel's story is the role of the founding fathers of Israel, the twelve sons of Jacob, the patriarchs of the twelve tribes of Israel. If Jesus' agenda is to replicate and renew that ancient template, to make all things righteously new, then this number of founding fathers is significant. I conclude that because Jesus' twelve disciples are male rather than female is due to the ancient originating story and is not a result of gender discrimination against women.

The question easily arises: Could not Jesus have "made new" the gender relationships in the kingdom then and there by including women in leadership from day one? Surely, he could. But he chose not to do so. It is beyond anyone's competence to declare why he did not do so, but, beyond the very real issue of public propriety perception, my own hunch is that Jesus did not include them in the inner circle because he fully expected his followers to do so in the days to come! Did not the prophet Joel announce that "in the last days it will be, God declares, that I will pour out my Spirit upon all flesh, and your sons and your daughters shall prophesy" (Acts 2:17). This passage is quoted by Jesus' "rock," Simon Peter, in the first Christian sermon, explaining the presence of the Holy Spirit among the apostolic band. Even if you think that the author of the Acts of the Apostles is responsible for this citation, rather than it being a direct quote from Peter's sermon, its very presence in this story indicates "daughters" were understood to be included among the Spirit-endowed prophets. Indeed, the balance of Acts goes on to tell us of numerous female leaders in the earliest church—Prisca, Lydia, Phoebe, and others. Multiple historians have subsequently documented that women were most certainly within the leadership cadre of the early church.[3] Most regrettably, in ensuing generations that place was denied them due in no small part to the weakness of males who craved power and/or who caved in to male-dominated cultural patterns.

The Visible Becomes the Authorized

Having noted the precedent of the apostolic church, consider next a Latin phrase from the church's later history that played and plays a significant role in this matter of gender bias. That phrase is *lex orandi, lex credendi*, which may be translated as the Rule of Prayer is the Rule of Belief. Further defined, this phrase means that what is observed and participated in as the church gathers for prayer (that is, for worship) becomes or sets the pattern for what is accepted as credible and true for belief. At its most basic level, *lex orandi, lex credendi* means "what happens during worship, matters." In this case, what people saw and heard on Sundays for centuries (males only in leadership) became what was believed to be God-ordained. Liturgical practice became theological dogma. And, of course, male priests were only too happy to supplement that impression with all manner of intellectual arguments for their all-male club.

In my own case, the idea of women as ordained deacons[4] was shocking when first introduced to me. No church I had ever seen had women deacons (my bunch took that "seven men" note in Acts 6:3 seriously!), and no church I'd ever seen had a female pastor![5] Well, okay, there was the exception of Sister Perkins, the pastor of the Pentecostal Holiness Living Way Tabernacle lovingly attended by my maternal grandparents. She was the one outlier. But then, I have already confessed to our Baptist practice of closely monitoring the excesses of the Pentecostal folks, so Sister Perkins' pastoral role was accepted by my parents as a forgivable aberration. After all, there was only one of her in a city of umpteen dozen male pastors. Meanwhile, we true-blue Baptists remained as committed to all-male leadership as the Pope.

While in my thirties, however, questioners of the existing *lex orandi, lex credendi* began to be heard. Once I began to think about it, the fact that half the human race should be excluded from the church's leadership did not sound very Jesus-like to me. Goaded by the challengers, I then began to read the historical materials and Bible studies they suggested and became convinced that what I had heard and seen all my life was not the only way church could be done. Even more to the point, I became convinced that the exclusion of women as partners in ministry was sinful, as discriminatory in its own way as racism. But my conviction was still a matter of theory.

Then I accepted a pastoral call to a church that had a female associate pastor. For the first time in my life I had opportunity to work alongside a vibrant, intelligent, called minister of God whose name wasn't Bill or Frank or Harry. From that day to this I give thanks for her, the Rev. Moray Loring. There was a gracious competence and compassion within Moray that put the lie to every slur ever spoken about women in ministry. She had me from hello, and I sincerely missed her when I eventually said goodbye to that congregation a decade later. Even more decades have now passed, decades in which I have been privileged to serve alongside many other "Morays" and to learn from and teach some wonderful female seminarians (some of whom could "out-preach" their male counterparts by a mile). One of my hopes is for the day when worshipers will consider it wholly unacceptable if women and men are not visible and vocal every Sunday in the ordained leadership of their church. *Lex orandi, lex credendi* should be telling worshipers that no one is excluded here. To see this in worship is to see the reign of God at work.

Sex/Gender: Below the Belt, Between the Sheets, and Beyond Reason

Beware of Monday Morning Visits

The other great challenge within the orbit of human sexuality today concerns the presence of gay, lesbian, bisexual, transgendered, and other people whose orientation doesn't fit a heterosexual norm. This challenge currently makes the struggle concerning women in leadership feel like child's play.

Perhaps the gist of what I have to say about this matter and of how my mind has changed is to tell you a story that comes into focus on a Monday morning years ago, a Monday following Easter Sunday. A lady I knew only socially called and asked to see me. As she entered my office her face told me she was in distress, and, indeed, she was barely seated when she began to weep. Eventually her story came out.

She had a son in his early twenties—who only recently had told her and her husband that he was gay. With his declaration a flood of understanding washed over her. Now she understood why her bright, handsome son had had such a rough adolescence. Why he'd had so few friends, why he had withdrawn from any social groups, why he was so often depressed, why he'd refused to go to church after his middle school years.

But the day before, Easter Sunday, she and her husband had prevailed upon him to attend Easter services with them at their church. All went well until, tragically, in the midst of the sermon, the pastor spoke of the Easter parades of yesteryear, but of how today those parades would be taken over by all the gays and lesbians and all their outlandish dress and behavior. Her son's body literally sagged when the pastor's condemnations filled the room. And at this point in telling her story this mother paused, looked at me with tear-filled eyes and said, "Dan, I know what the Bible says about homosexuality. But surely, it's not that simple ... or mean. Is it?"

I had no good answer for her—at least none that satisfied me. Like everyone else in the world at the time, I was aware of the spreading AIDS epidemic. The church I was serving even had an active AIDS ministry, helping those suffering from HIV-AIDS. But this ministry was an expression of compassion, not of advocacy for gay men (and "gay men" was the way it was then presented and popularly understood). That ministry of compassion had been for me a sufficient response. But this heartbroken mother was now confronting me with the deeper question of what I believed the Bible said—and in her mind, what God thought—about "gay men," about her son.

Truthfully, what I had to go on that morning was some culturally bequeathed uneasiness about homosexuality and a vague acquaintance of a few biblical passages I believed justified my feelings. Except for some consciousness-raising questions prompted by comments from my school counselor wife (which I will talk about in a moment), I probably wasn't that far from where my pastoral colleague was—other than that I, unlike him and his Easter pronouncement, would never have blabbed it in such a manner or forum. My ignorance and prejudice were hidden; his were hurtfully flaunted. But that mother's question sent me off on a long journey of discovery, biblically, theologically, personally, pastorally.

My trek began with the Bible, the point of the lady's question: "Surely, it's not that simple ... or mean. Is it?" I first confirmed that there were no biblical passages about sexuality that were friendly toward any sexual expressions other than those of heterosexuality. Had these disapproving passages been confined to the Old Testament, I might have inquired if they had been superseded by a kinder New Testament. But the New Testament was no less condemning. The words were there on the pages of both testaments and could not be erased.

But those words must still be interpreted. Thankfully, in the 1980s a spate of research on those words and the contexts that surround them began to give helpful and merciful light to these severe texts. Also, historical research about the church and homosexuality opened new avenues of understanding. One must-be-mentioned book in this regard was John Boswell's *Christianity, Social Tolerance, and Homosexuality: Gay People in Western Europe from the Beginning of the Christian Era to the Fourteenth Century* (1981). In light of this research many pastors and academics were content to dismiss the Bible's unfriendly texts as irrelevant to our present concerns; these texts, they concluded, were not talking about the same phenomena we now faced. I, however, found some of the assumptions and the exegetical tiptoeing of the researchers ultimately unconvincing and was unable to dismiss or rewrite the stern words I read in my Bible. Even some early advocates of acceptance and affirmation of gays concurred in my conclusion. As one of them, Walter Wink, Professor of Biblical Interpretation at Auburn Theological Seminary in New York City, summarized it: "... the Bible quite clearly takes a negative view of same-sex relations, even in those few instances where it is mentioned at all."[6]

The Women, Once Again!

The matter of homosexuality might have been laid to rest then and there had it not been for two women. One was that tearful mother and her unforgettable question. The other was my spouse. Working regularly with children in the public schools as my wife did, she would occasionally tell me of the problems she was dealing with as she tried to help this or that child. On more than one occasion she would shake her head and say of some struggling middle school child, "I really believe they are gay, but just haven't come around to understand that yet."

Admittedly, she was no psychotherapist and had no credentials to qualify her as an expert. But she is one of the most perceptive persons I know and had been working with kids for years. (She was also a participant in our church's AIDS ministry.) When she spoke about these children, I had to listen. And what I heard was that these children were wrestling with sexual orientation and were no more choosing their orientation than they

Sex/Gender: Below the Belt, Between the Sheets, and Beyond Reason

had chosen their skin color.[7] They were who they were, and whether they liked it or not, or were even yet aware of it, their sexual attraction was to persons of the same sex.

Her credible voice of experience, added to the weight of the research I was reading, pushed me into the column of those who could not buy the proposition that same-sex attraction was a lifestyle choice. It is an orientation, not a choice. Stated more forthrightly, some persons are created by God as homosexual.[8] I came to this conclusion because the evidence led me there, and because I cannot yet fathom why anyone would choose the rejection, the stigma, and the suffering that come with such a choice. Though I will readily admit that sexual perversion exists (across the sexual spectrum), to choose an identity certain to elicit slurs and condemnation makes no sense. Even if our society has grown more accepting since the time I was first wrestling with this, it still seems to me that if it is a chosen lifestyle then its selection is the most self-damning choice imaginable.

So, having come this far, where was I to go? On one hand I had my book, a book that held sacred value for me, and it stubbornly said No. On the other hand, I had this lady's son—but not just him. There were also those men our AIDS ministry worked with every week. There was a friend and a ministry colleague I knew or had reason to assume was gay. All of these were real people, human beings, and some were people whose values, beliefs, and hopes mirrored mine, yet their sexual orientation condemned them as less than whole persons—no, as vile persons. Was my love for the Book to outweigh my love for all these people?

There is an instructive story tucked away in the Gospel of Matthew about this dilemma.

> Jesus left that place and went away to the district of Tyre and Sidon. Just then a Canaanite woman from that region came out and started shouting, "Have mercy on me, Lord, Son of David; my daughter is tormented by a demon." But he did not answer her at all. And his disciples came and urged him, saying, "Send her away, for she keeps shouting after us." He answered, "I was sent only to the lost sheep of Israel." But she came and knelt before him, saying, "Lord, help me." He answered, "It is not fair to take the children's food and throw it to the dogs." She said, "Yes, Lord, yet even the dogs eat the crumbs that fall from their master's table." Then Jesus answered her, "Woman, great is your faith! Let it be done for you as you wish." And her daughter was healed instantly. (15:21-28)

The tension in this encounter is set up by the fact that this woman is a Canaanite woman. Even a cursory reading of the Old Testament will let you know that Canaanites were ancient bad news in Jewish opinion. They were the expendables. The biblical texts Jesus would have heard and read all of his life would have excluded them from the circle of God's mercy, and Jesus' own policy seems not to have varied from that pattern.

That is, he followed the custom of his people until this woman tearfully told him her story and in essence asked: "Jesus, I know what the Bible says. But surely, it's not that simple ... or mean. Is it?"

When Loves Collide

When faced with the choice of his love for the Book versus his love for the person standing before him, Jesus chose the person! Jesus chose to love and honor the person before him more than the words in his sacred book. Remarkable! Instructive!

In effect, Jesus was giving us another example of the principle he set when he said the Sabbath was made for us, for human well-being. In most minds it was just the opposite: the Sabbath was the great thing, and we were to serve it. Jesus, however, said the Sabbath was given for our good, and whenever Sabbath observance was twisted to become contrary to our good, then its divine intent has been lost—blind obedience to words on a page had overtaken concern for the welfare of real persons. Jesus would have none of it.

In this bold break from tradition, Jesus was following a precedent set by his Jewish ancestors. There is good indication that these earlier lovers of the book also had, in the interest of compassion, authorized revisions of stern words from the past. For instance, in the Torah's oldest collection of "legal" matters (which scholars have named the Covenant Code), the law requires the release of the male Hebrew slave (not the female slave) after six years (Exod. 21:1-6). However, in the next oldest collection, the Deuteronomic Code, the release of a Hebrew female slave is also ordered along with the duty to provide all freed slaves with start-up provisions for living (Deut. 15:12-17). Finally, by the time of the most recent collection, the Holiness Code, it is forbidden to enslave a fellow Israelite (Lev. 25:39-46). It seems clear that, for all their reverence for their scripture, Israel's spiritual leaders occasionally "nudged the received legal tradition toward a code at once more fitting to the circumstances and a little more worthy of the story of God's reign."[9] Jesus did the same.

In doing this, Jesus also set an example for those of us who today ask what to do when our love for scripture collides with our love for people. By reversing the exclusivist patterns of centuries of Jewish practice and granting mercy to the Canaanite woman and her daughter, Jesus chose the person over the text and the tradition. He chose, in the spirit and practice of his ancestors, to honor the larger, grander spirit of his sacred book and to claim that higher ground for his action.

Interpreting the Sentence by the Book

I have chosen to approach the stern words about homosexuality in my Bible by stepping away from the specific words and asking myself what this book in its entirety is about. Is this book about keeping everything neatly filed in kosher categories, or helping us live together as God's variegated family? What is this sacred book driving at? Where does the gospel lead us? In what direction does the kingdom nudge us? If I listen for the heartbeat of the whole book, seeking to understand where it seems to want to go, my wrestling with a few contrary words ends. The message of the Bible suggests how to handle what a specific verse says.

As a matter of historical record, this approach to biblical interpretation was used with good effect during our nation's struggle with human slavery. "What the Bible says" about slavery was unquestionably front and center in America from the 1830s to the 1860s. One example is a January 27, 1861, sermon titled "Scriptural Vindication of Slavery" preached by the Rev. E.W. Warren, pastor of the First Baptist Church of Christ in Macon, Georgia. In this sermon Reverend Warren took up most every verse in the Bible that mentions slavery and came to the conclusion that the Bible, though it rebukes and denounces all manner of injustice and oppression, nowhere rebukes or denounces slavery. To the contrary, he found that the Bible "establishes and perpetuates [slavery]" and therefore "slavery is neither, unjust, oppressive, nor wrong."[10]

Disappointingly, the man's conclusions are correct—*if* all that is needed is to cite chapter and verses. Like it or not, you cannot effectively argue from the Bible that slavery is evil if biblical interpretation is simply a matter of quoting printed words. There's just too much acceptance and even endorsement of it to condemn it on the basis of quotable sentences from the Bible.

So, what did those people who opposed slavery do to counter this? Well, they never tried to argue away or erase the sentences the Georgia pastor loved. Rather, they chose to interpret those words in the light of the entire book. They pressed their case on the merits of what the Bible as a whole was driving at, on the liberating character of the God revealed in the book as a whole.

At one point in E.W. Warren's sermon he declared that before slavery could be condemned, "a higher law than the Bible must be found." That is precisely what abolitionists did—they appealed to a higher law *within* the Bible to counter the specific words the slaveowners prized. I've come to believe their method is the one best suited for my response to homosexuality.

As the previous chapter on the Bible demonstrated, biblical authority is always much easier to talk about than to practice, especially when it comes to emotional "beyond reason" issues. The course most often followed is to think of biblical authority mathematically, as a simple 1+1=2 matter, a straightforward calculation of data or, in this case, assembling all of one's proof texts. In this model the team with the larger stack of words wins. But I and many others would suggest that we need to think of biblical authority less mechanically and more relationally. Indeed, to think of the Bible itself as a love letter from God. You have to sit with a love letter to read between the lines. You engage the heart rather than a computer when you're reading a love letter. Always, biblical authority is more than repeating what Bible verses say; it seeks to grasp and restate for today what the Bible means.

I now have a better answer to that mother's question than I had years ago. Now I can tell her that while I cannot erase "what the Bible says," I can tell her that "what the Bible means" is not as simple nor as mean as what it says in a few places. I can tell her that though I do not understand all the sexual confusion we confront today, I do understand that simplistic "yes" and "no" responses to the complexities of human sexuality are out of touch with the kingdom vision of Jesus. I can tell her that everything in the Book must be interpreted in light of the love of the God of the whole book, in light of where this God seems to be headed. I can tell her the God of the Bible is more interested in human community than in a few phrases in a thousand-page book.

Since women occupy such a prominent place within this chapter, here is a closing story about a hero of mine. In mid-September of 1877 a graying female crusader arrived in the remote silver-mining boom town of Lake City, Colorado, population 1,000—give or take a gambler, miner, saloon keeper, ruffian or two. The city was newborn, nestled in a valley in the San Juan Range of the Rocky Mountains, the smell of wood resin still lingering in most of its buildings, including the new county courthouse, not yet a year old. To get to Lake City, the wiry lady rode a burro seventy miles across the Continental Divide on the treacherous toll road from Del Norte, Colorado. The state had a general election slated for that fall, and on the ballot there was a referendum to approve equal rights for women, specifically the right to vote. Massachusetts-born Susan B. Anthony was determined to get it passed, even if it meant a 140-mile, roundtrip, mule ride to secluded Lake City.

On the evening of September 20, Ms. Anthony made her way to the county courthouse to give her scheduled lecture. So overcrowded was the upstairs courtroom that her speech was relocated to the steps outside the courthouse. There, for two hours, she pled her case, noting the discrepancy between the $8 per month salary for female teachers versus the $24 salary for male teachers, pointing out numerous other injustices suffered by women, and pleading that women be given the right to own and control themselves, their property, and their labor. The local newspaper reported she was heard respectfully, even receiving some cheers, though the editor opined it would nonetheless be best for women to continue "to be the rulers of men by the force of their womanly modesty and retiracy. These, in their hands, are far more potent instrumentalities than the ballot." On election day the editor's views prevailed; the referendum failed statewide by more than a two-to-one margin, and in Lake City's county only 322 of the 1,009 votes cast favored Susan Anthony's cause.

There the story might end, except for this note. Within the audience that night there was a 24-year-old attorney, J. Warner Mills, who was inspired by Susan B. Anthony's words. Sixteen years later, in 1893, Mills, now a practicing law in Denver, wrote the text of the Colorado Equal Rights amendment that was approved that year by 55 percent of the state's voters. Though the United States did not follow suit until 1920, fourteen years after Susan B. Anthony's death, her voice still spoke through J. Warner Mills' words and through Colorado's voters and eventually to an entire nation of people who finally did the right thing!

My hope is that the labors of those who labor for gender and sexual justice today—sometimes with so little success—may one day be rewarded with victory, and by the sweet encouragement that even now, every day you are making a difference, even if you know nothing about it. And with that hope, I ask you to give attention to a final hurdle: politics!

Notes

[1] Paul K. Jewett, *Man as Male and Female* (Grand Rapids, MI: Eerdmans, 1975), 174.

[2] Lee Airton, *Gender: Your Guide: A Gender-Friendly Primer on What to Know, What to Say, and What to Do in the New Gender Culture* (New York: Adams Media, 2018).

[3] Cullen Murphy, *The Word According to Eve: Women and the Bible in Ancient Times and Our Own* (New York: Houghton Mifflin, 1998) provides a journalist's non-technical review of this in "Prominent Among the Apostles?" ch. 9.

[4] Deacons in Baptist life are laypersons, not clergy, and are typically ordained to this lay diaconal ministry.

[5] Meredith Stone, *A Baptist Reflection on The Bible & Women in Ministry and Leadership* (Baptist Women in Ministry, 2019) is a concise review and affirming interpretation of the pertinent biblical texts.

[6] Wink, "Homosexuality and the Bible," in Walter Wink, ed. *Homosexuality and Christian Faith: Questions of Conscience for the Churches* (Minneapolis: Fortress Press, 1999), 37. See also ch. 16, "Homosexuality" in Richard B. Hays, *The Moral Vision of the New Testament* (HarperOne, 1996) for a similar exegetical finding with opposite conclusion.

[7] It is now customary to distinguish sexual identity (whether one sees oneself as male, female, or neither) from sexual orientation (whether one is attracted to a person of the same sexual identity as one's own). This helpful distinction was not recognized at the time of these conversations.

[8] Although it exceeds the boundaries of this discussion, I believe the rightness of same-sex marriage is affirmed within my judgment that homosexual persons are created as much in the image of God as heterosexual persons.

[9] Alan Verhey, *Remembering Jesus: Christian Community, Scripture, and the Moral Life* (Grand Rapids, MI: Eerdmans, 2002), 372. A prayer overheard in a Scottish church asked: "May we never be engaged in a war in foreign lands, Lord, but if it be so, and if our maps disagree with the terrain before us, may we trust the terrain."

[10] The sermon, to my knowledge, has not been published, but a copy is available in the archives of the First Baptist Church of Christ in Macon, Georgia.

CHAPTER 20

※

Politics: Avoiding the Pilate Syndrome

"We are going to take our country back. We are going to fulfill the promise of Donald Trump. That's what we believed in; that's why we voted for Donald Trump. Because he said he's going to take our country back. And that's what we gotta do."[1]
—*David Duke, former Ku Klux Klan grand wizard,*
Charlottesville, Virginia, 2017

You may recall that the birthing moment for this book occurred in early 2018 in a meeting to discuss what fidelity to the gospel ought to sound and look like in the days of Donald Trump's presidency. That question should be asked in every political season, of course, but it has certainly occupied my mind in every section of this book. So, in fairness, you might say this book was born and bred in politics. In some circles this would be enough to dismiss it as being not "spiritual." But the same judgment could be made about the Bible.

Many of us use and read our Bibles devotionally. This is good and necessary. But our devotional use of the Bible has its dangers, one of which can be a blindness to its public, political nature. In a moment I will tell you of my awaking to this realization, but let me introduce the idea by noting that even biblical passages we know by heart often have a political edge to them. For instance, the psalm (23) that testifies to the LORD's leading us to "green pastures" and "still waters" also tells us that life is lived "in the presence of my enemies." Now, most often the salvation the Bible refers to is rescue from enemies, from adversaries, not rescue from any flames of hell. Enemies are a reality in this life, especially so if you are a political figure as was the reputed author of Psalm 23, King David. Even this calming psalm carries the scent of awkward confrontations and hostility.

Indeed, the first thirty-nine of the Bible's sixty-six books are filled with stories of enmity, of empires and kingdoms rising and falling, of palace intrigues, of unjust policies and raging prophets—of kings reading the writings of the prophet and then throwing those writings, page by page, into his fireplace like "fake news" (Jeremiah 36). Again and again the Bible reports the clash of opponents, sometimes acted out in the violence of war but just as often enacted in politically loaded courtroom dramas. For me the trial of Jesus is the most intriguing of these. Eugene Peterson gave us this rendition of its conclusion:

When Pilate saw that he was getting nowhere and that a riot was imminent, he took a basin of water and washed his hands in full sight of the crowd, saying, "I'm washing my hands of responsibility for this man's death. From now on, it's in your hands. You're judge and jury."[2]

I am fascinated that this man Pontius Pilate, a governor appointed by the Roman Empire and a political animal from head to toe, suddenly felt himself in soiled circumstances and, wanting no part of it, bailed out. Perhaps that's why he had advanced to this high position—he had learned the politician's ancient art of ducking out the back door when it gets hot in the kitchen. Commenting on Pilate's hand-washing tactic, Richard Rohr tersely summarizes: "Pilate maintains his purity, and Jesus pays the price."[3]

Unfortunately, Pilate's tactic is also quite common among bona fide Christians, among those who sidestep responsibility for what happens in the public square, who prefer devotional readings of the Bible and the purity of stained glass sanctuaries over grim city halls and fetid county jails. Rohr names this trait the Pilate Syndrome and pointedly reminds us that Jesus and his sisters and brothers always pay the price when kingdom cries for justice go unuttered, when the enemy encounters no opposition.

Up to Our Steeples in Politics

If we dump all the activities in city halls, legislative chambers, mayors' offices, county jails, district courts, and tax assessors' offices into one big kettle labeled POLITICS, I think it then becomes clearer that politics and political engagement are mandatory for believers in the gospel of the reign of God. Though it is common to dismiss politics cynically as did Ambrose Bierce when he labeled them "a strife of interests masquerading as a contest of principles; the conduct of public affairs for private advantage,"[4] the truth is that politics is a crucial component of human life. We are obliged to engage it because, after all the barbs are spoken, politics remains the place where our society allocates the lion's share of earth's resources.

—Politics determines whose children cry themselves to sleep in hunger and whose children are tucked into warm beds with full tummies.
—Politics determines who spends how much time in what kind of jail for which kind of offenses determined by what kind of officials elected by what kind of voters.
—Politics determines whose garbage is picked up how often and whose water is safe to drink and whose streets are maintained and whose earnings are taxed.
—Politics determines whose skin color or sexual identity or ethnic origin has a better shot at getting a job or finding a decent place to live.
—Politics determines the price of medical care, the size of atomic arsenals, the content of our school rooms, and our chances of survival on a warming planet.

Politics: Avoiding the Pilate Syndrome

If any of this matters *to* us, politics is not optional *for* us! This, of course, could be said of any citizen of our nation. But for those who call themselves Christians, there are additional reasons for political engagement. Chief among them is that it must be so if we are to be true to our own story. Those who read the Bible only through a devotional lens likely miss this part of our story, but if you remove all the political scenes from our story, you miss too much.

It starts with Joseph in Egypt, emerging from the political intrigue of a foreign nation to be its prime minister, determining food policies for a world power. Then there is Moses before Pharaoh, championing the cause of Joseph's now-enslaved descendants and leading an exodus of aliens to freedom. Next there are statutes about hospitality to strangers and ordinances about redistributing land and wealth every seventy years, and commandments about justice even for the beggar in the land. This leads to scenes from Israel's royal palaces, its Ahabs and Jezebels, its Davids and Bathshebas, its finger-pointing Jeremiahs and told-off Amoses, and its far-seeing Isaiahs dreaming of a king raised up by God who will finally bring *shalom* to Israel and to this world.

The plot finds its surprising denouement when a peasant couple driven from home by a tax-seeking tyrant borrows a cow stall in a forgotten town for the birth of their child. That child will make refugees of them, aliens hiding in a foreign land, yet he will grow and do and say amazing, revolutionary things and one day be himself strung up by a kangaroo court as a seditious troublemaker. Nonetheless, his followers will persist, saying they must "obey God rather than men" by fashioning alternative (subversive?) communities bearing the peasants' child's name; communities in which Caesar's distinctions of race and gender and class and nation and previous record are all irrelevant; communities where the economy is turned upside down because no one claims private ownership of any possession but holds all things in common; communities where all is done in honor of the crucified Presence among them; communities that insist that the peasants' child, Jesus, is Lord over all, and when no one is spying, they giggle and cry with delight in Brother John's rip-snorting apocalyptic vision of "Babylon" (read Caesar) sinking into oblivion.

I'd say that is all pretty political! Always, always the governance of people and the struggle for freedom and justice is a between-the-lines story if not the primary storyline of our Grand Narrative.

Even the book that preserves this story comes from prophets pitched into dry wells by angry kings, from parchment scratchings by exiles weeping by the rivers of Babylon and from missionaries in county clinks and apostles banished to lonely islands. The best of our heritage comes from refugee camps, from martyrs, from the witness of the persecuted, from a Birmingham jail. The often-unrealized truth about us is that we were born and bred in politics and political hot water. *Up to Our Steeples in Politics*[5] is therefore more than the title of a good book from 1970. It's also a truth about the church in every age, even if Pilate Syndrome victims haven't yet understood this facet of our identity.

Discovering the Public Face of Personal Faith

I say this with a quiet voice because I am talking to myself. As the foregoing chapters might suggest, politics played no conscious role in my early life. The public, political dimension of the biblical story was never shown to me, and therefore political engagement was not an important component of my Christian outlook for many years. The only campaigning the people of The Plan approved was campaigns against liquor by the drink and pari-mutuel gambling (which were usually lost). Other than these issues, my church did not talk politics—ever. It was no different in my family.

I do not recall overhearing one conversation about politics or candidates during my growing up years ... well, with the possible exception of quoting Oklahoma's favorite philosopher, Will Rogers, and his quip that "the more you read about politics, you got to admit that each party is worse than the other." I do remember my grandfather's puzzlement when the Eisenhower administration paid him to deposit acres of his farmland into the Soil Bank and not grow crops; he never could get his head around the economics or politics of that. When Watergate erupted, I discovered my mother had voted for Richard Nixon twice—but that was the only knowledge I ever had of her political leanings. If my father had any political opinions within his ninety-six years, he never let on. In sum, from church and family and school I learned my duty as a citizen to vote. But any idea that politics might be a dimension of Christian discipleship was unknown to me.

However, with my gradual move into an appreciation for the gospel of the reign of God, I saw that the messy world of politics was one of the arenas where the struggle for a more just world must be waged. Philip Yancey's observation, with which I began this book, that "the gospel of Jesus was not primarily a political platform" remains true—but only to a point. I believe we must also add that Jesus' gospel is not apolitical! Throughout this book I have attempted to show that his gospel was good news for the entire created order. Surely that encompasses the necessary tasks of ordering our life within this world; and the name for that assignment is politics. Or, if you insist upon a more spiritual word, public stewardship.

As all of this began to clarify for me, I realized that for years I had been marveling at the deeds of Moses, Samuel, Elijah, Huldah, Isaiah, Ezekiel, Esther, and so many more, without appreciating that their courage and faith in God were often shown in deeds that were most certainly political acts. They were going head-to-head with the powers-that-be in pursuit of a better world. And was not Jesus also within that number? Surely, it was within his purpose to release us from our bondage to fear of all the two-bit tyrants and rulers of this world, and even the swagger and strut of the death threat of the big liar named Satan, and to restore to us our rightful role as stewards of this bountiful earth and God-symbols one for another, all in glad praise and service of the God who reigns over all. This is a political agenda! Politics with a twist, to be sure, but nonetheless it was the political threat Jesus posed that made Pilate and Herod know the Nazarene must die. You don't get yourself crucified simply for going about doing good.

All of this showed me that unless I wanted to continue to sit high up in the bleachers admiring my heroes from a safe distance—and watch as brothers and sisters of Jesus were trampled upon by today's injustices—I had to let Pilate-like "purity" go and grasp responsibility. Washing my hands and withdrawing from the public arena would not do. Like the novice cook who was told the very first thing to do was to "Stand and face the stove." I saw I had to "stand" and face the "heat" of the day's political issues. If I did not speak and act on behalf of what I understood to be God's cause, was I so naïve as to imagine that the money and power interests of this world were going to advocate for fairness and respect for all? Were the voices of the David Dukes of our society going to be the only white male voices raised? Politics was where the issues determining the health of my world were being debated and implemented. Politics had to be an intentional part of my kingdom citizenship.

Is Theocracy a Four-letter Word?

The crucial question thus became how was I to "get political"? It is one thing to reject the escapism of the Pilate Syndrome; it is another to become engaged wisely. The history of the Christian West is replete with lessons in how *not* to do it. The string of sad stories from Constantine's adoption of Christianity as the Roman Empire's state-endorsed religion to the Crusades to the Inquisition to Europe's endless religious wars to Cromwellian England to America's colonial witch-burnings, all in varying ways arose from well-intentioned Christians who were attempting to give political expression to their understanding of the kingdom of God on earth. Indeed, this very desire to establish "a city set on a hill" animated our Pilgrim ancestors and the same zeal fed the early twentieth-century Progressive Era of American politics as demonstrated by the Progressive Party's 1912 Presidential campaign song, "Onward, Christians Soldiers." More recently, the Moral Majority of Jerry Falwell Sr. drank from these waters and spoke its language.

At least outwardly all these were gestures toward a politics of, dare I say it, theocracy. Yes, it is a leprous word, and regardless of the inflection one gives to it, theocracy carries cringing overtones that few wish to sound. Yet the word remains the only one I know to indicate the heart's desire of those who pray "thy kingdom come, thy will be done on earth." If we dare use it the same cruciform disclaimer must govern its meaning as when we speak of the kingdom; the theocracy sought must be a cruciform theocracy, bearing the lowly pattern of the cross. No doubt another word needs to be fashioned. But in the meantime this is the best word we have at hand, and, in an extended exploration of it, Christian ethicist Allen Verhey[6] has offered three clarifications of it that permit me to introduce it in this discussion. I will, however, surround it with quotation marks to indicate the qualified nature of the kind of "theocracy" I believe ought not to be dismissed as a four-letter word.

First, Verhey says "theocracy" does not mean the political rule of a priestly or clerical hierarchy. The technical word for that is *hierocracy*, but it is apparent that even in the Old Testament's theocracy, the power of priests and clergy is always interplayed with that of kings and judges. Moreover, the king is always held to be responsible to God, not to clerics or to priests. "In theocracy religious leaders are neither identified with political leaders nor given authority over them."[7]

Second, "theocracy" must not be confused with what Verhey terms *bibliocracy*, that is, the rule of scripture. Bibliocracy would call for the enactment of law codes taken from the Bible. The teachings of R.J. Rushdoony and Greg Bahnson of the Reconstructionist ("theonomists") ideology is a present-day expression of bibliocracy. Reconstructionism calls for Old Testament law to become the law of the land—for example, unrepentant adulterers and homosexual activity would be considered capital offenses. Many persons mistakenly believe this kind of rule to be "theocracy." It is not. "Theocracy does not entail any particular legal code, and Christians must not suppose the Bible provides a timeless set of civil rules."[8] To say the Bible may be used this way would require the equivalent of a Supreme Court (a Protestant papacy?) to determine *the* correct meaning and importance of the code—and thus the contest would be on for who is to be the "Theo" of this theocracy!

Finally, "theocracy" ought not be identified with any of the historical instances where attempts were made to institutionalize God's reign. All of the failed enterprises I named above, and more, fall into this category, for none can be judged successful implementations of a perfect civil order. "To defend theocracy is not to defend, say, Calvin's Geneva or to propose that a contemporary state ape [William] Penn's "holy experiment" [in Pennsylvania]."[9]

How Cruciform "Theocracy" Works

If "theocracy" does not mean the state is to be ruled by clergy or by a biblical code or along the lines of some failed Utopian society from the past, what then does it mean? I would suggest that it means a certain posture, some fixed concerns, and a methodology.

With regard to our political posture, "theocracy" means seekers of the kingdom enter the political arena with humility, especially with what the philosophers call "epistemological humility." In simplest terms this means the kingdom of God is not well served by anyone who pretends to have God's cell phone number. Though we may seek to act and speak for a realm of God's rule, we also must confess our knowledge of God's will is always "in part." Our best efforts, politically and otherwise, inevitably are ignorant of some dimensions of every problem we seek to solve and just as inevitably will have unforeseen consequences for good or ill that mock our pretensions to be more than mortals. Therefore, political engagement for us is always done with humility, for the ways of God are seldom if ever copybook plain before our eyes. We will not play Theo nor present ourselves, our party, or our proposals as hand-delivered from Above and thereby nullify our endeavors through our arrogance. For us then, the practice of "theocracy" is ironically first of all a defiant statement that God alone is God, and that we will not pretend to be God or permit another to usurp God's place. I know no better summary statement of the humility that becomes our political involvement than Reinhold Niebuhr's classic words:

> Nothing that is worth doing can be achieved in our lifetime; therefore we must be saved by hope. Nothing which is true or beautiful or good makes complete sense in any immediate context of history; therefore we must be saved by faith. Nothing we do, however virtuous, can be accomplished alone; therefore we must be saved by love. No virtuous act is quite as virtuous from the standpoint of our friend or foe as it is from our standpoint. Therefore we must be saved by the final form of love which is forgiveness.[10]

Beginning with this posture of humility, "theocracy" nonetheless proceeds with open advocacy of certain fixed concerns. We do not know all, but we do claim some understanding of a few essential things. We dare to believe that we have some basic insights into human nature and need, the corruptions of power, and the aspirational standards of the *shalom* of God's reign on earth. It is not that we alone have knowledge of these things, but that these concerns are always the first and most important considerations for us.

Crowning them is the supreme value of truth. This flows from our understanding of God as the sovereign one whose word is altogether trustworthy and in whose character there is no shadow. This valuation also flows from our understanding that common life in a democracy is impossible without reservoirs of trust in one another, without some modicum of confidence that we will not egregiously misrepresent the truth. We enact this axiomatic tenet of our life together when we require elected officials to take solemn oaths at their installation and court witnesses "to tell the truth, the whole truth, and nothing but the truth." Our conviction about the supreme value of truth also finds especially poignant biblical anchorage in the gut-wrenching writings of Jeremiah, the "weeping" prophet, whose ministry spanned the final spasms of Judah's life as a nation. In the Hebrew Bible (Old Testament) the word for "falsehood" or "lie" (*shqr*) appears seventy-two times; half of those are in the Book of Jeremiah, pointedly revealing the deepest source of Judah's decline and death.

The death throes of truth in American politics today is undeniable.[11] It may be true that "all political parties die at last swallowing their own lies," but in my own lifetime I have seen respect for truth diminish to a shadow. I saw it wounded first from those who plunged us into bitter division by prolonged lies about Vietnam and then Watergate. This was followed by further shredding of the nation's fabric of trust by a last-minute admission of illicit sexual liaisons within the White House itself. The nation had been lied to by its own leaders, by representatives of both wings of our political dialogue. Next, even the existence of any semblance of objective truth itself began to be questioned by philosophers and novelists. "Perspectival" truth and "personally defined" truth became the new understanding, leading us to today's culture of "alternate facts" and the anomaly of "true facts" and the accusations of "fake news" by a president whose capacity for mendacity is demonstrably wide and deep. As a nation, we now expect to be lied to and find ourselves forlornly searching both for unbiased news sources and for truth-speaking public figures. A "theocratic" bedrock, insistence upon truth-telling in the public square, has never been more needed.

The practice of "theocracy" also prizes the necessity of freedom. Like our commitment to truth, our commitment to freedom flows from our understanding of the character of God as one who never coerces but grants to all the freedom to determine their way. Even if in a given moment of history the majority would endorse my particular view, I would want to be no more controlling than is God. Again I say, the kingdom I seek is a cruciform kingdom; it reigns through persuasion, not compulsion.

This valuing of freedom also flows from the conviction that our common life flourishes best when we grant each other as much individual freedom as respectful life together can provide. So, the freedom I cherish is not a life without restraint, but it is a freedom with keen attention to our inescapable relatedness to one another. A gospel of the kingdom will not permit me to espouse any school of thought that consistently prizes individual freedom over social responsibility. For example, because I value freedom and its continuance, I want to be taxed to provide the very best schools for my nation's children—even if I no longer have children of school age—because no society thrives without educated citizens and because every child created in God's image should be given the intellectual tools to flourish. Because "us" is central to my understanding of human thriving and my understanding of the gospel of Jesus, I reject individualistic and extreme *laissez-faire* approaches to public and economic life. The "*pluribus*" of "*e pluribus unum*" strikes a gospel note for me and is as important as is granting as much freedom as possible.

This is so in the realm of religion as well. I do not want the state to favor or to suppress any religion or any anti-religious entity or persons. Persons' religious beliefs and practices are not a matter of governmental concern—unless, as indicated above, they infringe upon the personhood and freedom of others.

Politics: Avoiding the Pilate Syndrome

I reject the idea that this nation is or ever has been a "Christian" nation, though it undeniably was birthed by patriots who were mostly professing Christians. Nor do I wish to make America a "Christian" nation now. Rather, I seek the kingdom of God on earth, which is a goal higher than a so-called "Christian" political state. I seek the attributes of God's righteous rule, many of which are as important to other world religions as to the Christian faith. And, because no one comes to any faith by coercion, I prize the practice of freedom of religion and the freedom of non-religion. It is up to believers, on turf other than politics, to win the affections and loyalty of others to the faith we prize.

Compassion also becomes a cardinal concern for people of the dawn. Rather than permit our politics to be driven solely by economic barometers, people of the dawn give attention to the well-being of neighbors. All too often special considerations are granted to so-called money-makers, using the justification that "a rising tide lifts all boats." But if you have no boat, this policy helps not at all. Indeed, if you are a shore-dweller, a rising tide can even destroy the livelihood that you have. So, for those who derive their vision of the good society from Israel's prophets and Jesus, it is mandatory to be concerned about the impact of any law or policy upon shore-dwellers. This is true in realms beyond economics, of course, because a politics of compassion is for us not a sign of bleeding-heart liberalism but of godly compassion and justice.

To these themes of truth, freedom, and compassion I could add others such as courage and empathy. Yet I hope these two suggest that the "theocracy" I think is appropriate to seek politically is not the kind of bigotry and suppression that this word so often connotes. Rather it is a practical implementation of Jesus' command to "*seek* the kingdom of God"—knowing its full presence is always within the mystery and timing of God alone. Thus, these themes, even if idealistic, are to inform and infuse considerations of any and all specific policy proposals.[12]

Finally, with regard to methodology, what are we to do with specific policy proposals? How is a "theocrat" to deal with the actual nitty-gritty legislative decisions that often consist, in John Kenneth Galbraith's words, of "choosing between the disastrous and the unpalatable"?

My response is that compromise is not, any more than "theocracy," necessarily a four-letter word. In our politics we strive toward approximations of the kingdom. We do not "insist upon our own way" (1 Cor. 13), but among the options before us we seek the alternative that seems to lean toward the goals we seek. When political engagement is appreciated as one means of approximating the kingdom, rather than of establishing it, there is space for respectful dialogue with those with whom we differ. Compromise becomes a moral good rather than a regrettable flaw. As a "secular" example, we might recall that the 1789 Constitution that continues to bind these United States into one people is a compromise document, each article debated and massaged by the Constitutional Convention's delegates, and that it was endorsed by only thirty-nine of the fifty-five delegates with not a one of them ever imagining that their watered-down, compromise work would survive for two centuries and become a model to be widely emulated.

By endorsing a methodology of permissible compromise, it is evident that my use of the word "theocracy" is more an indication of priorities than it is a serious proposal for a system of American government. Fortunately, we live in a democracy, and I have no wish to see it supplanted by anyone whose goal is a theocracy in the senses we have seen it in history. What I do wish to see is the values of the reign of God suffusing the life of our democracy, that is, nudging our democracy toward a society that more nearly reflects God's intent. Though we cannot make this kingdom arrive, we can be its voice and its watchmen, calling out even in the political arena: "Prepare the way of the Lord!"

Augustine held that to the end of history the world's *shalom* must be gained by strife, by the clash of "enemies." *Shalom* will never, therefore, be perfect in this history. "But it can be more perfect than it is."[13] So, with sober hope we labor in the present day, longing for the promised day when the new creation will appear as final grace from the now and future Sovereign of all things, seen and unseen.

Some years ago, I offered my own Eight Commandments (I'm not smart enough to come up with ten) for Politically Active Believers.[14] I repeat them now as something of a summary and extension of all I have said here:

1. Thou shalt believe in original sin. No facet of life escapes the blight of sin, and no political viewpoint is pure and free from bias or error, even your own.
2. Thou shalt not be a one-issue activist; society's well-being is multifaceted.
3. Thou shalt not bear false witness. Winning by smearing is a loss.
4. Thou shalt do thine homework. Quoting the Bible is permissible, but only if you have studied the issues and can cite other reputable authorities as well.
5. Thou shalt not neglect the poor or blame them for their poverty.
6. Thou shalt not trample on religious freedom or the religious views of others.
7. Thou shalt not whine when attacked by media or foes. Politics is a contact sport, proving once again that loving one's neighbor isn't child's play.
8. Thou shalt remember that "God 'n country" is *not* one word.

The Church as a Political Player and Coach

A footnote must be added to all of this, a reminder that the church has a crucial role to play in all our political engagement. The discipline of politics ought not be solely an individual journey. In the church's prayers, its educational programs, and in its sermons and forums, the public dimension of our life ought to be visible. Opportunities to weigh the merits of legislation from kingdom perspectives are critically important. On occasions it may even be fitting for a church to issue a statement regarding its conclusions concerning public issues.

If all politics is local, the most local of all places for Christians is the community of faith where we coach each other in the ways of the kingdom, where the themes of truth and freedom and justice and courage and compassion are always before us. When decisions about the church's life and ministry are being made, a laboratory for political education presents itself. While not forgetting the larger world, this smaller world of the church's life together is to be a model of how that larger world might and should look. We are to practice as well as to pray: "Thy kingdom come, thy will be done on earth as it is in heaven." Tending our own garden well trains us in the ways of political effectiveness and grants us credibility in the public arena.

Never, however, is the church to be the servant of any one political party. The occasionally heard charge that some churches are simply the local Republican (or Democratic) Party at prayer is a damning accusation. Our allegiance is to the kingdom of God, and we are its servants alone. Thus our political engagement is not a matter of political partisanship but of kingdom priorities. Our foundational purpose is to nurture faith in God and to model love for all God's creation, not to campaign for candidate X or Y. Rather, on the Lord's Day we gather as equals, each one a child of God's love, and together we sing hymns of praise to one who is beyond and yet involved in all our politics.

On the Lord's Day we listen attentively for God's directives through "green pasture" and "enemy presence" scriptures—and squirm and wince when we hear more or other than what we welcomed. We pray together for the healing of the world of God's care, and we greet each other respectfully at the table and receive broken bread and blood-red wine, as beloved family. These actions, rising from beliefs of two thousand years and more, are our weekly bootcamp in discipleship and always our best preparation for the political fray that awaits us outside the sanctuary. Here, every Sunday, within sacred walls, we hear the muffled drums and trumpet call to a kingdom already powerfully at work among us, yet waiting in the wings, seeking ambassadors of its coming.

Notes

[1] "David Duke: Charlottesville Rally Part of Effort to 'Take Country Back,'" NBC News, August 12, 2017, cited in Jon Meacham, *The Soul of America: The Battle for Our Better Angels* (New York: Random House, 2018), 5.

[2] Matthew 27:24, Eugene H. Peterson, *The Message* (Colorado Springs, CO: NavPress, 1995).

[3] Richard Rohr, *The Universal Christ* (Convergent Books, 2019), 94.

[4] Ambrose Bierce, *The Devil's Dictionary* (New York: Dover Publications, 1958), 101.

[5] Will D. Campbell and James Y. Holloway, *Up to Our Steeples in Politics* (New York: Paulist Press, 1970).

⁶See part 5, "Remembering Jesus in the Strange World of Politics: Revisiting Theocracy—A Continuing Tradition of Justice" in Allen Verhey, *Remembering Jesus* (Grand Rapids: Eerdmans, 2005), 333-507.

⁷Verhey, *Remembering Jesus*, 339.

⁸Ibid.

⁹Ibid.

¹⁰Reinhold Niebuhr, *The Irony of American History* (Chicago: University of Chicago Press, 1952), 63.

¹¹The literature here is vast but my own convictions stem from reading, in order, the following works: David Wise, *The Politics of Lying: Government Deception, Secrecy, and Power* (New York: Random House, 1973); Karl Menninger, *Whatever Became of Sin?* (New York: Hawthorn Books, 1973); Marilyn Chandler McEntyre, *Caring for Words in a Culture of Lies* (Grand Rapids, MI: Eerdmans, 2009); Michiko Kakutani, *The Death of Truth: Notes on Falsehood in the Age of Trump* (New York: Tim Duggan Books, 2018).

¹²A most helpful guide in this regard is Miroslav Volf and Ryan McAnnally-Linz, *Public Faith in Action: How to Think Carefully, Engage Wisely, and Vote with Integrity* (Grand Rapids, MI: Brazos Press, 2016). They discuss wealth, the environment, education, work and rest, poverty, borrowing and lending, marriage and family, new life, health and sickness, aging life, ending life, migration, policing, punishment, war, torture, and freedom of religion.

¹³Reinhold Niebuhr, *Moral Man and Immoral Society* (New York: Charles Scribner's Sons, 1932), 256. This quote and its surrounding paragraph paraphrase Niebuhr's concluding words in chapter 9, "The Preservation of Moral Values in Politics."

¹⁴J. Daniel Day, *If Jesus Isn't the Answer, He Sure Asks the Right Questions* (Macon, GA: Smyth & Helwys Publishing, 2015), 94.

Excursus:
Hitler's Reich (Kingdom) and the Church

Modern history's most notable demonstration of a flawed interface between politics and religion came in 1933-1945 in Germany's *Kirchenkampf* (church struggle) as Protestants and Catholics responded to the rise and rule of Adolph Hitler's Nazi Party. Hitler initially and deceitfully masked his contempt for Christianity and the churches (A typical candid comment, found in his *Table Talk*, is: "The war will be over one day. I shall then consider that my life's final task will be to solve the religious problem.... The final state must be: in the pulpit, a senile officiant; facing him, a few sinister old women, as gaga and as poor in spirit as anyone could wish."), and received overwhelming support from Germany's churches because of his strong conservative politics. However, as his power grew and the full import of his promised thousand-year Reich objectives became clearer, clergy and churches split in their support or chose, as the majority did, to follow the safest course: silence.

In the following essay (originally published in the July-August 2020 issue of *Nurturing Faith Journal*) I examine this horrendous chapter of church history as a case study in how not to fall to the Pilate Syndrome.

Deeply Entwined
Seven Marks of a "Christian Nation" in a Perilous Hour

"Without any doubt, we Germans are a Christian nation."

That pronouncement by Heinrich von Treitschke, an influential German political thinker, was received warmly as the twentieth century dawned. His fellow countrymen were pleased that he had perceived "how deeply Christianity is entwined with every fiber of the German character."

The Christian faith "inspired the nation's arts and sciences," he said, and its spirit "animated all healthy institutions of our state and society."

Germany was, after all, the land of Martin Luther, a nation of forty million Protestants and twenty million Roman Catholics—all of them "Christian"—with Jews numbering less than 1 percent of its population.

How, then, did this "Christian" nation become the home for a poison (fascism/Nazism) that snuffed the lives of six million European Jews, plunged the world into a war that took twenty-five million soldiers' lives (and perhaps an equal number of civilian lives), and consumed more than four trillion dollars of the earth's resources?

How was it possible for a "Christian" people to swear fanatical allegiance ("*Sieg Heil!*" means "Holy Victory!") to a dictatorial Führer who had no use for historic Christianity—a religion for weaklings mired in Jewish filth when what was needed was a muscular "positive Christianity" of pure German identity?

How can we explain church sanctuaries forested with flags depicting a twisted cross (the German word for cross is *kreuz*; the word for swastika is *hackenkreuz*, a hooked cross) and so few worshipers sensing something was horribly wrong?

How did German Christians not see that the nationalism of the Nazi slogan "*Deutschland über alles*" (Germany over All, Germany First) was a point-blank refutation of the primal Christian creed, "Jesus is Lord"?

The problem is complex and helpful answers equally so. But some understanding is crucial if we are to profit from the painful past and walk wisely in the political chaos of the 21st century.

At the risk of oversimplification, here are seven observations about the tragic devolution of the church in Germany between 1919–1945.

One: The Church was filled with frustrated, unrepentant citizens.

On Nov. 11, 1919 World War I finally slogged to its conclusion with inglorious defeat for Germany, a nation only forty-eight years old, formed from a federation of previously independent states.

Finding the Gospel

The hubris and miscalculation that led Germany into war ended with a humiliated nation saddled with punitive armistice terms exacted when the victors divided the war's spoils.

French leader Clemenceau said the only thing not demanded of Germany in the Treaty of Versailles was the Kaiser's britches. Herbert Hoover was less humorous when he wrote:

> Destructive forces sat at the Peace Table. The future of twenty-six jealous European races was there. The genes of a thousand years of inbred hate and fear of every generation were in their blood. Revenge of past wrongs rose every hour of the day. It was not alone the delegates that were thus inspired. These emotions of hate, revenge, desire for reparations, and a righteous sense of wrong were at fever heat in their people at home.

For Germany's role in The Great War even a democratic form of government was forced upon a people whose pattern of subservience to strong, authoritarian rulers was bone deep. Sadly, the inept political bungling of this enemy-mandated democracy (the Weimar Republic was further exacerbated within ten years by a worldwide financial collapse.

Thus, during the years of 1919–1933 the pews of German churches were filled by a proud, unrepentant people, raw with political embarrassment, financial deprivation, and cultural rage. They sought the consolations of their religion, surely, but they also sought a leader who could lead them to the international greatness they believed was due them.

Not seated among them, but busy formulating a response to their yearnings, was a young and opportunistic, bitter veteran of the Kaiser's army, Adolph Hitler. When the surrender had been announced, he said:

> Everything went black before my eyes; I tottered and groped my way back to the dormitory, threw myself on my bunk and dug my burning head into my blanket and pillow.... And so it had all been in vain. In vain all the sacrifices and privations; in vain the hunger and thirst of months ... in vain the hours in which, with mortal fear clutching at our hearts, we nevertheless did our duty.

Hitler wrote in his 1925 autobiographical Nazi manifesto, *Mein Kampf* (meaning, "My Fight"): "The more I tried to achieve clarity on the monstrous event ... the more the shame of indignation and disgrace burned my brow.... I, for my part, decided to go into politics."

Two: The Church was politically inexperienced.

From Martin Luther the Germanic people had received a nuanced concept of "Two Kingdoms" in which the spiritual dimension of life was represented in the kingdom of Christ and the mundane, secular concerns by the kingdom of the world.

In Luther's view these were mutually reinforcing expressions of God's two-handed way of nurturing personal piety and public order. Christians owed obedience to Throne and Altar.

Four hundred years later, Luther's Two Kingdoms concept meant in actual practice that the Altar was expected to preach a spiritual gospel and inculcate personal virtue—and leave the affairs of the state to the Throne.

There was little space left for the church to speak to the state, let alone criticize its actions. What today's activists would call "speaking truth to power" was not within this church's skill set.

Therefore, when the political winds dramatically changed direction, as they did upon Hitler's becoming chancellor in 1933, church leaders were ill equipped by church doctrine, practice or congregational expectation to oppose the Throne.

Preachers found that sermons dealing with the most basic Christian teachings of forgiveness and loving all persons were heard to be "political" sermons and the slightest negative references to current events were construed to be unpatriotic and anti-Hitler.

Pastors were expected to remain politically neutral or be openly pro-Nazi.

One "prophetic" voice, Pastor Paul Schneider, the first Protestant pastor to die in a concentration camp, protested to his wife in a letter written from his cell in 1937: "It is not that I and all the rest have said too much in our sermons, but rather that we have said far too little."

In truth, Schneider and the rest had few models to emulate other than the biblical prophets.

Three: The Church was financially compromised.

Another aspect of the unification of Throne and Altar was the financial dependence inherent within it. Just as the rulers of the separate Germanic states had previously appointed their ecclesiastical leaders and funded their activities, so during the Kaiser's and the Weimar administrations, Germany's churches were included within the nation's budget and supported by citizens' tax dollars.

Administratively, each branch of the Church (Lutheran, Reformed, Roman Catholic, etc.) determined its own leadership, but all were dependent upon the government for their financial livelihood.

The initiation of such church disagreement with Hitler as there was began with Hitler's desire to assume administrative control of the churches. A large group of Protestant church leaders, calling themselves the "German Christians," supported his desires, seeking "One Church for One Germany."

These "German Christians" also ardently supported the Fuhrer's larger agenda, but from a coalition known as the "Confessing Church" they encountered stout opposition to Hitler's push for a state-appointed bishop over all the churches. But both groups were understandably wary of offending the hand that fed them.

Four: The Church was plagued by unacknowledged racism.

The word "German" and its correlates became in those days Nazi euphemisms for a biologically pure Aryan race. There was and is no such thing as a pure Aryan race, but truth did not hinder propagandists from peddling the lie of a biological basis for the notion of "German" superiority.

From this falsehood they then further legitimated their denigration of all persons not of pure Aryan blood—such as gypsies, Africans, and especially Jews.

Although the number of Jews within Germany was miniscule, the Nazis saw (wealthy) European Jewry as being primary contributors to Germany's defeat in World War I—and thinkers such as von Treitschke gave scholarly credibility to that notion when he concluded his earlier quoted praise of Christian Germany by saying: "Judaism, on the other hand, is the national religion of a tribe which was originally alien to us."

Even in the now-famous Article 24 of its 1920 platform, the Nazis declared that the Party "combats the Jewish-materialistic spirit at home and abroad and is convinced that a permanent recovery of our people can only be achieved from within on the basis of the common good before individual good."

Once in power, the Nazis repudiated even the Jewishness of Jesus and sought a German "positive Christianity" free of all Jewish taint. But the odor of Auschwitz crematoria was within the Party's earliest platform; anti-Semitism was clear from the beginning.

Within the churches, however, the resistance to this arose only when the "German Christians," following Hitler's 1933 purging of all Jews from state employment, attempted to purge the handful of church leaders who had been born Jewish.

Their attempt ignited a struggle within the church that only a few people (for example, young Dietrich Bonhoeffer) understood to be a struggle about race; most viewed it as an issue of ordination, of baptism's efficacy, and of church authority.

The reason for this blindness was the embedded but unacknowledged anti-Semitism within the church.

Whereas the Nazi's anti-Semitism was racially based, the church's disdain was religiously based and its history reached back to the long venerated interpretation of Matthew 27:25 ("His blood be upon us and on our children") as an everlasting divine judgment against the Jews for the crucifixion of Jesus—not to mention the many other passages within the New Testament that bear an anti-"Jew" aura.

Even Germany's favorite historic "Christian," Martin Luther, had written many astonishingly anti-Semitic paragraphs. Given such a history and the scant number of Jews within the nation, the Nazi's racist rhetoric was easy to dismiss, if it was even seriously noted.

For church folk the issue wasn't justice for a minority; it was the attainment of a restored nation with international respect.

Five: The church mirrored the nation's endorsement of a strong leader with bold ideas.
As the darkness of the Great Depression fell upon an already prostrated nation, another seismic shock came to Germany. In the election of 1930, the Nazis astounded the nation's intelligentsia by garnering 6.5 million votes, granting them 107 seats, the second largest representation in the *Reichstag*.

No doubt this ascendancy was due in part to the Party's bold ideas. The Party was rabidly anti-Communist in an hour when the Red Scare was at fever pitch and its Russian homeland only a border away. But it was just as rabidly pro-Germany.

The Nazi promises of prosperity, its list of practices and groups detrimental to a restored Germany, and its avowed resolve to purify a soiled nation offered strong medicine indeed. Tragically, it was a medicine that proved fatal when in 1933 the Nazi's painter-turned-politician and his gang of thugs wrested complete control of the government.

In that pivotal election year of 1930 the president of the Weimar Republic, Paul von Hindenburg, was 83 years old, an overweight relic of an era that was as dead as the soldiers he had led to defeat in The Great War, and his chancellor, Heinrich Bruning, 44, was a thin-lipped, balding administrator who, according to British historian Piers Brendon, had "a habit of speaking quietly as though he were afraid of being heard."

The pair incarnated everything the forty-year-old Adolph Hitler despised—and dramatically reversed.

Contrary to their prim, monocle-wearing respectability, Hitler campaigned in common clodhoppers, blue serge suit, black fedora, and soiled overcoat, resembling "a suburban hairdresser on his day off," according to one admirer. But in the 1920s, politics was still more word than image-oriented.

In a 2006 study of *The Language of the Third Reich*, philologist Victor Klemperer noted the abundance of superlatives in Hitler's speech and Nazi propaganda; superlatives such as "greatest" and "bravest" and "most glorious" always attended Nazi ideas just as only denigrating adjectives were used for all others.

But Hitler used image too. "Only a storm of hot passion can turn the destinies of peoples," he had averred in *Mein Kampf*, "and he alone can arouse passion who bears it in himself."

Accordingly, Hitler's oratory was an explosion of passion. "An orgasm of words" flowed from the man, according to one observer, inducing ecstasy in his listeners who seemed not to care that even his frequent tactic of crushing his spectacles in his clenched fist as he neared his final sentences was scripted for effect.

Brendon noted that Hitler lost about five pounds in weight during every speech, though he drank small bottles of mineral water throughout. He sometimes took a block of ice to the rostrum to cool his hands.

But he sweated so profusely that the dye running from his suit stained his shirt and underwear blue.

Germany—indeed the political world—had never seen or heard his like. Overwhelmed by the spectacle he presented, the German people—including well-intentioned Christians—gave him just enough power to grab still more power until the world they had known was set afire and lost.

Six: The church was ruled by self-preservation concerns.

In one sense, this observation is a restatement of the earlier stated financial dependency of the church. But it is also more.

When the church opposed Hitler's desire to assume administrative control of the church, the objection was not to his wider program of German renaissance; it was a struggle for the theological integrity of the church, about the internal workings of the church.

Even the justly celebrated repudiation of Nazism found in the Confessing Church's Barmen Confession of 1934 (written primarily by Karl Barth) did not, for all its other merits, address the racist foundation of Nazi ideology.

Later, when the "German Christians" attempted to purge Jewish-born leaders from the church, the debate was focused on the status of Jewish converts to Christianity, not on the value and dignity of the Jewish people themselves.

In both instances, the conflict centered around the institution's life, not the life of the world. Even Barth admitted: "It confined itself to the Church's Confession, to the Church service, and to Church order as such. It was only a partial resistance."

Only in a 1936 document penned by a core of "Confessing Church" leaders (and perhaps never seen by Hitler) did Protestant church leaders repudiate the Nazi administration. The Vatican did so on March 4, 1937, in the papal encyclical *Mit Brennender Sorge* ("With Burning Anxiety").

But, by then, it was too late.

We can strive to contextualize and soften this disappointing record by placing alongside it the affirmation of the church given by the Jewish exile, Albert Einstein, who had looked to the universities and the nation's newspapers to offer great resistance. But they failed. According to Einstein,

> Only the Church stood squarely across the path of Hitler's campaign for suppressing the truth. I never had any special interest in the Church before, but

now I feel a great affection and admiration for it because the Church alone has had the courage and persistence to stand for intellectual and moral freedom. I am forced to confess that what I once despised. I now praise unreservedly.

Still, the church in all subsequent ages, must confront the confession attributed to Lutheran pastor Martin Niemoller, who spent 1937–1945 in Sachsenhausen and Dachau as Hitler's "personal prisoner":

First they came for the Communists, and I did not speak out—because I was not a Communist. Then they came for the Trade Unionists, and I did not speak out—because I was not a Trade Unionist. Then they came for the Jews, and I did not speak out—because I was not a Jew. Then they came for me—and there was no one left to speak for me.

Seven: The church was victimized by 'cheap grace.'

As Niemoller struggled in 1937 to accustom himself to solitary confinement in Sachsenhausen, he received a book, *Nachfolge* ("Discipleship"), just written by his younger colleague, Dietrich Bonhoeffer.

It contained an inscription in Bonhoeffer's hand: "To Martin Niemoller, who could have written a better book on this subject."

Bonhoeffer's work, later published in English as *The Cost of Discipleship*, has however become a classic. Its first section deals with Martin Luther's much beloved rediscovery of the doctrine of salvation by grace alone.

However, as Bonhoeffer surveyed the subsequent interpretation of Luther's insight and the spineless state of Protestantism in the reformer's homeland, he sadly concluded that "the result [is] that a nation became Christian and Lutheran, but at the cost of true discipleship."

"We gave away the word and sacraments wholesale," he wrote, "we baptized, confirmed, and absolved a whole nation unasked and without condition … We poured forth unending streams of grace. But the call to follow Jesus in the narrow way was hardly ever heard."

Written from the epicenter of the modern world's most climactic *de profundis* hour, Bonhoeffer's words must be pondered, not as interesting history, but as an admonition to Christians in all hours and places.

Sources

"Baptists and the Holocaust." *American Baptist Quarterly.* Spring 2018.

Barnett, Victoria. *For the Soul of the People: Protestant Protest Against Hitler.* Oxford University Press, 1998.

Brendon, Piers. *The Dark Valley: A Panorama of the 1930s.* Knoft, 2000.

Cochrane, Arthur. *The Church's Confession Under Hitler.* Westminster, 1962.

Conway, J.S. *The Nazi Persecution of the Churches, 1933–1945.* Regent, 1968.

Hockenos, Matthew. *Then They Came for Me: Martin Niemoller, The Pastor Who Defied the Nazis.* Basic Books, 2018.

Stroud, Dean G., ed. *Preaching in Hitler's Shadow: Sermons of Resistance in the Third Reich.* Eerdmans, 2013.

CHAPTER 21

❋

Coda: Here Ends the Status Report

I began this book by saying I wanted to share my notes of how I have changed my mind about several matters of the Christian faith, and principally about the message of the gospel itself. I hope I've accomplished that task. Now you can make of my journey what you will and use its findings as you wish.

In retrospect, I see that there are two passages of scripture that summarize all I have written. Both are attributed to Jesus. To the people of Galilee, Jesus said: "The time is fulfilled, and the kingdom of God has come near; repent, and believe in the good news" (Mark 1:14). And to a religious leader, Jesus said: "Do not be astonished that I said to you, 'You must be born from above—or anew'" (John 3:7).

Although I have said much about the first passage, I fear I have said too little about the latter. Yet Jesus' announcement of the kingdom is empty if divorced from his words about new birth, for, as he says, "no one can see the kingdom of God without being born from above—or anew" (John 3:3). These two verses are indissolubly wed. Divorced from new birth, the kingdom becomes only an attractive social goal, theoretically fascinating but not a living personal fire. Divorced from the kingdom, the new birth becomes a personal experience lacking context and calling. Married, the two enable a life of purpose, roots, and gratitude. The two, in tandem, provide a transcendent anchor and a tangible focus for a "saved" life. Yoked, they comprise the better gospel I have found and now commend. But they must be kept united.

Perhaps the connection has not been visible enough within these pages. If so, I must now emphasize that God's dream of the re-creation of the cosmos has a personal beginning point: the individual human heart. It would be folly to speak of the rebirth of all things but pretend that our spiritual innards, that we ourselves, are not in need of such or that we have no soul-work to do or accept. T.S. Eliot warned of those who attempt to side-step this essential, "dreaming of systems so perfect that no one will need to be good,"[1] and I want no part of that cul de sac.

The presence of the kingdom that Jesus released is to be both a matter of experience and a hope for our world. In its message those who have failed find the land of beginning again, and those who have succeeded find the highest goal for all their striving; both are "saved" through the power of this gospel. The better gospel I have found and tried to present here does not minimize the importance of the individual's experience of the grace of God. It does seek to interpret it as our introduction to the larger realm of God's dream for the whole creation.

The sad truth is that we have a notoriously difficult time keeping these truths in dynamic interaction. Churches that have heard the gospel of The Plan tend to preach only that gospel and offer the single gift of "getting saved." On the other hand, churches that have heard the gospel of a New Order tend to preach only a social gospel without equal attention to Jesus' power to re-create individuals. Consequently, God's call to be justice-seekers is never heard in one church and God's call to be "born again" is never heard in the other. We become either evangelistic churches or social justice churches—or nondescript ecclesiastical driftwood. And in all this sorting out, the great church is torn asunder once again, with believers embarrassedly acknowledging one another as distant cousins who seldom speak—and when we eavesdrop on one another, we shake our heads in disappointment at what we never hear mentioned.

In truth there is only one gospel, one gospel that is both deeply personal and profoundly social. The "better" gospel suggested in this book is meant to include and reconcile these personal and social polarities within Jesus' gospel of the reign of God. So, the good news I have tried to unfold in these pages needs to sing, with equal ardor, "Just As I Am" and "Where Cross the Crowded Ways of Life," songs of individual appeal and of social witness. It needs to teach persons how to speak of Jesus and invite others to follow him and also to teach them how to write letters to editors and elected officials, and to organize and pray and petition and picket for justice. This gospel will speak testimonies of persons coming to know Jesus and of his maturing them in his image; it will also report meals served, housing provided, legislative initiatives backed, injustices named and rebuked—kingdom "sightings." This gospel tells the artist, the scientist, the environmentalist, the musician, the journalist, the lawyer, the banker, the teacher, the parent, the social worker, and the garbage man to value their daily work as an expression of the same gospel preached on Sundays. This gospel authorizes us to do the two-fold work of new birth *and* of new creation. It is the gospel of the king who is making all things—and each of us—new.

The actuarial tables place me within those in the twilight of their life and thus include me among the elderly who predictably sit around and tell tales on winter evenings. Nonetheless, my great hope is that what I have shared with you is more than just a pastor's faith journey and certainly more than a grandfather's tale. It represents my best attempt to report what I believe to be altogether true and trustworthy—the gospel. I especially like the way Nikos Kazantzakis tells the heart of it in the final paragraphs of his classic *The Last Temptation of Christ*:

> His head quivered. Suddenly he remembered where he was, who he was, and why he felt pain. A wild, indomitable joy took possession of him. No, no, he was not a coward, a deserter, a traitor. No, he was nailed to the cross. He had stood his ground honorably to the very end; he had kept his word. The moment

he cried ELI ELI, Temptation had captured him for a split second and led him astray. The joys, marriages and children were lies; the decrepit, degraded old men who shouted coward, deserter, traitor at him were lies. All—all were illusions sent by the Devil. His disciples were alive and thriving. They had gone over sea and land and were proclaiming the Good News. Everything had turned out as it should, glory be to God! He uttered a triumphant cry: IT IS ACCOMPLISHED! And it was as though he had said: Everything has begun.[2]

Notes

[1] Choruses from "The Rock," VI, in Eliot, *The Complete Poems and Plays 1909–1950* (New York: Harcourt, Brace & World, 1962), 106.

[2] Nikos Kazantzakis, *The Last Temptation of Christ*, trans. P.A Brien (New York: Simon & Schuster, 1960), 495-496.

For Further Reading

Disappointment

Butler, Jon, Grant Wacker, and Randall Balmer. *Religion in American Life: A Short History.* 2nd ed. New York: Oxford University Press, 2011.

Balmer, Randall. *The Making of Evangelicalism: From Revivalism to Politics and Beyond.* Waco, TX: Baylor University Press, 2010.

Gaustad, Edwin and Leigh Schmidt. *The Religious History of America: The Heart of the American Story from Colonial Times to Today.* Rev. ed. New York: HarperSanFrancisco, 2002.

Leonard, Bill J. *A Sense of the Heart: Christian Religious Experience in the United States.* Nashville: Abingdon Press, 2014.

Discovery

McKnight, Scot. *The King Jesus Gospel: The Original Good News Revisited.* Rev. ed. Grand Rapids, MI: Zondervan, 2016.

Rauschenbusch, Walter. *A Theology for the Social Gospel.* New York: MacMillan Co., 1917.

_____. *Christianity and the Social Crisis.* New York: MacMillan Co., 1907.

Wallis, Jim. *Agenda for Biblical People: A New Focus for Developing a Lifestyle of Discipleship.* New York: Harper & Row, 1976.

_____. *The Call to Conversion: Recovering the Gospel for These Times.* New York: Harper & Row, 1981.

Wright, N.T. *How God Became King: The Forgotten Story of the Gospels.* New York: HarperCollins, 2012.

_____. *The Day the Revolution Began: Reconsidering the Meaning of Jesus' Crucifixion.* New York: HarperOne, 2016.

Discernment

Campbell, Ernest T. *Christian Manifesto.* New York: Harper & Row, 1970.

Diangelo, Robin. *White Fragility: Why It's So Hard for White People to Talk About Race.* Boston: Beacon Press, 2018.

Irving, Debby. *Waking Up White and Finding Myself in the Story of Race.* Cambridge, MA: Elephant Room Press, 2014.

MacLean, Nancy. *Democracy in Chains: The Deep History of the Radical Right's Stealth Plan for America.* New York: Penguin Books, 2017.

Verhey, Allen. *Remembering Jesus: Christian Community, Scripture, and the Moral Life.* Grand Rapids, MI: Eerdmans, 2002.

Volf, Miroslav and Ryan McAnnally-Linz. *Public Faith in Action: How to Think Carefully, Engage Wisely, and Vote with Integrity.* Grand Rapids, MI: Brazos Press, 2016.

Wink, Walter, ed. *Homosexuality and Christian Faith: Questions of Conscience for the Churches.* Minneapolis: Fortress Press, 1999.

Yoder, John Howard. *The Politics of Jesus.* Grand Rapids, MI: Eerdmans, 1972.

www.ingramcontent.com/pod-product-compliance
Lightning Source LLC
Chambersburg PA
CBHW070843160426
43192CB00012B/2294